The Religious World of Antislavery Women

WOMEN AND GENDER IN
NORTH AMERICAN RELIGIONS

Amanda Porterfield and Mary Farrell Bednarowski
Series Editors

The 1850 Fugitive Slave Law Convention in Cazenovia, New York. *Courtesy the J. Paul Getty Museum, Los Angeles.*

The passage of the Fugitive Slave Law spurred abolitionists on to even greater efforts. According to the *Liberator,* some two thousand persons, among them thirty fugitives, attended this antislavery meeting in Cazenovia, New York. The speaker in the forefront has not been positively identified, but she is likely Abby Kelley Foster. Other identifiable figures are Frederick Douglass and Gerrit Smith (to the left and behind Foster). The African American women wearing bonnets and shawls are likely the sisters Emily and Mary Edmondson, former slaves.

The Religious World
of Antislavery Women

SPIRITUALITY
IN THE LIVES OF FIVE
ABOLITIONIST LECTURERS

Anna M. Speicher

SYRACUSE UNIVERSITY PRESS

We acknowledge the following sources for their kind
permission to quote archival material:
American Antiquarian Society
The Center for American History, University of Texas at Austin
Department of Rare Books and Special Collections,
University of Rochester Library
Department of Special Collections, Syracuse University Library
Division of Rare and Manuscript Collections, Cornell University Library
Friends Historical Library, Swarthmore College
Library of Congress
Massachusetts Historical Society
Oberlin College
Phillips Library, Peabody Essex Museum
Quaker Collection, Haverford College Library
Schlesinger Library, Radcliffe College
Sophia Smith Collection, Smith College
Special Collections and Archives, Kent State University Libraries
Special Collections and Archives, W. E. B. DuBois Library,
University of Massachesetts Amherst
Trustees of the Boston Public Library
William L. Clements Library, University of Michigan Ann Arbor
Worcester Historical Museum

The paper used in this publication meets the minimum requirements of American National
Standard for Information Sciences—Permanence of Paper for Printed Library Materials,
ANSI Z39.48-1984 ∞

Library of Congress Cataloging-in-Publication Data

Speicher, Anna M.
    The religious world of antislavery women : spirituality in the lives of five
abolitionist lecturers / Anna M. Speicher. — 1st ed.
        p.   cm. — (Women and gender in North American religions)
    Includes bibliographical references and index.
    ISBN 0-8156-2807-2 (cloth : alk. paper). — ISBN 0-8156-2850-1 (pbk. : alk. paper)
    1. Women abolitionists—Religious life—United States—History—19th century.
2. Antislavery movements—United States—History—19th century. I. Title. II. Series.
BR525.S64   1999
261.8'34567'082—dc21
                                                                            99-16819

Manufactured in the United States of America

ANNA M. SPEICHER is an independent historian and consultant in the metropolitan Chicago area. She is a part-time instructor of American history at the School of the Art Institute of Chicago. She is presently editing an anthology of the diaries and other religious writings of the Grimké sisters.

Contents

Conclusion

Appendix

Illustrations

Acknowledgments

I AM GRATEFUL FOR the support and assistance of many people and institutions. James O. Horton directed my dissertation at the George Washington University and has continued to advise me through the stages of transforming a dissertation into a book. His dedication to his students—and former students—is unparalleled. I am most appreciative of his friendship and support. Lois Horton, too, has been most generous with her advice and assistance.

I have greatly benefited from the suggestions of those who have critiqued various ideas and drafts of this work: Harriet Hyman Alonso, Carol Kolmerten, Teresa A. Murphy, Phyllis Palmer, Amanda Porterfield, Richard Rabinowitz, Mitchell Snay, Deborah Bingham Van Broekhoven, and Dewey D. Wallace. Additionally, I am grateful to all the participants in the 1997–98 Newberry Fellows Seminar Program for their incisive and insightful comments on a draft of the Introduction to this book.

This work would not have been possible without the cooperation of the staffs of the many archival collections that are listed in the bibliography. In particular, Robert S. Cox, former curator of manuscripts at the William L. Clements Library at the University of Michigan, provided help again and again throughout the research and writing of this work.

My spirits have frequently been lifted by strangers who have not only asked, "What are you writing?" but have expressed enthusiasm for the ideas explored in this work. The support of my family and friends has been invaluable. I thank them for their assistance and for their willingness to listen to anecdote after anecdote about "my women." My husband, Paul Teetor, has shouldered major responsibilities on behalf of this project. I am most grateful for the innumerable ways he has helped me. My sons, Nathan and Everett Teetor, have allowed me to experience the complexities and rewards of combining family life with intellectual pursuits. They have brought balance and joy to my life. I am, finally, grateful to all those, including the subjects of this book, who have shared their visions of faith and community with me. I have benefited immeasurably from their voices; I hope this book has too.

The Religious World
of Antislavery Women

Introduction

"IN THE BONDS OF THE GOSPEL AND THE SLAVE"

IN HIS MEMOIRS THE Unitarian minister Samuel J. May recalled that when Angelina and Sarah Grimké began their 1837 antislavery lecturing tour in Massachusetts, he was "not a little disturbed in [his] sense of propriety." Then he heard them speak, an experience "which dispelled my Pauline prejudice. I could not believe that God gave them such talents as they evinced to be buried in a napkin. I could not think they would be justified in withholding what was so obviously given them to say on the great iniquity of our country, because they were women."[1]

The women who are the subjects of this book—Sarah Moore Grimké, Angelina Grimké Weld, Lucretia Coffin Mott, Abby Kelley Foster, and Sallie Holley—shared May's conviction about the God-given nature of their mission as antislavery lecturers. Whereas the entirety of this book explores the religious faith of these women and its relationship to their lifelong beliefs, choices, and actions, Angelina Grimké needed only a line to explain her commitments in 1837. In closing a letter to Theodore Weld, the man who was to become her husband, she used the phrase I have borrowed for the title of this introduction: "Farewell in the bonds of the Gospel and the slave."[2]

This book began as an effort to understand what factors have motivated and sustained some women who chose unconventional paths in their lives. Nineteenth-century women who demonstrated their opposition to slavery by public lecturing were ideal for this purpose because of their double marginalization: these women chose not only to advocate a controversial and generally unpopular political cause, but elected to do so in an unconventional, "unfeminine" way, by speaking in public to mixed or "promiscuous" audiences—those composed of men as well as women.

The women I selected for this study shared some significant characteristics: they were all of Euro-american descent; they were all raised in the eastern United States; they all had a socioeconomic status at least high enough to permit them the luxury of some education. There were some significant differences in their backgrounds as well. Unlike the others, the Grimké sisters were Southerners and originally Episcopalian; Mott and Kelley, more expectedly, were Northern Quakers; Holley, also a Northerner, was raised in an unorthodox Christian household. Kelley's parents were struggling farmers; Mott came from a hard-working whaling and merchant background; the Grimkés, from a wealthy and aristocratic plantation-owning family; Holley's father held an assortment of positions from Commissioner of the Erie Canal to truck farmer. Holley was amiable; Kelley, often caustic. Angelina Grimké was assertive; her sister, deferential. Sarah Grimké, having converted to Quakerism, worked unsuccessfully for years to try to earn the designation as minister that Lucretia Mott was granted almost as a matter of course. Nonetheless, in the lives of these women one can trace a similar pattern of conviction and action that led each one step by step toward the momentous decision to raise her voice publicly in the antislavery cause. (See the appendix for notes on how these particular women were selected for this study and for brief biographies of other female abolitionist lecturers.)

Although all the Northern states had acted to eliminate slavery (either immediately or gradually) by 1804, Northern views on the "slave question" were many and varied. They ranged from endorsements of Southern claims that slavery was the kindest and most effective way of civilizing and Christianizing an inferior and heathenish people to the most radical of calls for immediate, uncompensated abolition of all slaves coupled with measures to promote racial and gender equality in the North as well as the South. Between those two extremes were a multiplicity of positions, including moderate antislavery stands proclaiming that slavery would die a natural death in "God's time," and promotion of gradual emancipation often coupled with expatriation to other lands.

In addition to endorsing the most radical of positions surrounding this controversial issue, immediate abolition, the women who are the subjects of this study also flew in the face of social convention by advocating for their cause in the public arena. Public speaking was generally considered to be a masculine activity, particularly if the audience addressed included men as well as women. The unconventionality of such a forum for a woman was occasionally overlooked, as when Deborah Sampson Gannett conducted her post–Revolutionary War lectures on her wartime experiences as a soldier in masculine disguise. In Sampson Gannett's case, it appears that the mantle of republican loyalty was spread over her, protecting her from the bulk of criticism she might otherwise have faced. Frances Wright, the Englishwoman who spoke publicly against slavery in the early 1800s, did not meet with such forbearance. Maria W. Stewart, the free-born African American woman who gave four public lectures on the topic of moral reform and community uplift to African American audiences in Boston in 1832 and 1833, abandoned her speaking career owing to the public hostility directed toward her, hostility that she attributed to her gender.[3]

Contemporary scholarship, however, has convincingly challenged the perception that there was a rigid line drawn between the spheres of nineteenth-century American men and women. Historians have cogently demonstrated that the boundaries between public and private were far more fluid in practice than in theory. Nancy Hewitt and Lori Ginzburg, for example, have identified numerous examples of individuals and groups who did not adhere to the policy of separate spheres.[4] It now appears that the concept of separate spheres is more helpful as a prescriptive guideline than as an absolute statement of reality, and applied, additionally, mainly to white, middle- and upper-class women.

Nonetheless, women speaking in public to mixed audiences on such a controversial and political topic as slavery was a too obvious flaunting of gender roles for many. Many people were not sympathetic to arguments such as Samuel J. May's, or to the precedents of biblical women such as Huldah or Phebe, who are recorded in scripture as having served, respectively, as prophetess and preacher. Indeed, in an age when scripture was commonly used to justify social and political as well as religious positions, one clergyman carefully eliminated the loophole that some might perceive in such biblical tales. A decade before the Grimkés began their lecture tour, Ashbel Green asserted categorically that

> miraculous inspiration has long since ceased in the Christian church, [and] no such excepted cases as those we have mentioned, can any longer occur. The general rule, therefore, laid down by the Spirit of Christ, speaking by the mouth of St. Paul, is now in force, without an

exception. Women are, in no case, to be publick preachers and teachers, in assemblies promiscuously composed of the two sexes.[5]

So what to make of such women as the antislavery lecturers who openly flaunted public opinion and cultural norms? Initially, I expected to discover these women to have been motivated by a keen sense of social justice and bolstered by a will strong enough to withstand severe criticism. I suspected that religious faith would likely be a factor in creating both those conditions. The more I grew to know these women—largely through their own words in public speeches, writings, and private correspondence, but also through the eyes of their contemporaries—the more I realized that a commitment to discovering and acting upon religious truth was not simply one aspect of their lives, it was the fundamental organizing principle of their entire lives. This was in spite of the fact that four of the five severed (or had severed for them) their membership in organized religious groups. And even Lucretia Mott, the only one of the five who remained a lifelong member of a religious sect, the Society of Friends, saw herself as "a kind of outlaw in my own society."[6]

None of the faiths of any of these women, including Mott, has been examined in a systematic way. Gerda Lerner, whose excellent biography of the Grimké sisters was the first scholarly work published on these important women, refers to the mature faith of the Grimkés as "a vague Pantheism of their own devising" which led to their "liv[ing] their humanitarian convictions according to their own, very personal interpretation of the Bible." Katherine Herbig, whose unpublished dissertation on Sallie Holley remains the only major exploration of Holley's life, summarizes Holley's faith as "nondogmatic and centered on ethical problems." Keith Melder's recent essay on Abby Kelley describes her as attempting "to throw off religious authority," an effort that resulted in her "adoption of an unorthodox and highly personal religious stance." Dorothy Sterling's full-length biography of Abby Kelley, by contrast, does discuss Kelley's religious beliefs, although her primary interest is in exploring Kelley's reform activities.[7]

Both Lerner and Blanche Hersh (whose 1978 study of fifty-one "feminist-abolitionists" remains the only book-length analysis of such women as a group) refer to their subjects as having made, in Lerner's words, "a religion of reform."[8] Hersh goes on to claim that "ultimately, the religious needs of the feminist-abolitionists were met by their work—reform became their religion." She provides details of how these women abandoned ortho-dox faiths and doctrines, but her discussion of any evolving faith is limited to statements such as the previous one and to comments that these women maintained religious views that were "eclectic" and "nonconformist."[9] This literature conveys the impression of a religious identity consisting of idio-syncratic leanings that, for all intents and purposes, was synonymous with the reform work of these women. This impression has in turn bolstered the impression that religion played a diminishing role in the lives of these women reformers.

This was not so. Although these women became progressively more radical politically and honed their philosophical positions accordingly, they not only continued to view their reform work as a religious mission, they also gave a great deal of thought to the theological foundation of that mis-sion. Their criticisms of American Protestantism were critiques in the high-est sense of the word; they exposed the church's failures to adhere to what they saw as basic Christian ideals, and they continued to formulate and articulate religious principles based on their conception of those ideals. But because these women, for the most part, distanced themselves from rec-ognized religious groups and movements, and drew their beliefs from a variety of sources, their religious views are difficult to analyze.

This is not to say that churches or movements did not influence them. On the contrary, one can identify strains of Quakerism, transcen-dentalism, spiritualism, premillennialism, Unitarianism, and universal-ism in their religious views, as well as evidences of romanticism and Enlightenment thought. The nature of that relationship is less clear. Whereas one can point to Lucretia Mott's Quaker upbringing as a reason for her to embrace the concept of the inward light, it is less clear why Sallie Holley, who identified most closely with Unitarianism, would hold essen-tially the same view. Be that as it may, the religion of these women cannot be analyzed simply on the basis of participation in such groups; thus, the resort to vague mentions of individual and eclectic religious philosophies. Rather than attempt to place these women within a predefined category of faith, or to be content with a vague description of their views, I have looked for clues to define religion as they themselves did, rather than to impose a definition on them. In so doing I have uncovered a richness of religiosity that is largely hidden when religion is thought of in terms of institutions and movements.

In recent years, numerous explorations of popular religion have broadened our understanding of religiosity by including noninstitutionally sanctioned beliefs and practices such as some of the revivalist camp meetings, spiritualism, folk healing, and occult practices. They have paid attention also to religion as experienced by lay people rather than by clerical elites.[10] This study expands these significant efforts by exploring religion as an essentially personal phenomenon, existing independent from affiliation with religious organizations, grassroots movements, or folk practices.

Further, the women in this study had no hesitations about merging their religious and their political convictions, nor was this merging in itself a problem within a culture and a political system that accepted the premise and legitimacy of divine will as an authority for action. These women's difficulties came in challenging the identification of religion with church and creed. Such a linkage seems only to have been strengthened by the nineteenth-century trend toward denominationalism and the corresponding competition among sects for members. This trend in turn led to the staking out of religious turf among sects; one result may have been increased definition of the boundaries between sects, but another was an increasing separation between those aspects of life viewed as sacred and those seen as secular. This development was undoubtedly exacerbated by the trend toward the feminization and privatization of religion as a partial result of the advance of industrial capitalism and the corresponding segregation of public and private spheres.

In examining the religiosity of these women, this study explores a particular style of nineteenth-century religion that was transformative and directed toward worldly reform, rather than sentimental, self-absorbed, and enervating. Here religion was clearly a radicalizing factor, not the sickly, enervated liberal religion Ann Douglas has contended that nineteenth-century women helped create.[11] The women in this study, though they did not depend on church and clergy (which may explain some of the differences between Douglas's conclusions and those offered here), found religion to be liberating, a source of inspiration and strength.

Other scholars have addressed the issue of the radical and transformative potential of religion in the nineteenth century. In *Radical Spirits,* Ann Braude examined the relationship between the nineteenth-century movements of spiritualism and woman's rights and took issue with Ann Douglas's view of nineteenth-century religion as sentimental and ultimately disempowering for women. Braude found that "the identification of piety with femininity could aid in the expansion of women's options and contribute to the potency of a comprehensive moral idealism." She claimed that "More women stepped beyond conventional female roles because of Spiritualism than they would have without it. In mediumship and in its inherent individualism, Spiritualism held up a model of women's unlimited capacity for autonomous action to the men and women of nineteenth-century America." Like the abolitionist women examined in this work, Braude found that, despite their withdrawal from denominational religion, spiritualists maintained their religiosity throughout their lives.[12]

Robert Abzug came to a similar conclusion in *Cosmos Crumbling,* a fascinating exploration of the religious dimension of reform from the early national period to the 1840s. Historians such as Gilbert Barnes have emphasized the evangelical roots of the abolition movement and deplored the secularizing influence of its radical wing, headed by that "figurehead of fanaticism," William Lloyd Garrison. Abzug, by contrast, finds religion to have been a key ongoing influence. In fact, he argues, radical reformers sought to maintain and strengthen the religious aspect of everyday life in the face of societal attempts to partition the sacred and the secular into separate spheres.[13]

Like the men highlighted in Abzug's study, these women were intent on preserving the integration of the sacred and the secular, a relationship which they viewed as endangered by rigid adherence to sect and sectarian doctrines and rituals. And certainly the history of the hundred-plus years since their passing has not contradicted their fears. For example, the importance of religion for these women can hardly be overestimated, but it has frequently been misunderstood at best and sometimes ignored. I suggest that part of the problem is due to a difficulty that contemporary historians have in transcending the secularism of our own age in order to interpret accurately the religiosity of a previous one.[14]

In previous centuries, religious language was used as widely outside religious meetinghouses as inside and biblical scripture was commonly employed to justify political positions. Today, confessing to sincere religious conviction is often viewed as appropriate only within designated sacred space. (One significant exception to this rule has been the example of the African American community in which religion has been much more integrated into the "secular" aspects of the community, such as social welfare and politics.) In the broader American society, however, as James Moseley states, religion has become "a special aspect of life with its own institutions, leaders, and theories, rather than remaining the symbolic center of a holistic world." He concurs with sociologist Thomas Luckmann, who

> has hypothesized that progressive institutional differentiation leads to the privatization of religious consciousness. The process of institutional specialization allows religion to coexist with other increasingly distinct public institutions, such as political and economic structures. But as other institutions—big government and big business—wield increasing influence on one's public life, an individual may find that his or her religion, if it is to survive, becomes an internal, private affair. Even in one's own mind, religion may become compartmentalized and remote from the rest of life.[15]

Likewise, Stephen Carter argues convincingly that people today who admit to operating from religious principle are dismissed as sentimental and irrational, not really fit to interact in the world of business and politics.[16] The most visible societal exceptions to that segregationist rule are often affiliated with conservative religious groups whose efforts to impose their religious views on the secular realm are often viewed by others with suspicion and distaste.

It may be that this situation is changing. In the retrenchment of government support for social welfare programs, much has been made of the necessity for community organizations, and particularly religious groups, to pick up the slack. Further, the upsurge of interest in a gamut of spiritual disciplines that are often lumped together as "New Age" may signal an emerging synthesis of the religious and the secular. But that is still a trend that may be predicted for the future rather than a present reality, particularly in the scholarly world.

The difficulty of contemporary secular historians in accepting the religiosity of a previous era is supported by a comment made by Gerda Lerner in the preface to her 1993 work, *The Creation of Feminist Consciousness.* Lerner states there that in her long career as a women's historian it was only recently that she began "fully [to] appreciate the depth and urgency of the search of Jewish and Christian women for connection to the Divine. . . . The insight that religion was the primary arena on which women fought for hundreds of years for feminist consciousness was not one I had previously had."[17] This comment helps to explain her minimization of the significance of religion in her biography of the Grimkés, published nearly twenty years prior to this revelation.[18]

More recently, Nell Painter's insightful biography of Sojourner Truth explores the way scholars, feminists, and the public at large have preferred the symbol of Truth to her reality. Painter suggests that one of the most important aspects of the neglected Truth is her religiosity. This, Painter claims, has been due to Truth's memory having fallen "into the hands of successors to abolitionists and woman suffragists, politically minded reformers whose religions or lack thereof were far from the beliefs she [Truth] held most of her life. Linked inextricably to feminists and insurgent blacks, her persona lost the religion of her free woman's life."[19]

I attempt, then, in this study, to place religiosity into its appropriate position of preeminence in the lives of these five women reformers. In so doing, another aspect of these women's lives comes to the fore, that of their collegiality—sorority is perhaps an even more appropriate word—and their leadership within the larger community of antislavery reformers.

The noninstitutional but quite specific religious principles to which these women adhered, which included a commitment to gender and racial equality, led them to broaden the scope of the abolition movement. They were helpful, for example, in extending the human rights issue of equality for African Americans to include, both theoretically and practically, equal rights for women, black and white, as well. They squarely addressed racial prejudice and discrimination as issues inseparable from slavery itself. The ideas propounded by these women were influential in developing the ideologies of the antislavery and woman's rights movements and in the choice of tactics used to promote the goals of those movements.

Whereas the abolition movement has frequently been credited with providing the inspiration and the political expertise for the nineteenth-century woman's movement, the effect of the woman's movement on the antislavery movement has most often been considered in terms of its divisive impact. Abzug, for example, discusses women's contributions to the reform movement mainly in terms of their political actions to secure equality, which contributed to the splintering of the antislavery movement in 1840. Thus, although his book provides an insightful analysis of the radical reformers' interest in sacralizing everyday life, the activist women are viewed mainly as political actors. In this he echoes the view taken by Lawrence Friedman in *Gregarious Saints*.[20] These are interesting shifts from the usual representation of women as domestic and religious and men as oriented toward business and politics; however, the five women reformers studied here embraced the sacred in all aspects of their life. Their religious convictions led them to embark upon their political reform activity, and further, their own experiences of gender marginalization contributed to their understanding of religious truth. Their theories of women's equality, founded in religious principles, gave depth to the antislavery movement.

Although in some ways the entire group of abolitionist women can be regarded as a community, the antislavery lecturers were set apart by virtue of their public work. In this communal environment, they served as symbols of dedication and were looked to as leaders. Their ideas were adopted, criticized, and refined by one another and by the wider body of abolitionist women and men.

The type of community that grew up around these antislavery leaders was not a traditional one. Historians have addressed the existence of women's community in the nineteenth century in various ways. Carroll Smith-Rosenberg's analysis of the correspondence of nineteenth-century women has revealed a "female world" in which women's most intimate alliances were to each other rather than to the men in their lives. The unabashedly intimate language of the letters transcribed and edited by Smith-Rosenberg reveals the deep emotional commitment of these female friends and relatives. Smith-Rosenberg's intention was to illustrate the flexibility and responsiveness of "the supposedly repressive and destructive Victorian sexual ethos";[21] Nancy Cott took the possibilities of this sisterhood a step farther. She suggested that "[w]omen's reliance on each other to confirm their values embodied a new kind of group consciousness, one which could develop into a political consciousness."[22]

In this study I build on Cott's claim. But rather than use the term "group consciousness," as Cott does, I use the word, "community," to connote not just an acknowledgment of mutuality of interest, identity, and purpose in the abstract, but more intimate personal and emotional bonds. This definition of community accurately describes the relationships of these antislavery women to one another and to their extended networks of families, friends, and supporters.

These women were not linked by family or geographic proximity or, initially, friendship. Their community was founded on conviction and occupation. Although this may seem to indicate that they were simply business acquaintances, which is the impression Friedman conveys, their relationships were in fact far more intimate. The extent of their association was somewhat unexpected, as they have been evaluated by scholars mainly as individuals or included in larger and more general studies of antislavery and feminist women.[23] Although neither their religious nor their political views were unique, their public exposition of abolitionism marked them in their own and others' eyes as a select group of leaders. They had an enormous impact on one another. From this perspective, it becomes apparent that the bonds forged by religious and political commitment were extraordinarily strong.

Studying their interaction gives us insight into how nineteenth-century activist women worked together. Their networks were weblike. Each of these women had friends and sometimes family as well, who supported them and looked to them for direction. Various members of these groups related personally to more than one of these lecturing women, and the lecturers themselves interacted, merging the personal and the professional in their relationships without difficulty—unlike the male abolitionists described by Friedman. Other scholars have suggested the importance of the supporting role women played in the abolition movement, in terms of fund-raising, petition drives, and organizing.[24] This study points to another level of organization in which a few women, along with their networks of supporters and correspondents, affected the ideology and tactics of the movement as a whole.

The first chapter and the last two chapters of this book are primarily biographical. Here my purposes are to provide some background for readers who have not encountered one or more of these women previously, and to offer a new perspective on some significant periods in their lives by paying close attention to their religiosity. In chapter 2 I describe their impact on the wider antislavery community. In the third and fourth chapters I analyze their religious views, in terms of both their reaction against orthodox Christianity and their vision of what true Christianity might be. In chapters 5 and 6 I deal with the relationship of their faith to social action, specifically to their antislavery activism and their commitment to women's rights.

My goal throughout has been to present these women as fully and fairly as possible. In recognition of their gifts as writers and speakers, I have chosen to quote extensively from the voluminous collections of their writings, believing that their own words often provide the most complete and indeed, the most interesting articulation of their views.[25] In some instances I have chosen to juxtapose quotes from various years. Whenever I have done so it has been from the conviction, developed after reading and rereading manuscripts, published writings, and other contemporary accounts, that this juxtaposition, although chronologically awkward, most faithfully represents their views and will aid in the reader's understanding. Bearing in mind that truth and justice were lifelong goals for these women, I hope that I have succeeded in according them some measure of that for which they themselves labored so diligently.

1 &

"A Heart to Work a Tongue to Speak"

THE CALL TO MISSION

NGELINA GRIMKÉ ONCE described her fellow abolitionist Maria Weston Chapman as "one of the noblest women I ever saw," saying, "there is real antislavery here, a heart to work a tongue to speak."[1] Those lines also aptly describe her own commitment to antislavery work, and that of the other four women discussed in this book. These women, educated, articulate, and interested in the world around them, wanted to use their abilities in accordance with what they intuited was God's will. In so doing they all gradually focused their attention on the issue of slavery. Following are sketches of the paths that led them to their decision to become antislavery lecturers.

SARAH GRIMKÉ: "CALLED TO THE WORK OF THE MINISTRY"

Sarah Moore Grimké, born in November 1792, was the second daughter of John Faucheraud Grimké, a South Carolina judge and plantation owner, and Mary Smith Grimké, also of Southern aristocratic background, a woman who bore fourteen children and managed the large Grimké households. The Grimkés were regular churchgoers, members of the Episcopal Church. They expected their children to conform to the conventions of their region and class, the boys to embrace respectable professions and the girls to marry well and care for their families and households. Up to the age of twenty-seven, Sarah Grimké did, for the most part, conform to expectations. One exception was her expressed desire to study law as her beloved older brother Thomas did. Although her father was impressed by her mind, commenting that "had she been of the other sex she would have made the greatest juror in the land," he quickly squelched that unfeminine aspiration. And Sarah Grimké obediently gave up her dream of studying law and continued on the path laid out for her, entering Charleston society and enjoying the pleasures it afforded.[2]

In an account of her spiritual development, penned in mid-1827 at the age of thirty-four, Grimké described herself in this earlier period as living a life of "dissipation and folly."[3] Occasionally, in the midst of her social engagements, she suffered bouts of religious remorse for her self-indulgence. At the age of eighteen she encountered a Presbyterian minister, the Reverend Henry Kolloch, who impressed her with warnings about the sinfulness of a frivolous life. But like those of many other young women of her time, her path to religious conversion was a halting one. At times she vowed "to purchase heaven at any price." These moments of repentance were inevitably followed by a return to the social life that Rev. Kolloch had condemned. In her 1827 account she described herself at these times as having "returned like the sow to my wallowing in the mire, having disregarded this call to arise and shake myself from the dust of the earth."

Grimké's process of religious conversion was typical for Christian Protestants, particularly women, of her day. Although the details of individual conversions differed, the broad outlines of the experience almost always followed the same lines. There were a number of recognized steps leading to conversion. First came an awareness of sinfulness and of separation from God. This was often a protracted period in which, like Grimké, an individual would become convinced of his or her sinful state and determine to reform, but would then slip back into sin, only to repent and return to sinfulness again. This period could last for years, but at last the individual would report a final crisis of repentance, generally involving a realization of the omnipotence of God and of his or her own worthlessness, and an understanding that the only possible resolution was to surrender completely to God.[4]

In Grimké's case, her final break from her society lifestyle came after she accompanied her dying father to Philadelphia in 1819 for medical consultation and then spent several months with him at a seaside resort in New Jersey. Her spiritual reflections were particularly intense during her father's illness and at this propitious time she became acquainted with the Society of Friends. Her father's physician was a Quaker and she and her father boarded with a Quaker family in Philadelphia. At that time she "saw nothing to recommend the[ir] profession as to Religion tho' they were very kind," but she was increasingly drawn toward their faith.[5] She was quite affected by the volumes of John Woolman's writings that some of her Quaker acquaintances had given her.[6] After her return to Charleston, her reflections upon religion and her father's death resulted in a social withdrawal so pronounced that her mother sent her to stay with her Uncle James Smith and his family on their Cape Fear River Plantation in North Carolina. This experience did rouse her from her lethargy, but not in the way her mother had hoped. For lack of any other religious fellowship there, she attended a Methodist church "and under their loud and alarming preaching, together with associating with some truly spiritual minds I became revived from the state in which I was, and a little spiritual life being revived I was enabled to approach the throne of grace and to deliver at one of their love Feasts a public testimony to the Truth." She did not, however, convert to Methodism, for having "carefully examin[ed] their principles and doctrines . . . found them as faulty as all the others which from time to time I had investigated."[7]

She concluded that she would remain an Episcopalian despite her objection to its "lifeless forms," for "no change I then saw would afford me any satisfaction." She added, though, in her 1827 account, that "I have reason to believe that the Lord was even then preparing me for admission into this Society of which I am now an unworthy member."

Her mother having acquiesced in her departure from the South, on 15 May 1821, Sarah Grimké boarded the ship that was to carry her to a new home with Catherine Morris, a Quaker related to the Philadelphia Friends she had met previously. By that time, she had gone beyond simply deciding to attend Quaker meetings and, in time, to petition for membership in the Society of Friends. She recorded these reflections in her journal: "I desire ere I depart once more to dedicate my self to the service of God, carefully and with tears have I sought the will of my heavenly Father and I believe I am acting under the immediate influence of his holy spirit and in compliance with his will in going to Pennsylvania. . . . A strong impression is at times upon my mind that I shall be called to the work of the ministry."[8]

So it was with high hopes for a life of service in the ministry, a non-salaried vocation open to women as well as men in the Society of Friends, that she took up her new life in Philadelphia. Unfortunately, the fifteen years that followed her move did not fulfill her hopes. Although she was accepted as a member of the Arch and Fourth Street Quaker meeting in

1823, her tentative offerings as a preacher were for the most part rebuffed. Her diary for these years is an almost unbroken lament of her spiritual difficulties, which she attributed as much to her own unworthiness and faithlessness as to the lack of receptiveness and downright hostility from the senior members and elders at her meeting. On 31 December 1825 she recorded in her diary:

> Another year has nearly run its round, and what hast thou to render to the Lord, nothing but a faithless heart, the past year has been to me a season of much suffering, disappointment and death have marked its progress, and deep inward trials have been my portion, surely it requires double diligence to keep the heart when love and good will seem to have fled from it. . . . I have said within myself my punishment is greater than I can bear.

Grimké attributed her problems in good part to the fact that she was not a birthright Quaker, that is, had not been born into a Quaker family. But it also appears to have been true that she was not an entirely gifted speaker. One of her friends gave her some telling advice:

> I do believe that if thou could'st speak more slowly, and divide thy sentences, and paragraphs by suitable pauses, it would add greatly to the weight and dignity of thy communications, both ministerial and supplicatory. There is something of a hurried appearance in thy manner, and thus keeping the sentences in close connection, causes them to seem like repeating what has been previously stored in the mind."[9]

Prepared speeches, of course, were anathema to Quakers, who believed that only spontaneous utterances in response to divine prompting were legitimate.

Her mode of speech was not Sarah Grimké's only problem. In spite of her avowed humility, she could never quite bring herself to surrender completely to the judgment and authority of the Quaker hierarchy, which might have made her a more acceptable member. Her diary reveals that for quite a while after committing herself to the Society of Friends, she dressed simply, like a Quaker, but in black, a departure from the typical Quaker gray. It seems odd that someone who professed to be so humble and so in need of guidance would refrain from acquiescing in such a small matter. Her application for membership in the Society was refused initially because the committee "could not feel it the right time to proceed in this matter." Although she publicly accepted the committee's verdict, she wrote in her diary that "having carefully sought the truth I cannot feel as if I had made the application at a wrong time." She was resentful when Catherine Morris, the woman with whom she boarded, cautioned her against praying out loud, even within her own room. It was, however, only to her diary that she asked, "Where does Jesus tell his disciples to cease from vocal prayer, he used it himself." Perhaps most importantly, she rejected an opportunity for social legitimacy within Quaker circles by refusing the offer of marriage made to her by Isaac Morris, a Quaker widower and the brother of Catherine Morris.[10]

It is clear from her frequent painful recollections about this matter that although she considered Morris "her dearest earthly friend," and agonized over and over about her decision, in the end she felt obligated to answer a higher call, that of the ministry. Four years to the day of his proposal, she acknowledged that "to the individual there was sufficient attachment. . . . But I feel peaceful in the surrender I have made and if I can only have the F[rien]d. of sinners for my F[rien]d, the bridegroom of souls for my husband, I shall have all I have craved."[11]

As time went on, her anguish continued, although its cause changed. She increasingly viewed herself as being faithful but wronged. Sometimes she despaired because "trials seem to cluster round me so thickly" and asked, "Is the mercy of the Lord clean gone forever[?]" She did occasionally find satisfaction in expressing herself in meeting as when she "had to speak a few words to advocate the cause of a crucified Redeemer[.] [T]he language has been sweetly and encouragingly with me, 'I have set before thee an open door and no man can shut it.'" More typical though is her comment that "I think I have seldom experienced a greater conflict in meeting, or endured more suffering on account of the little I have to do in the Ministry than I did last 1st day morn[in]g." She felt like one condemned, and her sabbaths, rather than being a source of comfort or inspiration, became "seasons of such suffering."[12]

There were two catalysts for Sarah Grimké's eventual break with Quaker authority. The immediate cause was a final humiliation from Jonathan Evans, one of the most powerful of the Philadelphia Quaker elders. In attending a Quaker meeting, Grimké felt moved to speak, and rose to do so according to custom. She had not gotten far before Evans interrupted her, saying, "I hope the friend will be satisfied." She "immediately sat down and was favored to feel perfectly calm." Her break from the authority of the Society of Friends, a few months before her forty-fourth birthday, was accompanied by an abandonment of the journal in which she had for seventeen years recorded her often painful spiritual progress. As she continued in this final journal entry:

> [A]ltho' I am branded in the public eye with the disapprobation of a poor fellow worm and it was entirely a breach of Discipline in him publicly to silence a minister who has been allowed to exercise her gift in her own meeting without ever having been requested to be silent, yet I feel no anger towards him, surely the feelings which could prompt to so cruel and unwarrantable an act cannot be the feelings of Christian love but it seems to be one more evidence that my dear Savior designs to bring me out of this place[. H]ow much has his injunction rested on my mind of latter time "When they persecute you in this city flee ye unto another." I pray unto thee oh Lord Jesus to direct the wanderers footsteps.[13]

Sarah Grimké could now assert her faithfulness to God and turn her back on the Quaker authority to which she had deferred for so many years. She prayed to Jesus to direct her footsteps, but her destination does not really seem to have been in doubt at this point. Without hesitation she declared her readiness to accompany her sister Angelina in her proposed parlor talks to women on behalf of the American Anti-Slavery Society—a course of action against which she had previously counseled Angelina.

While her father's death began a spiritual conversion, Grimké's break with the Society of Friends helped her claim her public voice and her sense of mission. A year later, she put her experience in perspective: "I still feel I am thankful that what was intended to crush me to the earth, was the means of setting me free from the spiritual bondage in which I had groaned for years, under the ecclesiastical power of our elders and was the means of my mouth being opened to plead the cause of the dumb."[14] For the first time, Sarah Grimké began to feel confident about her ideas and her direction. Angelina noted the difference in her sister, commenting that Sarah

Although a Grimké relation by marriage was a professional daguerrotypist, this image of Sarah Moore Grimké is one of the few extant photographs of either of the Grimké sisters, and is, like the photograph that appears in chapter 7, undated. *Courtesy Clements Library, University of Michigan.*

This, perhaps the only extant photograph of Angelina Grimké, probably does not do her justice. It certainly does not reflect the vitality and enthusiasm she exuded. *Courtesy Library of Congress.*

"enjoys more real comfort of mind than I ever saw her enjoy before."[15] As Sarah Grimké's story is now entwined with her sister's, we shall continue it after returning to Charleston to consider Angelina's early years.

ANGELINA GRIMKÉ: PUTTING ON "THE GOSPEL HARNESS"

Born in 1805, Angelina Grimké was Sarah Grimké's youngest sister.[16] She too encountered numerous obstacles along her path, but her self-confidence was far greater than her sister's and she was never so tortured with self-doubt. (Until, that is, she married, had children, and wrestled with feelings of frustration and inadequacy about her maternal role. For more on this, see chapter 7.) Her spiritual path was, however, more complicated than that of any of the other women here.

At an early age, Angelina Grimké established a reputation for independence of mind in regard to religion. She refused to be confirmed in the Episcopal Church because, she later stated in an autobiographical manuscript, she had "determined never to join any Church until . . . [she] had real, heart-felt piety." She did continue to attend Episcopal services with her family but claimed in the same manuscript to have "passed near 19 years in entire indifference as to my eternal welfare" when her brother and his daughter were lost at sea. Appropriating their deaths as a sign to her, she exclaimed to her aunt, "I deserve it for I have always said that nothing but affliction would ever bring me to God."[17]

Several months later she and her mother and sister began attending some mid-week Presbyterian services. The minister's

> communications were sent so powerfully to my heart that I was at times exhausted with weeping and this language was impressed on my mind "this is a teacher sent from God" and as I listened for the first time to the truths of the Gospel from his lips I inwardly exclaimed "this is a new doctrine" for I had been accustomed to nothing but moral discourse.[18]

At first, Grimké "continued to go to the E[piscopal] Meetings on first days and 4th days and the P[resbyteria]n on 5 day evenings." Then, feeling called to that fellowship and receiving no objections from her family, she became a member of the Third Presbyterian Church in Charleston in 1826 (five years after her sister Sarah's departure to Philadelphia).

In describing her attraction to the Presbyterians, Grimké noted that she particularly appreciated their "principle of liberality" toward those of other denominations: "Our Pulpits are open to all Christians and as I have often heard my dear Pastor remark our communion table is the Lord's table and all his children are cheerfully received at it. I have seen a good deal of other denominations but I do not find among any such a desire of union with all others and not even among them to the extent I earnestly desire to see."[19]

Grimké attended services regularly, as often as three or four times a week, and taught a class of children in the Sabbath school. Her Presbyterian enthusiasm did not last long, however. Within two years, she had become disillusioned with the church's sectarianism (a reversal of her earlier approval of its ecumenical tolerance). Her commitment to ecumenism, that is, respect for and cooperation among Christian bodies had, if anything, increased. In February 1828 she noted: "My mind has been brought to feel of late the necessity of Union among Christians—not members of the same Church or Denomination only, but of *every* Church and Denomination— Christians are like the rivers which flow thro' and fertalise our land, taking their rise[?] in different parts but all losing their waters in the same great Ocean and mingling them together there—"[20] Such an ecumenical focus set her apart from the Protestant trend of her day, which was toward the building of denominations and denominational barriers rather than the effacing of them. In addition, Grimké objected to what she viewed as the ostentatious dress and manners of the members of the Presbyterian Church. This was undoubtedly largely due to the influence of her sister Sarah, who returned to Charleston in November 1827 for a visit of several months.

In January 1828, Angelina, like her sister, began keeping a diary that was largely a record of her spiritual journey. In her first entry she reported that:

> Today I have torn up my Novels. My mind had long been troubled about them—I did not dare either to sell them or to lend them out, and yet I had not resolution to destroy them until this morning when in much mercy strength was granted. A great deal of my finery too, I have

put beyond the reach of any one. My hat also I untrimmed and have put nothing but a band of ribbon round it and taken the lace out of the inside. I do want *if* I am a christian to *look* like one.[21]

Although she claimed first that she was "violently opposed to Quakers" she was also "forcibly struck with the holiness of her [sister's] life and the gentleness and humility of her manner," adding that "very soon after she came I saw that I must be a Quaker."[22]

Also important was Grimké's own developing stand on church theology and doctrine, again obviously quite influenced by her sister's Quakerism. She wrote that some of her friends in the church "heard me with suspicion advocate the Doctrine of Universal Grace, Perfection and some tho't I was going to turn Methodist. My Pastor also desired a conversation with me and found I was no longer the zealous promoter of Presbyterianism and that I disapproved of many things among them I regarded Baptism and the Sacrament to say no more at least [as] quite unnecessary."[23]

Finally, Grimké came more and more to the conclusion that she had outgrown her church and she no longer felt the need to defer to the authority of her pastor, whom she had earlier declared to be "a teacher sent from God." "I felt," she wrote, "like a child who after having learned his Alphabet perfectly was still kept in it by his teacher whilst he was anxious to be taught some more advanced lessons." She had begun to feel that her internal sense of God's word was more accurate than her minister's preaching: "sometimes during the Sermons I would feel so plainly that the Minister was not preaching from the life that I desired to close my ears to his words and to listen to Him who spake in my heart and to my heart as never man spake. The outward preaching often disturbed the inward voice and I was much tried."[24] In fact, by March, Grimké flamboyantly announced to Elizabeth Bascom that the Reverend William McDowell "can do nothing more for me, and if I lean on him any longer he will be a broken staff to pierce me."[25] Again, it is most likely that this conclusion originated in Sarah Grimké's sharing with her the Quaker concept of the "inward light," the idea that there is, in the words of George Fox, the founder of Quakerism, "that of God in every man."[26]

Angelina Grimké then began a rather tortuous process of severing her membership from the Third Presbyterian Church. Her pastor and several members of the congregation made strenuous efforts to keep her in their fold. She remained adamant. To Elizabeth Bascom she wrote that although

> [i]t seemed strange that I should be called out of a Church in which I believe I have been permitted to grow in knowledge and grace . . . it was plainly shewn to me that when an infant in Jesus I needed to be taught by outward instruments, for when I was a child I spake as a child, I thought as a child, I understood as a child, but the time had now come when I must put away childish things, for I had come to the mountain which could not be touched and now the anointing [sic] which I have received of Him abideth in me, and I need not that any man teach me.[27]

Angelina Grimké now asserted, with a confidence reminiscent of her embrace of Presbyterianism: "I feel that my proper place now is in the silent meeting of Friends. I believe them to be the most spiritual of any sect—the most obedient, the most crucified to the world. They look like Christians and carry Religion into everything."[28]

Angelina Grimké visited Philadelphia from June to November of 1828, and her stay confirmed her in her desires to join the Society of Friends and to leave the South. She was dissatisfied with her life in Charleston and for the first time in her journal mentioned an antipathy toward slavery, exclaiming, "when shall I be released from the land of Slavery"? Like her sister, she was increasingly convinced that she had a spiritual mission to fulfill, which in her case was explicitly linked to the sufferings of the enslaved. She prayed to God to "prepare me in any way *thou* pleasest for the work thou has set before me—purify me like silver and make me just what thou wouldst have me to be."[29] (Her confident albeit submissive tone stands in stark contrast to Sarah Grimké's related but despairing question during the same years, "How can the vile become pure? . . . How can the tin, and the dross and the reprobate silver be destroyed?"[30]) Lacking an outlet in Charleston for her emerging antislavery convictions, she devoted herself to her own meditations and to improving the conduct and spiritual life of her family, friends, and acquaintances—often to their annoyance. She chastised her brothers for not supporting themselves financially and for their attitudes on slavery. They were particularly hostile to her intervention, her brother Charles once going so far as to tell her that "he wished I never would speak to him for it would be far pleasanter to live on terms of silence with me."[31] Angelina's mother, whom Angelina criticized for her coldness, her accommodation to the (in Angelina's eyes) unprincipled lifestyle of her children, and her unchristian ostentatiousness in serving elaborate meals and redecorating her rooms, wavered between a desire to placate her daughter and exasperation with her demands. Angelina Grimké also described in her diary various well-meaning interventions with friends, generally successful from her point of view, and a singularly unappreciated attempt to reconcile the two feuding (and only) members of the Quaker meeting that she attended in Charleston. In this instance, her efforts were repulsed, one of the disputants going so far as to call her "a busy body about other men's business."[32]

Increasingly, though, her attention became focused on the plight of slaves. Although she prayed for a release from the land of slavery, she also declared her willingness to remain in South Carolina if that was God's will.[33] After recording her horror at an incident in which she observed a black woman being dragged by two white boys to the workhouse for punishment, she wrote that she felt her unwilling presence in the South

> was preparing me for future usefulness to them and this *hope*, I can scarcely call it, for my very soul trembled at the solemn tho't of such a work being placed in my feeble and unworthy hands, this idea was the means of reconciling me to suffer and causing me to feel something of a willingness to pass thro' any trial if I could only be the means of exposing the cruelty and injustice which was practiced in this Institution of oppression . . . —above all of exposing the awful sin of professors of a meek and merciful Master who left us an example that we should walk in his steps.[34]

Although Angelina Grimké's concern for the spiritual and physical well-being of others was undoubtedly sincere, her ability to interpret tragedy with herself as the central character is at the least disconcerting. She became adamantly opposed to slavery, but in the diary passage above, it is her pain in having to witness this distressing scene, rather than the pain of the slave woman, upon which she dwells. This is reminiscent of her reaction to her brother's death, which she seemed to view as a spiritual catalyst directed at her. Her youth, her passionate and spontaneous nature, and the fact that she was for the most part addressing herself to her own journal, necessarily casting herself as the central character of events, provide some excuse for her self-absorption, although it is difficult to absolve her completely.

Angelina Grimké was not, however, entirely passive in her antislavery position, even in Charleston. She interceded with her brother in his punishment of slaves. She reported one conversation with a woman who was defending the institution of slavery. Grimké finally asked her, "[W]ould thou be willing to be a Slave thyself?" When the woman eagerly answered No! then said I thou hast no right to enslave a negro, for the Master expressly says "do unto others as thou wouldst they should do unto thee."[35] She spoke her mind on the issue of slavery on social occasions, discomfiting the Grimké circle of acquaintances, who did not find discussion of the propriety of slavery or even the treatment and rights of the enslaved appropriate parlor talk.

Throughout 1829 Angelina Grimké thought often of moving to Philadelphia, and was encouraged by her sister Sarah. She wrote on August 13, "I do not think I pass a single day without apprehension as to something painful about the servants," and two days later, that were it not for her mother and for the belief that her presence restrained her brother in his treatment of his slaves, she would leave home.[36]

Finally, in September Sarah wrote saying that Catherine Morris had agreed to house Angelina as well as Sarah. Her mother was saddened but did not oppose her going, and in November of 1829, eight years after Sarah's departure, Angelina, too, took ship for Philadelphia. She was enormously relieved to be leaving the South, regarding this move as her entrance into the Promised Land. She wrote: "I think that the children of Israel could not have looked towards the land of Canaan with keener longing than I do to the North."[37] Like her sister, however, she did not find her life among the orthodox Philadelphia Friends entirely satisfactory.[38] Interested in current events and desiring to be useful within the world, she chafed at the restrictions imposed on her by the Quakers, who frowned on interaction with "the world"—that is, anyone and anything not directly related to the Society of Friends. She gratefully acknowledged the receipt of some literary correspondence sent to her by her brother, saying: "We mingle almost entirely with a Society which appears to know but little of what is going on outside of its own immediate precinct. It is therefore a great treat when we have access to information more diffuse and which introduces our minds in some manner into the general sensation which seems to have been excited in the Religious [World]."[39]

Angelina Grimké was struck also by what she termed "the inconsistency of the people," which apparently occasioned the thought that perhaps she "was too good to be one of them"; another clear contrast to her sister's reaction to criticism. Still, at this point, she attributed her concerns to a satanic temptation to keep her from serving God, rather than to evidence that she should break with the Society of Friends.[40] Part of the reason for her forbearance may have been her interest in marrying Edward Bettle, a young man from her meeting. The two conducted a not entirely promising courtship; his family strongly disapproved of her interests outside the meeting, such as her visit to Catharine Beecher's seminary with the view of training to be a teacher. His death from cholera in 1832 both terminated their relationship and lessened Angelina's interest in accommodating the restrictions of her Quaker society.

So despite Quaker disapproval of mingling with the world and her sister's deep reservations, Angelina Grimké became involved in the antislavery movement in the early 1830s. She began reading the *Emancipator* and the *Liberator* (two prominent antislavery newspapers), attended an antislavery lecture by the British abolitionist George Thompson in March 1835, and by May of that year was enrolled as a member of the Philadelphia Female Anti-Slavery Society.[41] In August she wrote a strong letter of support to William Lloyd Garrison, declaring that "The ground upon which you stand is holy ground; never—never surrender it."[42] This letter established her as a public voice against slavery after Garrison published it in the *Liberator* the following month.

Her impulsive action resulted in condemnation from her sister Sarah as well as her Quaker meeting. Sarah urged Angelina "to surrender herself to the guidance of Friends," not accepting any more than they did that Angelina was pursuing a path directed by divine will.[43] On the contrary, Sarah Grimké wrote in her diary:

> The suffering which my precious sister has brought upon herself, by her connection with the anti slavery society which has been a sorrow of heart to me, is another proof how dangerous it is to slight the clear convictions of Truth, but like myself she listened to the voice of the tempter and oh that she may learn obedience by the things that she suf-

fers. Of myself I can say the Lord brought me up out of the horrible pit and my prayer for her is that she may be willing to bear the present chastisement patiently.[44]

Angelina was affected enough by all this disapproval to agree "to go to no more Anti Slavery Meetings for one year, and then try whether she had been indulging self-will, or really following the leadings of the Holy Spirit."[45] At the end of her self-imposed probation, however, Angelina Grimké concluded that she was indeed called by God to this antislavery work. She promptly sat down to write her *Appeal to the Christian Women of the South* in the summer of 1836. This period of her life closed with her realization that

> The door of usefulness among others seems to have been thrown open in a most unexpected and wonderful manner, whilst the door of usefulness in our S[ociet]y seems as if it was bard [sic] and double lockd [sic] to me. I feel no openness among f[rien]ds, my spirit is oppressed and heavy laden and shut up in prison. What then am I to do? The only relief I experience is in writing letters and pieces for the Peace and AntiSlavery causes and this makes me think my influence is to reach beyond our own limits.[46]

Unlike her sister, Angelina Grimké no longer thought that her reservations about the Society of Friends might be the result of satanic temptation. She believed that the sect was doomed, not because of its principles, but because of its lack of faithfulness to them, as well as its reliance on an autocratic and rigid discipline. "I have no doubt," she wrote to her sister, "that our S[ociet]y will be given over to death, because we are too whole in our own eyes to allow the good physician to heal us."[47] She saw her own belief in the necessity of individual spiritual conscience not as a departure from Quakerism or from Christianity, but rather a return to it. Elizur Wright, secretary of the American Anti-Slavery Society, invited Angelina to speak on abolition to small groups of women in New York, and after some soul-searching, she decided to do so. She informed her sister Sarah, expecting to hear more reproaches from her. Much to her surprise, Sarah, having encountered her own final crisis in her relationship with the Friends, announced that she would accompany Angelina in her new work. By November 1836 the sisters were attending a training session for antislavery agents in New York.

The Grimkés began their antislavery talks in January 1837, launching their notorious Massachusetts lecture tour that summer. Gerda Lerner estimates that the two spoke at "at least eighty-eight meetings in sixty-seven towns, . . . reach[ing] a minimum of 40,500 people."[48] That tour concluded abruptly with Angelina Grimké's severe illness in November. In February 1838, however, she addressed the Legislative Committee of the Massachusetts legislature and in March the sisters gave a series of lectures at the Odeon in Boston.

In May 1838, after a brief and mainly long-distance courtship, Angelina Grimké married Theodore Weld, a fellow abolitionist and one of her chief mentors since her New York training. The two intended to continue to work faithfully in response to God's call, whatever that might be; in fact Weld's description of their marital commitment was determined to the point of grimness:

> We marry Angelina, not merely nor mainly, nor at all comparatively to enjoy, but together to do and to dare, together to toil and testify and suffer, together to crucify the flesh with its affections and lusts, and to keep ourselves and each other [unspotted?] from the world—to live a life of faith in the Son of God, pilgrims and strangers, ready, yea rejoicing if called to it, together to lie upon the rack, or clasp the faggot, or walk with steady tread the scaffold—looking to Jesus.[49]

The following chapters will provide more details on the antislavery activities and the later lives of Sarah and Angelina Grimké. We turn now to the backgrounds of the other women in this study.

LUCRETIA MOTT: CONSECRATING HERSELF TO THE GOSPEL

Lucretia Coffin Mott's path to becoming an antislavery activist and lecturer was considerably less tortuous than that of the Grimkés. Lucretia Coffin was born on Nantucket in January 1793, less than two months after Sarah Grimké's birth. She was the second of eight children born to her parents. At the time of her birth, her father, Thomas Coffin, was a whaler, who in 1800 managed to purchase his own vessel, the *Trial*. During his prolonged absences, her mother, Anna Folger Coffin, managed both her house and family and the "shop of Goods" which she, like other wives of whaling men, opened to supplement the family income during her husband's absences.[50] Lucretia Coffin Mott never lost the respect she acquired for her mother and other such women of Nantucket. As she wrote in 1853:

> I can remember how our mothers were employed while our fathers were at sea. The mothers with their children around—'twas not customary to have nurses then—kept small groceries and sold provisions that they might make something in the absence of their husbands. At that time it required some money and some courage to get to Boston. They were obliged to go to that city, make their trades, exchange their oils and candles for dry goods, and all the varieties of a country store, set their own price, keep their own accounts; and with all this, have very little help in the family to which they must discharge their duties. Look at the heads of those women, they can mingle with men; they are not triflers; they have intelligent subjects of conversation.[51]

Anna Coffin's nontraditional work, along with the Quaker upbringing that emphasized the equality of gifts among men and women, surely contributed to her daughter's assurance of a wide range of possibilities for her life.

Thomas Coffin abandoned his whaling career after a dispute in South America forced him to leave the *Trial* there.[52] In 1804 the family moved to Boston, where Thomas Coffin established a merchandising business. In 1806 the Coffins decided to send Lucretia and her younger sister Eliza, to Nine Partners Boarding School, a Quaker school near Poughkeepsie, New York. She did so well in her studies that after two years she was offered and accepted a position as an assistant teacher of "Reading, Grammar and Arithmetick."[53]

Mott claimed that her interests in abolition and women's rights were established early on. Not only did she receive no salary for her work as an assistant at Nine Partners, she found that women teachers received only half of what was paid to the men. She said later, "The injustice of this distinction was so apparent that I early resolved to claim for my self all that an impartial creator had bestowed." Her concern for the enslaved was established when she and other students were shown books and pictures depicting the horrors of the Middle Passage and the treatment of slaves; as a result, she claimed, "my sympathy was early enlisted for the poor slave."[54]

The painter Kyle succeeded in capturing Lucretia Mott's calm self-assurance in his 1841 portrait of her. *Courtesy Friends Historical Library of Swarthmore College, Swarthmore, Pennsylvania.*

It was also at Nine Partners that Lucretia Coffin met her future husband, James Mott. Mott was also teaching at Nine Partners, having been a student there since the age of nine. In 1809 Lucretia Coffin left Nine Partners and moved with her family to Philadelphia, where Thomas Coffin

James and Lucretia Mott, 1842. Lucretia Mott was the only one of the five women in this book to have married prior to the beginning of her speaking career. She and her husband James were devoted to each other. Prior to one of her preaching journeys in 1834, he wrote to a cousin, "Lucretia will be absent about three weeks, and I am not a whit better reconciled to a separation than I was a year ago,—but must make the best of it" (James Mott to Phebe Post Willis, 23 May 1834). *Courtesy Friends Historical Library of Swarthmore College, Swarthmore, Pennsylvania.*

had purchased a profitable cut nail factory.[55] Shortly thereafter, James Mott followed the Coffins to Philadelphia and Thomas Coffin offered James Mott a partnership in his firm, which he then renamed Coffin and Mott, Merchants. (James Mott later went into business on his own, becoming a domestic commissions merchant.)

After their marriage in 1811, Lucretia and James Mott resided in the Philadelphia area for most of their lives. Like her mother, Lucretia Mott combined her domestic responsibilities, which by 1817 included caring for two children, Anna and Thomas, with work outside her home. That year she and her cousin, Rebecca Bunker, organized a Quaker girls' school under the auspices of the Women Friends of Philadelphia for the Southern District.[56] Shortly thereafter, tragedy struck her family with the sudden death of their son Thomas in April. Mott continued to teach, but eventually resigned her position in February 1818, six weeks before the birth of her third child, Maria.

It was to the death of her son that Mott attributed the beginning of her preaching ministry: "To one of her descendants who asked her, in her old age, how it happened that she became a preacher in the Society, she said, with tears, even then, that her grief at the dear boy's death turned her mind that way, and after a small beginning, meeting with sympathy and encouragement, the rest was gradual and easy."[57] Mott's first recorded public words were in the form of a prayer she offered in her Twelfth Street Meeting that all recognize the necessary presence of the holy spirit in "all our efforts to resist temptation, and overcome the world." In 1821, her Quarterly Meeting concurred with the Monthly Meeting of Women Friends for the Western District of Philadelphia that Lucretia Mott had "a gift in the ministry committed to her" and she was officially designated a Minister in the Society of Friends.[58] Mott received considerable encouragement for her preaching ministry from her own and her husband's family, as well as from other Quakers—a striking contrast to the reception accorded to Sarah Grimké. In one 1818 letter from James Mott's grandfather to his parents, his grandfather asked with interest, "How does Lucretia come on in the preaching line?"[59]

When the American Society of Friends divided in 1827, the Motts became Hicksites, the progressive faction affiliated with Elias Hicks. James was ready to take the Hicksite side immediately; Lucretia hesitated. Her granddaughter's comment was that she was considered so valuable a member that no pains were spared to keep her in the old communion. She hesitated; dear and valued friends were on both sides; and it may be, judging from her experience in her own Society, that she already had some misgivings as to the trammels of all religious associations; she may, perhaps, have sympathized with the feeling that prompted a liberal-minded Friend, who, when asked why he remained in connection with the Orthodox branch, replied, "For the short distance you propose to move, it seems scarcely worth while to get up."[60]

Lucretia Mott was involved in many causes throughout her life, including abolition, temperance, woman's rights and peace. She believed, however, that those most in need of help were the "millions of down-trodden slaves" who were the "greatest sufferers" in the land. So, she said, "when I consecrated myself to that gospel which anoints 'to preach deliverance to the captive,' 'to set at liberty them that are bruised,'" she felt also that she had bound herself "to plead their cause in season and out of season . . . and to give all my aid in my power in every right effort for their immediate emancipation."[61] This belief was strengthened by her first tour of Quaker religious meetings made with another minister, Sarah Zane, in 1818. The two of them traveled to Virginia, and in Mott's first view of plantation slavery, she reported that "the sight of the poor slaves was indeed affecting."[62]

Mott was one of the founders of the Philadelphia Female Anti-Slavery Society in 1833 and served as its president for many years. While her children, who eventually numbered five,[63] were young, she spoke mainly to local assemblies, either Quaker meetings or meetings "with the coloured people at their several places of worship."[64] After her children were older, she traveled more widely around the North and as far south as Washington, D.C., and northern Virginia, visiting other meetings and speaking on the issues that concerned her, slavery being one of the foremost.

Although Lucretia Mott had difficulties with the Society of Friends, she had several advantages that the Grimkés did not. As a birthright Quaker, she probably had more latitude within her meeting. Having her gift as a preacher formally acknowledged also gave her more authority. And, unlike the Grimkés, who severed themselves from the support of their Southern, slave-owning family both geographically and ideologically, Mott's family remained close-knit and supportive of her. Her husband James, although also an abolitionist, seemed to view his role as primarily one of support for his wife's activism. In a comment more typically made of a wife than of a husband, their granddaughter stated that "although he [James Mott] was not so widely known as she, and his field of usefulness in consequence might seem more restricted, yet no one can contemplate [their] lives . . . without realizing that *his* life made *hers* a possibility."[65] James Mott had an immense respect for his wife's judgment, counseling one minister with whom she had disagreed that, "If she thinks thee wrong, thee had better think it over again."[66] Mott's extraordinarily active career, although still remarkable, becomes somewhat more understandable given the support she received from her family.

ABBY KELLEY: "IF HE SENDS ME . . ."

Abby Kelley was born in 1811 in Pelham, Massachusetts, the daughter of Wing and Diana Daniels Kelley.[67] Her father had had two daughters from a previous marriage; Abby was the fifth daughter born to Diana Kelley. Shortly after her birth, her father purchased farmland near Worcester, Massachusetts, and she was raised there. As a child, Abby Kelley was released from many household chores because her parents thought she had a delicate constitution. Encouraged to be outdoors, she gained a reputation as a tomboy, and enjoyed helping her father with his chores.[68]

Like Mott, Abby Kelley was raised a Quaker, receiving religious instruction from her mother, "the strictest of Orthodox Friends."[69] Work and weather permitting, the family attended a Quaker meeting in Uxbridge. In 1822, Wing Kelley sold his farm and bought another, complete with sawmill, in Tatnuck, also near Worcester. Unfortunately this venture did not prosper, and the family struggled to make a living.[70]

At the age of fifteen, Abby Kelley left home for the New England Friends Boarding School in Providence, Rhode Island, determined to help support her family by becoming a teacher. She borrowed her initial tuition money from one of her sisters. Her daughter claimed that she had been told that her mother had "work[ed] so hard over her lessons that the perspiration would stand out on her face as if from hard physical exertion."[71] After her first year she returned home and taught school for two years, earning enough money to repay her sister and pay for an additional year of school.

In 1829, at the age of nineteen, Abby Kelley returned to the Kelley farm and, now the oldest daughter at home, helped support the family by teaching in a nearby school. She also paid for her younger brother and sister's education at the Friends School. Her father's farm continued to do poorly, and with his daughter's encouragement he sold it, raising enough money to pay off his debts and buy a smaller farm in Millbury, six miles from Worcester. Abby Kelley taught at a school in Millbury until she learned of an opening at a Friends' school in Lynn, Massachusetts. So in 1836, at the age of twenty-five, she moved to Lynn, boarding with the Chase family.

Lynn was a town with an active abolitionist contingent. In 1832 Kelley had heard William Lloyd Garrison speak in Worcester, but had had little outlet for her antislavery sentiments there.[72] In Lynn Kelley promptly joined the newly formed Lynn Female Anti-Slavery Society and was elected corresponding secretary. One of her first responsibilities was to go door-to-door collecting signatures on a petition to Congress calling for the prohibition of slavery in the District of Columbia. This was hard work, but by the end of 1837, the society had collected the names of nearly half the women in Lynn.

Toward the end of 1836, Wing Kelley died, and this event, as with the deaths of Lucretia Mott's son, Sarah Grimké's father, and Angelina Grimké's brother and niece, resulted in more intense spiritual reflection. "Father's death," she wrote to her sister Olive, "taught me the necessity of looking beyond earthly things for support."[73] But her spiritual outlook was even then tied to social reform. She continued in the same letter: "My variety is made up in watching the progress of moral enterprises. The temperance reform, embracing Grahamism and Abolition and Peace—and these three questions are sufficient to take up all spare time. 'Tis great joy to see the world grow better in any thing. Indeed I think endeavors to improve mankind is the only object worth living for."

The Grimkés, particularly Angelina, heavily influenced Kelley. Kelley met the sisters at the first Anti-Slavery Convention of American Women held in New York City in May 1837, and persuaded them to make Lynn their first stop in their Massachusetts lecture tour that summer. Later that year, she attended two antislavery meetings with them and, years later, recalled her disappointment when Angelina Grimké refused to raise her voice on some disputed points because, "The brethren will not like it." Kelley, with her deeply instilled Quaker belief in responding to the promptings of the inward light, challenged Angelina: "Is it better to listen to the brethren or to the divine voice in our own souls?"[74]

Kelley began to feel that her active participation in the Lynn Society was not enough and started to consider lecturing herself. Confiding this possibility to her family, she met with disbelief and opposition. She reported that one of her sisters "thought I should render myself quite contemptable [sic] and should not be able to accomplish any good . . . that I have nothing to recommend me to the public." Kelley turned to scripture to meet that objection: "I wish she would read her bible and see if the *great* have ever been the special laborers in the Lord's vineyard. Who were the twelve apostles?—poor fishermen. He who throws his own strength entirely away and puts on the better strength, shall find himself girded for the fiercest battle."[75]

By 1838 Abby Kelley was not yet speaking in public, but she was continuing to devote much of her time and energy to the abolitionist cause, while still teaching in Lynn. As she said,

> I did whatever I could to carry forward the work; circulating petitions
> to the State Legislature and to Congress, distributing our publications,
> soliciting subscriptions to our journals, and raising funds for our soci-
> eties; in the meantime, by private conversation in season and out of
> season explaining our principles and measures, taking more and more
> of the time left from my school duties.[76]

In May 1838 Kelley attended the Second Anti-Slavery Convention of American Women held at the newly built Pennsylvania Hall in Philadelphia. At a public meeting held in the evening she joined Angelina Grimké and Lucretia Mott on the platform and delivered her first public address. Acknowledging the mob outside which was angrily protesting the assembly, she said:

> I have never before addressed a promiscuous assembly. Nor is it now
> the maddening rush of those voices nor the crashing of those windows,
> the indication of a moral earthquake, that calls me before you. No,
> these pass unheeded by me. But it is the still small voice within which
> may not be withstood, that bids me open my mouth for the dumb; that
> bids me plead the cause of God's perishing poor.[77]

After her brief remarks, she left the platform. She was later joined by Theodore Weld, who immediately urged her to enter the lecturing field, saying, "Abby, if you don't, God will smite you!"[78]

Kelley eventually found that "my whole soul was so filled with the subject that it would not leave me in school hours, and I saw I was not giving to this duty what was its due."[79] She resigned her teaching position, a momentous step for one who needed to support herself financially. She went to stay for a time with her mother, who was in poor health. Still uncertain as to her future, she opened the Bible one morning to read a passage at breakfast, and the verses she turned to were First Corinthians 1:26–27. She read: "Not many wise men, after the flesh, not many mighty, not many noble are called; but God hath chosen the foolish things of the world to confound the things which are mighty, and base things of the world, and things which are despised, and things which are not, to bring to naught things that are, that no flesh should glory in his presence."[80] Kelley said later that

> I closed the book and said to my mother: "My way is clear now; a new light has broken on me. How true it is, as history records, that all great reforms have been carried forward by weak and despised means! . . . I will go out among the honest-hearted common people, into the highways and byways, and cry, 'Pity the poor slave!' if I can do nothing more."[81]

From that time on, Kelley dedicated herself almost totally to antislavery work, beginning her lecturing career in Connecticut in 1839. She held sixty-five meetings in her first nine-month tour.[82] In 1845 Kelley married abolitionist Stephen Symonds Foster; their daughter, Paulina Wright (Alla), was born in 1847. Kelley Foster continued to lecture and raise funds for most of the next twenty years, often traveling to the West as well as around the Northeast. Her continuing career will be discussed more fully in the following chapters.

SALLIE HOLLEY: CALLED BY A DIVINE VOICE

The last member of this group is Sallie Holley. In her path to becoming an antislavery lecturer, Sallie Holley had several advantages: she began with religious views that were already unorthodox; also, by the time she began to lecture in the early 1850s, people had become more accustomed to hear-

Lithograph portrait of Abby Kelley Foster in 1846, the year after she married Stephen Foster and the year before she gave birth to their daughter Alla. *Courtesy American Antiquarian Society.*

ing women speak before mixed audiences. Holley's buoyant and appealing personality was yet another factor in her favor.

Holley was born in February 1818 in Canandaigua, New York. She was named for her mother, but that appears to have been one of the few legacies she claimed from her—she even changed the spelling of her name

Sallie Holley, about 1852. Just beginning her lecturing career, she reported from Wilmington, Delaware, that "a crowded town hall listened with great respect; some slaveholders present; collection $7.06! Quite a surprise to the anti-slavery folks here" (to Caroline Putnam, 31 Oct. 1852, Holley, *A Life for Liberty*, 98).

from Sally to Sallie. We know little more about Sally House Holley than that she bore twelve children, raised eight of them to adulthood, and remained a Methodist while her husband and daughter espoused a form of Unitarianism. Although Sallie Holley continued to visit her mother long after her beloved father's death, she rarely mentioned her mother, either in praise or blame, in her extant letters. Our knowledge of Sally House Holley's death is gained not from her daughter's correspondence but from John White Chadwick, the editor of her daughter's letters, who commented that she died in June 1868 at the age of eighty-two "suddenly ending a life of splendid health and practical efficiency."[83]

Sallie Holley's silence about her mother is more puzzling given her loquaciousness about her father, to whom she was clearly devoted. Myron Holley was a man of apparently meager business aptitude, avid political conviction, and unorthodox religious persuasion. He was one of the founders of the antislavery third party, the Liberty Party. He pursued a variety of occupations, from bookstore owner to commissioner of the Erie Canal to truck farmer. Having taken on the additional responsibility of acting as treasurer of the Canal project, he left that position in disgrace in 1824 after being unable to account for a missing $30,000 of canal funds. In 1821 the Holley family had moved to a pleasant home in Lyons, New York, one of the new villages that grew up along the Canal. After Myron Holley's fiscal disaster, the family stayed in Lyons but moved to a smaller house, while he attempted to clear himself of criminal charges. Four years later the New York State Assembly voted to exonerate Holley, and the assets that he had assigned to the state in the interim were returned to him. His business problems did not lessen his daughter's devotion to her "dear sainted father."[84]

Myron Holley was described as being Unitarian, but he was not affiliated with any congregation. Instead he regularly held his own religious services for the benefit of his family and others. Sallie Holley attributed her own deep religious faith to her father's influence. "Nothing," she said, "impressed me more, as I grew into young-womanhood, than my father's earnest religious conviction, ever ardent, alive, and all-controlling."[85] Myron Holley also eschewed the popular revival conversion experiences. When the teacher at Sallie's day school in Lyons brought in exhorters to convince the girls of their sinful state and their need for repentance, Myron Holley wrote her a scathing letter. He demanded that she confine herself to academics and not fill his daughter with the "fear, grief, or gloom" of

Calvinism.[86] In her teens in the early 1830s, Sallie Holley went to Rochester to live with the Child family, where she served as a companion to Mrs. Child, an invalid. There she began to learn about the antislavery movement, reading a local antislavery newspaper, the *Rights of Man*. At the same time her father became more involved in the abolitionist cause. Having moved the family to their new truck farm in the Rochester area, Myron Holley sold vegetables during the day and lectured as an agent of the New York Anti-Slavery Society in the evenings. Diverging from the Garrisonian path of abstention from party politics, Holley also campaigned on behalf of the Liberty Party.[87]

Myron Holley continued to accumulate debts as he worked on behalf of his causes. Having moved his family again in December of 1840, this time into a rented house in Rochester, Holley died unexpectedly in March 1841. Sally House Holley, his widow, moved near Buffalo to live with one of her married sons. Sallie Holley stayed in Rochester, now living with the Porter family, and began to teach school.[88] Her first class was a group of sixty immigrant Irish girls. Interestingly, one month after her father's death, she also chose to be baptized in a Unitarian church in Buffalo, New York. Because of the lack of records, we do not know why she did this at this particular time. Perhaps her father's death stimulated her religious consciousness, as was the case with the other women here. She may have been looking for a substitute for the religious inspiration her father had provided. Or perhaps the death of her father, a man who had chosen not to affiliate with an institutional religious body, simply freed her to seek membership in the denomination whose theology most closely paralleled hers.

Sallie Holley taught for several years, and also, according to Chadwick, lived for a time in Monroe, Michigan, with one of her brothers. In 1847 she accepted the suggestion and the financial support of some of her New York friends, and enrolled in the Female Department at Oberlin College. This was over the objections of at least one of her brothers who urged her not to attend that "nigger school" (Oberlin having made the decision to admit African American as well as Euro-American students).[89] Like Kelley, she worked to help finance her education, washing dishes, baking bread, caring for children, sewing, and tutoring.[90]

Holley's experience at Oberlin highlights the religious tensions within the abolitionist movement. Oberlin was founded in 1833 as a missionary outpost for education in the West. On the verge of collapsing because of lack of students, it was saved by an influx of students from Lane Seminary in Cincinnati—abolitionists who left Lane under the guidance of Theodore Weld. Despite this early history of radical political commitment, Oberlin resisted some of the more radical impulses within mid-nineteenth-century Protestantism and remained a stronghold of evangelicalism.[91] In the abolitionist schism of 1840, Oberlin, with its strong ties to the Tappans, sided with the conservative, more evangelical faction rather than with the Garrisonians, who were more likely to be comeouters than staunch church members. Comeouters were those who applied to the Christian churches of their day the Apostle Paul's dictum to "be ye not unequally yoked with unbelievers" but rather "come out from among them, and be ye separate."[92] Their view was that the corruption of the churches was so complete as to make reform from within impossible.

Among the radical abolitionists, Oberlin acquired an aura of theological conservatism and rigidity. Sarah Grimké wrote of a friend who was sending her children to Oberlin: "I hardly understand how her [Esther Wattles] free mind and elevated spirit can brook the strict, hard, old theology of Oberlin."[93] Lucretia Mott told Sallie Holley that Mrs. Gage had written to Oberlin "with a view of sending her daughter there. She received an answer saying they would 'be very happy to receive her daughter and particularly at this time, as a very interesting revival was in progress and the daughter might be hopefully converted.' That decided Mrs. Gage against sending her daughter there."[94]

Despite its position as the first coeducational college in the nation, Oberlin did not support greatly expanded roles for women.[95] Oberlin had strong ties to Lewis Tappan, one of the foremost of the evangelical abolitionists, who held traditional views about women's roles. Chadwick even speculated that, had the schism in the antislavery movement, which allowed Tappan and others to dissociate themselves from the endorsement of women's expanded roles, occurred prior to the founding of the college, women probably would not have been admitted at all.[96] Nonetheless, despite the restrictions imposed on them, women like Sallie Holley (and also Lucy Stone and Antoinette Brown Blackwell) profited from their years there; Holley referred in 1863 to her Oberlin experience as "the grandest event of my life."[97] Sallie Holley's unorthodox religious background made her conspicuous at Oberlin. Chadwick notes, commenting on the difference between her faith and the typical revivalist conversions against which her father had railed, that the "orthodox people at Oberlin, teachers and students . . . could not understand how anyone so earnestly religious [as Holley] could be so without their experience of enmity against God and rejection of his Son"—anger and rejection of God being a common and expected step in the conversion process. She seems, though, to have been comfortable at Oberlin, asserting her independence when necessary and emphasizing her concurrence with the prevailing views where possible. On one occasion she assured some other students, to their surprise, that she intended to take communion—if, that is, she were allowed to pray with the other communicants. She told them, "[n]othing is so sacred as prayer, and if you allow me to pray with you I shall certainly take the communion, and nothing but Mr. Finney's coming down from the pulpit and seizing the bread and wine shall prevent me."[98] At other times she challenged the status quo, as when she protested that dancing was no more sinful than the calisthenics taught at Oberlin. She also objected to her boardinghouse mistress attending prayer meetings twice a day, thinking it "poor religion for her to do these things and neglect her family and boarders, leaving for them skimmed milk and scanty food while she was drinking in 'the sincere milk of the Word,' and battening on the bread of life."[99] Holley's earnest desire was, she said, "to be established immovably in the very spirit and principles of the Divine Master. My life falls far short of my ideal, yet I think I can apprehend something of the beauty and glory of a truly Christian life."[100]

Meeting Caroline Putnam was undoubtedly one of the "grandest events" of Holley's Oberlin career.[101] Putnam had been raised in a more Calvinist tradition, but her views on abolition and women's roles matched Holley's. Together they rented a carriage and attended the woman's rights convention in Akron in 1851. They also attended antislavery meetings together.

Like the other women in this study, Holley could not separate faith from worldly events, and she felt particularly strongly about slavery. Despite her father's Liberty Party affiliation, Sallie Holley moved toward the Garrisonian position. Her decision to become an antislavery lecturer was a spontaneous one. In the summer of 1850 she attended an antislavery convention in Litchfield, Ohio, and heard Abby Kelley Foster make an "urgent appeal in behalf of the wronged and fearfully outraged slave women." At that moment, Holley "felt called by a Divine Voice to plead her cause—and with instant yieldings to the hitherto undreamt-of command, said 'I *will*.' After the meetings she spoke with Mrs. Foster, and told her she would answer that call!"[102]

Kelley Foster invited Holley to accompany her immediately; Holley declined, promising to join Kelley after finishing her studies at Oberlin. Kelley Foster was skeptical of Holley's burst of enthusiasm, but Holley did as she promised. She continued to attend antislavery meetings, and spoke at one in Litchfield in 1851.[103] In August of that year she accepted an invitation from the free black community in Sandusky to speak at their celebration of West Indian Emancipation Day. She submitted a request to the Ladies' Board of the College for permission to attend. Permission was granted with the proviso that she not stay "in a colored man's house" for fear of adverse publicity for the school. Holley replied that she felt it to be her duty to accept such an invitation "as a testimony to my principles and, really, to those professed by this institution"—and she did so.[104] That year she also resigned her Unitarian membership, believing that the church supported Millard Fillmore, who had become president upon Zachary Taylor's death in office. "I think," she wrote to Caroline Putnam, "that I cannot consent that my name shall stand on the books of a church which will countenance voting for any pro-slavery presidential candidate. Think of a woman-whipper and a baby-stealer being countenanced as a Christian? My anti-slavery sympathies burn stronger and stronger."[105]

In the fall of 1851, after her graduation from Oberlin, Holley began her lecturing career. Although she had reservations about her own skill as a speaker, she plunged into her work. She began as an independent lecturer, but her earnest and pleasant manner made her so popular that by November the American Anti-Slavery Society invited her to become an official agent. Holley accepted the offer, which included a salary of ten dollars per week plus expenses, and her first official tour was launched the same month.

Caroline Putnam accompanied her on her first two tours but then returned to her family home in Farmersville for the next two years. Holley continued her travels, reporting the following fall that "[t]oday I was entertaining myself making out a memorandum of all the places and times I had lectured. I made out one hundred and fifty-six times."[106] She loved her work and her encounters with other abolitionists. During her first tour she wrote to friends that "My love and interest in the great cause increases and swells and brightens every hour. It does seem to me that I have at last found out my 'sphere.'"[107]

2 ❧

"A Bodyguard of Hearts"

THE ANTISLAVERY LECTURERS AND
THE BUILDING OF ABOLITIONIST COMMUNITY

NGELINA GRIMKÉ WROTE to Sarah Mapps Douglass after her second address to the Legislative Committee of the Massachusetts
legislature in February 1838: "It has been an inexpressible comfort and strength to me to find how deeply the Abolitionists here have sympathized with me and how they have been bound in exercise and prayer
with me. I did not expect it to the extent to which it has been manifested. I
feel that when I am speaking I am surrounded by *a body guard of hearts*
faithful and true and by the atmosphere of prayer."[1] Likewise, Sallie Holley
wrote, "You cannot know how richly rewarded I feel, how full my enjoyment is, in going about with these anti-slavery friends."[2]

Other abolitionists shared in this sense of camaraderie. John White
Chadwick, the editor of Holley's letters, described an evening he passed at
the home of John and Hannah Cox in Longwood, Pennsylvania. Lucretia
Mott was there; also, William Lloyd Garrison. Chadwick noted: "There
never was a happier company, and I am well assured that it gave a very just
impression of the average gathering of anti-slavery leaders and followers
when they were in the thick of the fight. They were no solemn, sour-faced
Puritans, but folk of kindly disposition, serenely confident that they were
engaged in a good work and that the good time was 'coming right along.'"[3]

Although becoming an antislavery activist in any capacity opened
the door to participation in this community, women who became antislavery lecturers were a unique group. These women shared a bond they themselves acknowledged both professionally and personally. They socialized
with one another and corresponded to and about one another as peers.
Though the details of their biographies differ, certain themes are repeated
again and again in each of their lives. Each woman was committed to seek-

ing religious truth. Each came to an understanding of divine purpose that included attention to the physical well-being of others as well as to her own personal piety. Each believed herself called to a mission focused, although not exclusively so, on racial justice. Although these women had already developed a commonality of intellectual and spiritual convictions, their lives began to converge in a visible way as each adopted public speaking as a fundamental part of her mission.

The developing primary relationships among the subjects of this book are revealed in their personal correspondence. Throughout their careers, all these women casually mention encounters with one another. Abby Kelley socialized with the Grimkés before and after Angelina's marriage. She also corresponded with Lucretia Mott and Sallie Holley. The Grimkés often visited with the Motts when they were in Philadelphia. Lucretia Mott's daughter, Maria Mott Davis, also mentioned an occasion in 1838 on which the Grimkés failed to attend an evening party hosted by the Motts at which the Grimkés—the "lions," as Davis referred to them—were to be the guests of honor.[4] Sallie Holley visited the Grimkés, the Fosters, and the Motts. Sarah Grimké wrote after one such occasion: "We had a delightful visit from Sally Holly [sic]. It is so kind in such women to come and see us. She is a noble looking woman and I should very much like to hear her lecture."[5]

A significant reason for the development of their camaraderie was their shared religious convictions. After visiting the Grimké-Welds, Abby Kelley confessed that she had been moved by the "spirit of love pervading all their daily [work?] and conversation—a broad mantle of charity which to me is pretty good evidence that they are seeking to walk in the right way. . . . I think I never passed a week more profitably. It was a school which called into exercise almost every better principle and feeling of the heart."[6] Sallie Holley visited the Grimké-Welds in 1852 and wrote disparagingly of their looks and dress, but glowingly of their conversation:

> Angelina and Sarah are full of mental vigour. They talk much of the great principles of life—how human life can be made harmonious and beautiful. . . . Sarah is deeply interesting in conversation but *shockity* in personal appearance. She reminds one of Charles Lamb's "Mrs. Conrady," where he attempts the refutation of the popular fallacy, "Handsome is that handsome does." Neither can you say of Sarah Grimké "I think I have seen that face before, somewhere, but can't tell where." Seeing her

is an event of your life. It is like seeing Stonehenge. Both the ladies wear the "American costume." Such forlornities! But then their talk! Oh, it is angels' food! Not coarse, earthly fare, such as most people set before you. How you would expand and grow under such ideas.[7]

Their acceptance of the bond they shared shows itself in the way these women felt free to advise and chastise as well to support each other. Even their casual references to and about one another show an acknowledgment of a particular relationship. With Angelina Grimké's belief that it is "right that we should be tried in every way in order to prove our faithfulness," her reactions to the persecution faced by her colleagues should not come as a surprise. Upon hearing that Lucretia Mott was having difficulties with the Quakers, Grimké wrote that she was glad, for "I *know* it is good to suffer thus, the heart is made more single and cleaner—still closer to the blessed cause, when we have bought the privilege of laboring in it by sacrifice."[8] She responded the same way in 1838 when Abby Kelley faced difficulties, saying, "Perhaps it was all for the best that Abby had to stand alone. I know how strengthening it is to feel that we have no arm of flesh to lean on, and for her sake I rejoice in her loneliness."[9] Sallie Holley, who did not share Grimké's view of the salutary effects of martyrdom, wrote in 1852 that she had hoped to attend a Quaker meeting in Philadelphia because "I hear the Quakers are tightening the ecclesiastical screws upon Lucretia Mott more than ever. She will continue to be a faithful witness to all their shortcomings, to their excessive annoyance."[10]

These women found it natural to move between the personal and the professional in their relationships, readily acknowledging a social intimacy as well as holding one another to a high standard of responsibility within the antislavery movement.[11] In 1839 Abby Kelley visited the Grimkés in order to "rebuke them severely for absenting themselves from the N.Y. meeting." She withdrew her professional demand, however, in light of her personal concern in finding that "Angelina is truly very feeble" and Sarah was needed within the household.[12] In June of the same year Lucretia Mott came to see Angelina Grimké Weld while the latter was visiting in Philadelphia. Mott read Grimké Weld "an exceedingly interesting letter" from C. C. Burleigh, who had been asked to take a position with a new Massachusetts Antislavery Society. Grimké Weld not only opposed that step because of Burleigh's poor health, she also held Lucretia Mott somewhat accountable for his condition: "I told L. very seriously that I did not think she had ever felt as deeply as she ought the responsibility which rested upon *her* about CCB. He looked up to her as a mother and she never had restrained his speaking as she ought."[13] The Grimké-Mott chiding went the other direction as well. From the World's Anti-Slavery Convention in London in 1840, Elizabeth Cady Stanton passed along a message to the Grimkés from Lucretia Mott "which condensed is that she thinks you have both been in a state of reticency [?] long enough, and that it is not right for you to be still, longer; that you should either write for the public or speak out for *oppressed* woman. Sarah in particular she thinks should appear in public again as she has no duties to prevent her."[14]

Another significant role these women played for one another and for other women was that of mentor. The Grimkés, along with Angelina's husband, Theodore Weld, sponsored and encouraged Abby Kelley in her decision to begin public speaking. When the Grimkés were catapulted to leadership within the women's abolitionist movement in 1837, Abby Kelley was one of a number of young women who looked to them for direction. Early that year, Kelley had written to Angelina Grimké, telling her of the good effect her *Appeal to the Christian Women of the South* had had in Lynn. Grimké responded with thanks, and shared some comments on her disillusionment with the Society of Friends in regard to racial equality.[15] Later in the year, Kelley, an increasingly ardent activist, not only attended one of the Grimkés' meetings, but conveyed them to and from it in a carriage.[16] She was invited to and attended Angelina Grimké's wedding in May of 1838.

Soon after, Kelley began to think seriously of lecturing herself, and it was the Grimké-Welds to whom she turned for advice. From their new home in Fort Lee, New Jersey, Sarah Grimké commended Kelley for having spoken up at the Fifth New England Anti-Slavery Convention: "[i]t seems to me very important that some N[ew] E[ngland] women should practically assert the right to speak in public."[17] Kelley confided to the three her hesitations about public speaking: "I have prayed most earnestly that this cup might pass from me, not feeling that I could drink it. . . . I have not the gift. How can I make bricks without straw? I have waited thus long, hoping that I should be excused. No excuse comes. I *must* go and yet *how can I*?"[18]

Angelina Grimké Weld responded in a long letter, addressed to "My Dear Abby." In it she described her own initial fears and hesitations, adding, "This will show thee that thou art not alone in the opposition and difficulties thou meetest, nor in the feeling of *inability* for the work."[19]

A similar relationship developed between Sallie Holley and Abby Kelley. Kelley served as inspiration and mentor to Holley, just as the Grimkés had for Kelley. Holley revered Kelley; Kelley, for her part, was extraordinarily grateful to have found another woman willing to take up lecturing in the antislavery cause. Caroline Putnam described the occasion when Abby Kelley Foster first heard Sallie Holley speak: "Mrs. Foster was in the front pew with me. She frequently drew her handkerchief from her muff to her face—as I tho't, because of the cold she had taken."[20] Afterward, however, Kelley Foster came to their hotel room and

> poured forth her gratitude and benediction—in words like these—"I could but weep, and *weep,* and WEEP all the evening! I have laid prostrate before the throne, thanking God and rejoicing, that when my voice had grown so husky, and I was so nearly worn out, we had at last raised you up so fresh, so earnest, so devoted, and so well prepared for a powerful work." She said "I had expected a great deal from you—but this is a great deal *more,* you have far exceeded all my expectations!"[21]

The relationship between Holley and Kelley Foster did not end with this occasion. Holley repeatedly begged Kelley Foster to travel with her, saying that Kelley Foster was one of the few lecturers before whom she did not mind revealing her own inadequacies. Holley visited Stephen and Abby Kelley Foster at their home in Worcester and enjoyed her acquaintance with their daughter Alla. Her letters to Kelley Foster generally consisted of a mixture of professional concerns and personal anecdotes. In one letter, she spoke of some of her concerns about the antislavery movement but then went on to share a story from her recent travels:

> Now I will try to amuse you a little. Just before we left N.Y. State we staid where our hostess *smoked* indefatigably. In an apologetic explanation, she told us it was for the Quinsy to which she was subject, and reported the following gratifying result. Formerly she had *four* attacks in the year. She has smoked *14 years* and for the *last two years,* she has had only *three a year!!* Don't you think the case ought to go in the Medical books[?][22]

The influence of these women also extended farther out into the world. Although they related to both women and men, it is their impact on women that is most apparent. Elizabeth Cady Stanton corresponded with both the Grimkés and Lucretia Mott. Elizabeth Smith Miller, daughter of Gerrit Smith and a women's rights activist, corresponded with Sarah Grimké and Sallie Holley. Lucy Stone, the women's rights and antislavery activist, was a correspondent of both Abby Kelley Foster and Lucretia Mott. Angelina Grimké Weld's closest confidante, Jane Smith, provided a connection to Philadelphia friends. Abby Kelley kept in close contact with Maria Weston Chapman, her link to the Boston network. Caroline Putnam corresponded with many of the antislavery activists, keeping them informed of Sallie Holley's work and reporting their communications as well. Lucretia Mott maintained a long and intimate correspondence with her sister Martha Coffin Wright in which family matters were intertwined with reform issues.

The Mott home was the scene of many convivial gatherings. The Motts frequently entertained out-of-town guests; Lucretia Mott wrote to her cousin once that "[w]e have had less company than usual this winter more than a week has passed repeatedly without a lodger."[23] In 1837 the Motts moved to a home in which the dining room could seat fifty people. In her letters to her sister Martha, Lucretia Mott frequently conveyed both her personal enjoyment of her guests and her appreciation of the spiritual and intellectual stimulation they afforded.

The Grimkés in particular excelled at merging the personal with the professional. Writing to Queen Victoria to enlist her support for the American antislavery movement, Angelina Grimké did not hesitate to address Her Majesty as "sister."[24] Likewise, she admonished the acclaimed historian George Bancroft, as did Sarah Grimké the well-known Unitarian minister William Ellery Channing, for their errors on the subject of slavery. Their letters to these men were, however, couched in a kind but stern manner more reminiscent of authoritative elder sisters than of biting social critics.[25]

The relationship between Sallie Holley and Caroline Putnam is perhaps the most striking example of a transcendence of boundaries between the personal and social and the professional and political. After becoming intimates at Oberlin College, they spent much of the rest of their lives together. Putnam often traveled with Holley, although she herself declined to take any part in public speaking. She did, however, keep the broader antislavery movement abreast of Holley's activities, and also proselytized on a smaller level, visiting homes as a colporteur (a distributor of tracts) on behalf of the cause. As one correspondent to the *Liberator* put it, "Miss Putnam has a mission to visit families, as clearly as Miss Holley to address public assemblies."[26] They corresponded frequently while apart. Holley referred to Putnam by two different nicknames, the logical "Carrie," and more familiarly, "Putty."[27] Among an assortment of loving exchanges between the two is a letter Holley wrote to Putnam in 1861. She exclaimed that "my heart yearns toward you this morning, and the heaviest disappointment of my life would fall if you should die. Again and again I thank you for all your love to me. . . . How I should love to put my arms around your neck and kiss you!"[28]

For her part, Caroline Putnam idolized Sallie Holley. One of the reasons for this was her respect for Holley's religious convictions. "I never have in all my life," she wrote,

> felt more fully the extent of my obligation to you, how large is my indebtedness to the Truth you had received before me—and of which you became the Interpreter to me, nor never have I so earnestly longed to make such a personal expression of love and thankfulness, as I do now. . . . I believe you will "see, (some day) of the travail of your soul" with me, and "be *satisfied*"! At all events, I intreat [sic] your farther— and always (never ending) friendly faithfulness towards me, however ungraciously I may receive it at the time.[29]

When she was asked by one woman if she did not get tired of hearing Holley speak, Putnam answered by "asking her if she got tired of hearing the New Testament." Putnam believed that the questioner "would not have queried thus had she ever shared one of these consecrated hours."[30]

Holley offered another glimpse into her relationship with Putnam in a letter to Abby Kelley Foster. Foster evidently had written of her admiration for the absence of differences between Holley and Putnam. Holley replied, "I must say you were never more mistaken. As Charles Lamb said of himself and [his] sister, 'we have our bickerings, as should be among such near friends.'" She went on to describe how their relationship precluded their humoring each other with that "unmeaning, lazy sort of intercourse that passes in society under the gracious name of *amiability*, when in reality it is only mock virtue."[31] These two women clearly had the closest of relationships, holding each other to a high standard of emotional intimacy and integrity while they both worked on behalf of the antislavery cause.

Ironically, an important factor in unifying the women lecturers was the opposition they faced. Sarah Grimké remarked that "the ministry are in many places our warmest opposers, even where they profess abolition, they are generally averse to women's preaching."[32] The other women also shared in the Grimkés' experience that "[s]ometimes a sermon would be preached after we left a place to prove how grossly we were violating Bible principles and female delicacy. Sometimes they were preached when it was rumored we were coming to such or such a town."[33] Sarah Grimké once reported that they had "had the promise of a large Cong[regational] Ch[urch] for our meeting on 6th day, but the minister who had been absent returned and said if *we* went into his pulpit *he* never would again, so of course we could not obtain it."[34]

Abby Kelley, who was known for her blunt and uncompromising—that is to say, unfeminine—speaking style, received a considerable amount of abuse. On one occasion in Washington, Connecticut, she was received so positively that she agreed to return in two weeks. In the meantime, a local minister returned to town. Learning about Kelley's visit, he "preached a sermon on the text, Rev. 11–20, 'I have a few things against thee, because thou sufferest that woman, Jezebel, which calleth herself a prophetess, to teach and to seduce my servants to commit fornication.'" When Kelley returned as promised, she attended a prayer meeting and was not invited to speak. When the meeting ended, "not one of those whom I had met on my former visit [with one exception] . . . gave me a hand or a look, but passed me as if I had been a block."[35] On other occasions Kelley was publicly condemned as an infidel. Once she was told that a minister had described her—prior to having ever seen her—as having "brass enough in my face to make a fine-pail kettle."[36]

Unlike the others', Lucretia Mott's preaching ministry had been endorsed by the Society of Friends and she spoke most often to groups of Quakers rather than to the general public. But she, too, met with hostility. In 1840 she traveled to Delaware to hold a series of meetings, accompanied by Daniel and Rebecca Neall.[37] In Smyrna, where "reports of their being 'abolitionists' and 'dangerous and incendiary characters'" had circulated, stones were thrown at their carriage. At their lodging at a local Friend's house, a group of men came to the door and took Daniel Neall away, saying that they wanted him to "answer for his disorganizing doctrines." Mott wrote later, "I pled hard with them to take me as I was the offender if offense had been committed . . . but they declining said 'you are a woman and we have nothing to say to you'—to which I answered 'I ask no courtesy at your hands on account of my sex.'" Her appeals seemed to have had some effect, though, because "after a very moderate tarring and feathering, they allowed him to rejoin his friends without further persecution."[38] In this case, Lucretia Mott's courage and the disinclination of these men to deal with a woman saved her and her companion from serious injury. The threat of violence, however, was always present for the antislavery agents, male and female.

Opposition to Mott's preaching ministry came from within as well as without the Society of Friends. Orthodox Quakers shunned her because of her Hicksite affiliation. When she and other women delegates were denied their seats as delegates to the World's Antislavery Convention held in London in 1840, it was thought that this was due at least as much to her being a Hicksite as to her being female. And even her fellow Hicksites often did not approve of her antislavery activism. On one of her journeys a Quaker physician refused to treat her for an illness, saying, "Lucretia, I am so deeply afflicted by thy rebellious spirit, that I do not feel that I can prescribe for thee."[39]

Some of their opponents structured their arguments on the elevated ground of divine intention and scripture. Other reactions were more coarse or more directly aimed at particular individuals. Some journalists vented their anger in ridicule. In 1837, after the first Anti-Slavery Convention of American Women, the *New York Commercial Advertiser* mocked the absurd aspirations of the participants:

> Yes, most unbelieving reader, it is a fact of most ludicrous solemnity, that "our female brethren" have been lifting up their voices. The spinster has thrown aside her distaff—the blooming beauty her guitar—the matron her darning needle—the sweet novelist her crow-quill; the young mother has left her baby to nestle alone in the cradle—and the kitchen maid her pots and frying pans—to discuss the weighty matters of state—to decide upon intricate questions of international policy.[40]

"A BODYGUARD OF HEARTS" ∽

When Angelina Grimké made history by addressing the Legislative Committee of the Massachusetts state legislature in 1838, the *Pittsburgh Manufacturer* commented that "Miss Grimké is very likely in search of a lawful protector who will take her for 'better or worse' for life, and she has thus made a bold dash among the yankee-law-makers."[41]

The charge that Angelina Grimké was searching for a husband was minor compared to the accusations of sexual licentiousness sometimes directed toward women lecturers, as though the indecency of public speech went hand in glove with all other forms of perceived misconduct. In 1853, the usually indomitable Kelley Foster reported from Plymouth, Michigan, that had she known how she and her husband would be received, she might not have come: "It is only a few days since a member of a Pres[byterian] church who was at one of our Sunday meetings, was overheard by one of our friends, to say that I had formerly taken up with a 'great buck nigger,' and after getting tired of him, took up with Foster, and by and by, I should get tired of Foster and take up with somebody else."[42] Kelley Foster was a particular target of such rumors. In 1857 Lucy Colman reported a woman's response to her assurance that Colman was indeed a "Kellyite": "'Why,' said she, 'do you think she is right, or can be trusted upon this question, when she boldly advocates no marriage, lives sometimes with Stephen Foster, and sometimes with other gentlemen?'"[43]

Unfortunately for the critics, instead of silencing these women, the public persecution of them resulted in their drawing together as a group around which supporters mobilized. One prominent abolitionist minister, for example, wrote scornfully to his wife of the fears raised by the Grimkés among his fellow clergymen: "They are all agog because two quaker women *talk in meetings*! . . . Poor souls! They would do well to put on petticoats and [be] done with it. Indeed I suspect *diapers* would not be amiss on some of them! It is really humiliating to see *men* behave as some of our good ministers do."[44]

The reactions of many others also displayed their support. A letter from a Miss Gould gives some idea of the depth of positive reactions to Abby Kelley. After Kelley's visit to her town, she wrote that Kelley was accused of "corrupting the minds of the youth; enticing them from the path of rectitude; beguiling them from the church; and so perverting their understandings by thy sophistry, as to lead them to discard all religion, etc." Gould's indignant response was: "Corrupting the minds of the youth—Ah yes! some of the youthful minds in this vicinity, have become so corrupted, so perverted, that they begin to look with suspicious eyes upon the Church, recreant and reprobate to the cause of Christ; and are beginning to undervalue a birthright, from such a Parent." Miss Gould, who had not been "prepared to love . . . not even to respect" Abby Kelley because of the "calumny and slander" that had preceded Kelley's visit was clearly a convert both to Kelley's point of view and to Kelley herself. Having heard one of her church's Elders say, "All I wish is, Abby Kelly [sic] had never come here," she responded simply: "All I wish, said my soul in reply, is that she had come before, and would come again."[45]

Lucy Stone was another Abby Kelley convert. When the Fosters spoke at Oberlin College, which Stone was attending at the time, Stone wrote soon after, saying that she could "never feel sufficiently thankful that you came to Oberlin." She closed her letter with sentiments very similar to Miss Gould's: "I wish I *could tell* you, how much *good*, I received from your visit here. My heart dances gaily at the remembrance—it will be *long* before I shall be *so cheered* again.—but never mind, this is not a world to sit down, and *whimper* in, though it is *very pleasant* to have kindred spirits to sympathise with us. With *much love,* and a *kiss* for *both.* Your friend, Lucy Stone."[46] At a much greater physical distance, the Philadelphia abolitionist Esther Moore wrote, "I love Abby Kelley tho unseen my heart responds to every word she utters so far as I know them."[47]

Sarah Mapps Douglass, a black Philadelphia school teacher who felt that most white abolitionists continued to be prejudiced against African Americans, was particularly appreciative of the friendship of Abby Kelley and the Grimkés. Of the Grimkés she wrote: "Did all the members of Friends Society feel for us, as the Sisters Grimké do, how soon, how very soon, would the fetters be stricken from the captive and cruel prejudice be driven from the bosoms of the professed followers of Christ! . . . [T]hey saw our low estate. . . they lifted us from the dust and poured the oil of consolation . . . into our lacerated bosoms."[48]

Encouragement for these women was provided not only by individuals, but by organized groups. Female Anti-Slavery Societies provided the backbone of support for the women lecturers, particularly in the case of the Grimkés, issuing numerous letters commending their work. Their speaking was endorsed by the larger societies, such as the Boston and Philadelphia Female Anti-Slavery Societies, as well as by smaller societies. Their supporters were particularly conscious of the courage of their public actions and honored them for it.[49]

The proceedings of the three Anti-Slavery Conventions of American Women, held in 1837, 1838, and 1839, also indicate that the largest assemblies of antislavery women elevated the lecturers to positions of authority and followed their lead on particular issues. At the 1837 convention, for example, Lucretia Mott served as chair, Sarah Grimké as vice-president, and Angelina Grimké as one of the secretaries. Abby Kelley attended as a delegate. This first convention was led by these women and by Lydia Maria Child, well known because of her published antislavery works. The latter set the underlying religious tone for the convention by introducing the first resolution, establishing antislavery as the "cause of God." Of the thirty-two substantive resolutions introduced and adopted, Child alone introduced fourteen; another fourteen were introduced by Lucretia Mott, Angelina Grimké, or Sarah Grimké; one was introduced by Abby Kelley. Only three resolutions were introduced by the other 169 participants.

The resolutions passed at this convention laid the theoretical foundation of women's antislavery activism. Among other things, they called on "woman to move in that sphere which Providence has assigned her . . . to do all that she can by her voice, and her pen, and her purse, and the influence of her example, to overthrow . . . slavery." Other resolutions introduced by the Grimkés established that economic causes underlay the institution of slavery and that prejudice was a "pillar" supporting it.[50]

In 1838, at the Second Convention of American Anti-Slavery Women, again Lucretia Mott, Sarah Grimké, and Angelina Grimké Weld served as officers of the convention, and Abby Kelley attended as a delegate. Again these women had a large impact on the business of the convention. Lucretia Mott opened the meeting; Kelley and the Grimkés proposed seven of the nineteen resolutions adopted by the convention. This year also the resolutions tended to stress the religious foundation of their antislavery convictions, their objection to sectarianism and to sectarian passivity on the slavery issue, and the duty of abolitionists to combat prejudice as well as slavery itself.[51] By 1839, the leadership of the convention had become more diffuse (owing to illness, the Grimkés did not attend) but the tenor of the resolutions remained the same, indicating the widespread acceptance of the path laid down by the earlier leaders.[52]

Across the Atlantic, the lecturers had a similar impact. In December of 1836, an English Quaker named Elizabeth Pease penned a deferential letter to Angelina Grimké on behalf of the newly formed Darlington Ladies' Anti-Slavery Society. "Dear Friend," Pease began,

> Altho' personally unacquainted I feel something like an assurance that my motive will be accepted as a sufficient apology for thus venturing to trespass on thy time and attention. Thy name is become so familiar to us in connection with the noblest object which can engage the attention of mankind, the cause of the enslaved, that I am ready to believe thou will kindly forgive even a stranger for addressing thee on a subject which ought to be dear to every Christian heart.

Pease asked for guidance from Grimké in determining the direction of their new society:

> We are few in number but [so] anxiously desirous to direct our feeble efforts to the most advantage, that any hints from one so competent as thyself to give advice and information would be invaluable, and would be most gratefully received. . . . Accept my heart felt desires for the prosperity of the great work, and my sympathy with thee in thy labors and sacrifices in its behalf, and allow me to subscribe myself
> thy very sincere friend Eliz'th Pease[53]

In response to Pease's letter, Angelina Grimké penned a firm reply delineating actions Englishwomen might undertake in support of American abolitionism (as she had in her *Appeal to the Christian Women of the South*).[54] She began with a request for prayer on the part of her English sisters:

> Give to the Slaves of Republican Americans your sympathy and your prayers. I have great faith in the power of prayer to move the arm which wields the destinies of worlds. I have *no* faith in any efforts without this spiritual scaling ladder by which we can ascend in spirit to the very throne of Jehovah and present our petitions through the mediation of Jesus for his suffering representatives on Earth.[55]

Her other requests included "keep[ing] the subject of American Slavery continually before the British public," and convincing them that this slavery was an idolatrous horror worse than any heathen act because it was being committed by those who claimed to be Christians. Grimké asked that the Darlington society pass resolutions opposing slavery and direct them to American female antislavery societies; women at large; churches and clergy; and even children, whom she said might "be addressed with great effect now, for they are beginning to form themselves into associations to lisp the wrongs of the slave, and to throw their pennies into the coffers of the National Society."

The Darlington society did act on Grimké's suggestions. Pease continued her correspondence with the Grimkés, along with numerous other American abolitionists. She asked for more details of the racial prejudice exhibited by American Friends, and received in response, Sarah Grimké's lengthy document, "Colorphobia exemplified, Letter on the Subject of Prejudice Against Colour amongst the Society of Friends in the United States." Profoundly shocked by the evidence it contained, Elizabeth Pease incurred the wrath of the Quakers on her side of the Atlantic by editing and publishing it in England. Pease had hoped this pamphlet would convince British Quakers to send a formal rebuke to their American peers, but instead she was herself accused of "being an enemy of the Society of Friends."[56]

Although they never met, the Grimkés and Pease continued their correspondence across the Atlantic and considered themselves friends as well as colleagues in the fight against slavery. Another transatlantic friendship developed between Lucretia Mott and Richard and Hannah Webb, two Irish Quakers she met while attending the 1840 World's Anti-Slavery Convention. Richard Webb corresponded also with Sarah Pugh and Abby Kimber, two other Philadelphia Quakers who had been in England with Mott. In one reply to Webb, Mott mentioned to Richard Webb that "Sarah Pugh is so kind as to bring her letters here to open them, so that we may read them together" and in another commented that "Sarah Pugh brought your last after Abby Kimber had had it, for us to enjoy puzzling it out together. She always allows me to look over her shoulder while reading, and 'best fellow' finds out the hard words first—James Mott sitting by, profiting by our united facility of deciphering illegible characters, and really enjoying every word as much as we do."[57]

From East to West and across the ocean to Great Britain, the antislavery lecturers had a profound impact on the antislavery movement. As we have seen, they focused the attention of abolitionists, and particularly antislavery women, on specific issues they deemed of importance. Beyond that, they served as leaders around whom the antislavery community coalesced. A great part of the reason for their success lay in their ability to win over the hearts as well as the minds of their supporters. Their success was also due to the respect and admiration they were accorded as women who attempted to live out their understanding of religious truth in spite of the hardships they encountered.

The scholarly literature, although often commenting on the heightened awareness of women's rights issues due to the public presence of antislavery women, has frequently noted the negative effect of these women on the unity of the abolition movement. The 1840 schism within the antislavery movement is, for example, often attributed to the persistence of Abby Kelley and other women in taking leadership roles within the American Anti-Slavery Society.

Some of their effect was indeed divisive, contributing to the schism within the antislavery movement in 1840. But the personal charisma and ideological stands of these women also united many behind them, resulting in a radical abolitionist community that was linked both by their personal connections to these women and by their adoption of principles articulated by them.[58]

3 ❧
The "Outsideisms of Religion"

PROBLEMS AND POSSIBILITIES OF
THE CHRISTIAN CHURCH

D R. C. B. JUDD WROTE bitterly of Abby Kelley: "She passes from place to place among us, attacking every institution we cherish as the Civil Government, the Church, the Ministry, our Fathers, and in short all parties, sects and men without reserve of any and with defference [sic] to none."[1] Such criticisms were not uncommonly directed toward the most radical abolitionists, whose comeouterism (the abandonment of the Church as incorrigible), nonresistance, no-government, and women's rights positions made them harshly critical of religious and political institutions. These attacks concerned Sallie Holley, who frequently asserted her "liking for positive affirmative statements, rather than for negative assertions."[2] She was unhappy that "the people have become better learned in what Mr. Garrison [who was for many the personification of radical abolitionism] *does not believe* than in the great world of sanctities that his faith comprehends."[3] Radical women abolitionists were even more suspect because of their violation of traditional gender boundaries.

I will explore in this chapter the views of these antislavery activists on various aspects of organized religion, specifically within American Protestantism. Though these women valued religious association, they faulted Christendom for failing to live up to its own Christian precepts. They questioned the authority and validity of many other Christian institutions: doctrines, rituals, the salaried ministry, and, as will be discussed in the following chapter, the status of Jesus as Messiah and the authority of scripture. They rejected some of these out of hand; others they dismissed as irrelevant but harmless; still others they reinterpreted. They were particularly distressed by sectarian rivalry and intolerance, which they saw as detrimental to Christianity and to the progress of social reform in general and of antislavery in particular. Their fundamental belief was that organized religion was a tool only, and as a tool was useful only insofar as it furthered the growth of individual faith.

"THE MIDNIGHT DARKNESS OF SECTARIAN THEOLOGY"

Sarah Grimké enjoyed recounting the story of her aunt, who took, she said:

> a mischievous pleasure in bedecking herself with jewels, and then placing herself in a conspicuous situation at methodist camp meeting. After meeting she would invite the minister home to dine. They did not spare her either in the pulpit, or the parlor, and one day being somewhat roused by their remarks, she said, "Well I suppose you think if I take off my ornaments I shall be a christian." "No madam" replied one of them, "if you become a christian they will fall off."

Grimké did not, as one might expect, tell this story to emphasize either the perspicacity of the minister or the virtues of simple living. Instead she applied it as a metaphor to religious institutions such as sects, doctrines, and rituals. She referred to these as "the outsideisms of religion" which "fall off when the spirit no longer needs them." Instead of venerating such institutions as the sources of religious truth, she called them "leading strings for infancy," which could and should be outgrown and "dropt when the spirit realizes that they are hindrances instead of helps." Rather than being "painfully exercised on dogmas and doctrines," which "are of no importance to spirit progress," one should "strive to attain the one thing needful—*Love* to God manifested by love to his creatures."[4]

The simplicity of Grimké's vision of Christianity was shared by the other activists discussed here. Lucretia Mott emphasized what she saw as the foolishness of binding oneself to any creed, when all sects had modified their creeds over time.[5] As an example, she noted that "now that a large class of Unitarians are moving forward and leaving the fathers of that reformation behind, these in their turn are raising the cry of 'heresy,' which dying orthodoxy seizes as a straw whereon it may rest its expiring hope."[6]

For her part, Sarah Grimké counseled Elizabeth Smith Miller to "be not troubled" about church doctrines such as the Trinity, for "no theologian that I have ever met with, can give a rational understandable explanation of that dogma, and hence I cannot receive as a truth what is utterly repugnant to reason." She added,

> Let us give up these scholastic doctrines, to those, who vainly seek religion thro' the head, instead of the heart. Let us endeavor to illustrate in our lives the belief that God is Love, and that religion is an absorption into him, such an absorption, as renders us his representatives on earth. You have the all of religion, in what you say you are sure of— "There is a God and he is a being of love and purity. He requires us to be holy, and our happiness lies in regarding his requirements." This is all I know and this is sufficient for the present, if more is needed for our advancement, it will surely be given. Doctrines, which occupy so prominent a place in Christianity have eaten out the life of pure love. Let them go dearest.[7]

Likewise, according to Caroline Putnam, Sallie Holley once told Antoinette Brown, studying theology at Oberlin College in the hopes of becoming a Congregational minister, "Antoinette, all this false theology will fall right off you in time."[8] In regard to such doctrines as the Trinity, Holley agreed with her uncle, who said, "the Orthodox people attempt to dignify the doctrine of the Trinity with the name of Mystery, but there is no mystery about it. It is a plain contradiction, a flat absurdity."[9] In her move away from Presbyterianism, Angelina Grimké concluded that her sister Sarah was correct that in reading a book on church doctrine given to her by her minister she was "seeking the living among the dead."[10] Abby Kelley claimed to have no patience whatsoever with theologizing. She announced at one meeting that she "had no time to theorize, had never been able to understand the theological speculations of the Orthodox Church, her only idea of salvation being salvation from the sin of trampling on God's moral laws. She had no leisure for speculations or aesthetics. While Lazarus lies at the gate, who can sit at speculative study in his library or revel in the cultivation of his tastes[?]"[11]

These women's most vehement criticisms were reserved for the doctrine of human depravity and the concept of eternal damnation. Lucretia Mott believed the former, along with the concept of a "vicarious atonement," to be "a mistaken and paralysing dogma."[12] Sarah Grimké called the idea of eternal punishment a "blasphemy against the mercy and justice of God."[13] She believed rather in the universalist principle that all souls were destined for salvation; "'All souls are mine' saith the Lord," she quoted, "and 'none shall be able to pluck them out of my hand.'"[14]

Other doctrines they viewed as unnecessary but innocuous. Lucretia Mott, for example, did not share Sallie Holley and Sarah Grimké's repugnance for the concept of the Trinity. In her mind, that doctrine was too trivial to warrant concern: "As to the mere opinion of 'Trinity' or 'Unity' or any such purely speculative indulgence, affecting not the life or practice, 'the long-headed, reasoning man,' and 'the warm, enthusiastic, poetic-minded man' may each follow his convictions harmlessly."[15]

"THE BITTER FRUITS OF SECTARIANISM"

Perhaps the most fundamental religious assertion of these women was that it was not they but rather the churches of their day that were unfaithful to the principles of Christianity.[16] As Angelina Grimké wrote in 1837: "O! when will the *Christian* world (as it is called) be ready to embrace Christianity[?] What kind of Religion have we now, a mere *theoretical* skeleton, almost entirely destitute of purity of practice."[17] They attributed many of the evils of American Christianity to rampant sectarianism—to the tendency, in Mott's words, "to proselyte to sect rather than to Christianity!"[18] In theory Protestant denominations agreed that "all societies who profess Christianity and retain the foundational principles thereof . . . are in reality but one Church of Christ, but several branches . . . of one visible kingdom of the Messiah."[19] In practice, however, sectarian intolerance flourished, as did competition for members. This was particularly true in the nineteenth century when many new denominations were formed and some grew at an astonishing pace. The Methodist Episcopal Church, formed with 14,000 members in 1784, had become by 1844 the most popular Protestant denomination in the country with over one million members.[20] The growth of Methodism was aided by the use of such unorthodox methods as circuit riders and camp meetings. By 1851 the Baptists, another former minority group, were the second largest denomination with 1,105,546 members. These upstart denominations were followed more distantly by older groups such as the Presbyterians, with 487,000 members, and the Congregationalists, with 197,000.[21] Such rapid changes not unnaturally provoked tensions among Protestant denominations. One interesting study of such conflicts is David Kasserman's *Fall River Outrage,* in which he proposes that the 1833 murder trial of Methodist clergyman Ephraim Avery, in Fall River, Massachusetts, had as much to do with conflicts between the entrenched Congregationalist establishment and the upstart Methodist community as it did with the individuals concerned. As noted earlier, one of Angelina Grimké's reasons for joining the Presbyterian Church was its openness to other Christians, behavior she did not see evidenced by other denominations.

The Society of Friends, of which all the women but Sallie Holley were members at some point in their lives, practiced exclusivity in a different way. Its vision of itself, after its early history in America of evangelism and martyrdom, was of a body set apart from the world, including the rest of the Christian world. The Friends were, indeed, among the first religious bodies to speak against slavery and to outlaw it among their members. Further, many individual abolitionists had Quaker backgrounds. The Society as a whole, however, frowned on activities that brought its members into close contact with non-Quakers. This included disapproval of social activism such as abolitionism as well as a ban on marriages to outsiders.

The Grimkés' decision to enter the antislavery arena, then, was not taken lightly either by them or by their meeting. Sarah Grimké reported that Angelina Grimké's initial interest in the movement was discouraged by Friends, who told her "that the Meeting for Sufferings had the charge of this weighty matter, and that *whenever the way opened, they* would do all that friends could do. All individual effort on her part was discouraged." On Sarah Grimké's part, "finding that Friends disapproved . . . of her [Angelina] doing any thing in the A. S. cause, I did *all* that I could by remonstrance and entreaty to induce her to abandon *all* active co-operation with Abolitionists," urging her "to surrender herself to the guidance of Friends, and give up her responsibility as a moral being, to be taught and ruled and exonerated by them from individual obligations. This," she added, "was the creed I had been taught and I was not an unapt scholar."[22]

After Sarah Grimké's change of heart and commitment to follow Angelina into antislavery activism, the sisters never again let Quaker disapproval affect their course of action. They declared themselves faithful to a higher authority; as Angelina Grimké said, "the more I reflect on the exclusiveness of our Society, the more I am convinced its constitution must be radically wrong, for any thing which cuts us off from Christian communion with Christians of any name and cooperation with them in works of mercy and faith, must be of *man's* invention and does partake of the nature of that spirit which divides in Jacob and scatters in Israel." She compared the actions of Friends in "crushing and treading down every thing which opposes the peculiar view of Friends" to "the powerful effort of the Jews, to close the lips of Jesus." She finally concluded that "I do consider the restrictions placed on our members as so very antichristian, that I would rather be disowned than to be any longer bound by them." She declared her liberation from such limitations, saying, "I have borne them as long as I possibly could with peace of mind, and now that my Master has burst my fetters and set me free, I never expect to suffer myself to be manacled again."[23]

Given Quaker disapproval of their work, the sisters expected to be disowned, that is, to have their memberships in the Society of Friends revoked, at any time. They were, indeed, eventually disowned; the precipitating factor, however, was not their antislavery activism but their disregard of the Quaker dictum against marriage to outsiders. Angelina Grimké was disowned for marrying Theodore Weld, a non-Quaker; Sarah Grimké was disowned at the same time for attending the wedding. (The Quaker poet John Greenleaf Whittier also attended the wedding but avoided disownment by stepping out of the room while the wedding vows were being exchanged. Abby Kelley, though, attended the wedding and suffered no ill consequences.)

Lucretia Mott remained a member of the Society of Friends throughout her life, but she, too, had her difficulties, even in the more radical Hicksite branch to which she belonged. At the 1840 Yearly Meeting in Philadelphia, the minister Rachel Barker warned "the young people present to avoid being led by false prophetesses into 'the mixtures, the whirlwind, and the storm' of reform movements. They must instead keep in the quiet." Lucretia Mott was of course the particular "false prophetess" to whom she referred.[24] After 1847 Mott's meeting would no longer issue her a Traveling Minute for any of her journeys, essentially refusing to endorse her travels or her words. In fact, according to a memorial article appearing in the *Free Religious Index* after Mott's death, "for thirty years there was a large portion of the society which would have gladly seen her quit its membership. Some, indeed, would gladly have disowned her, but she knew her rights; and, though never suspending her ministry or her attendance at meeting, the opponents of her anti-slavery work could never catch her in the wrong."[25] Mott, whose own daughter was one of the disowned, also strongly protested the practice of expelling members for marrying outside the Society.

Abby Kelley was likewise opposed to the restrictions imposed on Friends, particularly those discouraging antislavery activism. Rather than waiting to be disowned, however, she herself publicly disavowed the Society of Friends in 1841. With her usual vehemence, she announced that "I hereby disown all connection or fellowship with the Society of Friends, feeling it a duty to 'come out and be separate, and have no communion with the unfruitful works of darkness.'" She added, perhaps not very convincingly, that "I would assure you that, in performing this act of obedience to the Divine will, I do it with the most tender regard to all in the Society."[26] When her meeting did not publicly acknowledge her action, she forwarded a copy of her letter of disownment to William Lloyd Garrison for publication in the *Liberator.*

Sallie Holley was the only one of the five who was never affiliated with the Society of Friends. Baptized by a Unitarian minister after her father's death, she never joined a congregation, and maintained a more detached outlook on sectarian practices. In one of her letters she reported with some amusement that "Parker Pillsbury says, 'The reason why the younger religious sects are not as cruel, oppressive, and persecuting as the older ones are, is because their teeth and claws are not yet grown.'"[27] A friend recounted a conversation in which Holley was told that one of the Fosters [Abby or her husband Stephen] had said the Methodist Church was "'worse than the worst brothel in New York.' 'Well' said she in her pleasant serious way, 'I do suppose that is a fact' and went on with considerable more."[28]

Holley was alternately amused and exasperated by her dealings with Quakers, who often asked her personal questions, criticized her for accepting money for her speaking, and were prejudiced against any special education for ministers. She described one encounter as follows:

At the close of my meeting yesterday afternoon, held in Friends' Meeting-house, an old withered crone of a Quaker woman made her way up to me with the following: "Is thee a married woman? How old is thee? Does thee live in Massachusetts? Thee resides with relations?" And for the thousandth time I answered those questions. Don't you think it would save time and trouble if I were to furnish the *Liberator* a list of questions that are constantly put to me, with all my answers, and thus forestall future interrogations?

You would laugh to hear all the criticisms these Quakers are guilty of regarding me. One said she thought I dressed too gay; another that I laughed too much; a third that I did not visit enough. A fourth wished I would speak oftener, and a fifth said I did not eat enough, and that I had large self-esteem. Still another said I ought not to receive money; to her mind it was just the same as a "hireling ministry."[29]

After another such encounter she wrote to Abby Kelley Foster: "I can exclaim with Charles Lamb[,] 'I am willing to meet a Quaker occasionally in the street, but I dont care to live with them.'"[30]

Both Kelley's and Holley's letters mention the rigidity and hostility of the Methodists more than that of any other denomination. Holley, for example, reported that when she was asked at a Methodist meeting to "declare the unsullied counsel of God . . . never," she said, "did I more zealously open up the shortcomings and wickedness of the Methodist church."[31] It would be unfair, though, to conclude from this that the Methodists were less supportive of abolition than other sects; the fact remains that many antislavery meetings were held in Methodist meetinghouses, indicating some openness to abolitionism. Other denominations may not have been singled out so much in their correspondence simply because the antislavery lecturers had little or no contact with them on their travels.

"HOW THESE MINISTERS FEEL THEIR DIGNITY":
A CRITIQUE OF CLERICAL AUTHORITY

Church hierarchy was another aspect of organized religion that these women criticized. The authority assumed by the clergy was a particular sore spot. Those with Quaker backgrounds were especially sensitive to the issue of the "hireling" ministry; in the Quaker view, the ministry was not a salaried profession to be chosen as a career, but a simple acknowledgment and exercise of a particular spiritual gift. Sarah Grimké recounted how this process worked for one Quaker minister she had known; "'I never preach' said he, 'until I can't help it.'"[32] But the Quakers had their own hierarchical system, and these women were critical of that as well. Lucretia Mott objected to the policy of "[c]lothing a few of our equal brethren, with power to judge the ministry—selecting here and there one to ordain for the ministry, and placing these in elevated positions, [for] it is no difficult matter for them to regard themselves 'the heads of the tribes' and to act accordingly."[33]

Sarah Grimké had a more fundamental critique of the ministry in general: "My convictions for several years past have been that the ministry as now organized is utterly at variance with the ministry Christ established."[34] She and her peers were skeptical about the motivations of the clergy, particularly in the clergy's general (although certainly not universal) resistance to abolition and women's rights. In Angelina Grimké's view, the cause of their resistance was not based in spiritual conviction, but rather in their fear of seeing their positions diminished or eliminated. In 1837 she commented to Jane Smith: "The Clergy are alarmed and they have great cause to be so and they will cling with a death-grasp to their pay and their power, but their doom is sealed I believe."[35] Likewise, Abby Kelley wrote scornfully: "How these ministers feel their dignity. They can't come on to a level with *women* and *'niggers.'* Mr. W[hiting] says 'The blacks must be colonized. It is of no use to think of elevating them.' I suppose he would go for the colonization of women unless he could keep his foot upon them."[36]

These women all rejected the assumption that the clergy by definition were privy to more profound spiritual insights than others. The root of their criticisms lay in their objection to external authority over individual religious conscience, of which more will be said in the following chapter.

"THE GOSPEL IS NOT IN THESE OUTWARD THINGS": A CRITIQUE OF RELIGIOUS PRACTICES

These women were not the only ones who critiqued American Christianity. Others, however, did so from a different perspective. Lyman Beecher, for example, attacked what he saw as the chief obstacles to the maintenance of a Christian society: "The name of God is blasphemed . . . ; the bible is denounced; the sabbath is profaned; the public worship of God is neglected."[37] But to these women, such "sins" were simply erroneous definitions of piety and not the practical expressions of Christ's love for humankind that were central to Christianity.

These women objected to many commonly accepted religious rituals and practices, or "forms," as they called them. Here their criticisms were slightly different than those directed at the dogma that they tended to regard as wholly pernicious. Forms, such as Sabbath observance, public worship, plain dress, communion, and baptism, were "legitimate, acceptable, noble" if it was understood that they were a "means to an end" rather than the end itself, obedience to God.[38] Generally, they viewed such practices as aids toward religious development, valuable insofar as they contributed to spiritual growth, but pointless in and of themselves: hence Sarah Grimké's comment comparing the "outsideisms of religion" to "leading strings for infancy" that were no longer necessary when the child learns to walk unaided. As Lucretia Mott stated, "the gospel is not in these outward things" such as "plain dress, or formal speech, or observance of times, or stated reasons of vocal prayer."[39]

Sallie Holley was once asked what she thought of the Unitarians adopting a liturgy; she responded that it seemed to her to be "an affectation." I should not enjoy it. I think it deadening to spiritual vitality. I used to laugh over what Henry Ward Beecher said in a public meeting to discuss the question,—'Why, I should as soon think of going a-courting with my father's old love-letters as prayer to God out of a book.'"[40]

Lucretia Mott also objected to certain common uses of prayer. She commented that "[t]o pray that health may be restored to a city, to have a national fast on account of the cholera and to humble ourselves for our sins and pray for a mitigation of these evils, without observing the laws by which health shall be restored, is the darkness of superstition."[41] Rather than pray to God for supernatural relief, people should accept that they are largely responsible for the situations in which they find themselves and should act accordingly.

The Sabbath also was for them no more sacred than any other day, worship not to be confined to any one day or hour. In this they concurred with the radical reformers profiled by Robert Abzug, who wished, he claims, to incorporate the spiritual into every aspect of life, rather than to isolate religion into a separate sphere delineated by Sabbath-day worship and assent to creed. Their intent was to preserve or intensify the realization of the sacredness of everyday life. Henry C. Wright was one of the radical reformers who best expressed this view when he commented in his diary that "praying, reading the Bible, going to Church, Baptism, the supper, singing, preaching were no more *religious* exercises than baking bread, knitting stockings, cooking a dinner, sweeping the room or the streets."[42]

These women believed, however, that a day set aside for rest and relaxation was important, particularly for laborers, who needed time away from work.[43] Sarah Grimké explained that the sabbath should be observed "as a day of rest, instruction and gathering in of the mind to God." Nonetheless, she added, if "our regard for that day prevents us from performing a duty then it is superstition."[44]

Such views on ritual and liturgy were radical for the nineteenth century, but they were not unprecedented. Much earlier, the Puritans had had similar objections: they rejected "conceived prayer" such as the Lord's Prayer and the Book of Common Prayer. Quakers, too, objected to vocal prayer not spontaneously offered in response to the leadings of the spirit.[45] In the nineteenth century, evangelical Protestantism moved away from structured worship to the more spontaneous prayers and exhortations such as those offered at camp meetings by new converts and exhorters.[46] As Abzug has convincingly argued, one of the hallmarks of the radical reformers of the nineteenth century, typified by the Garrisonian abolitionists, was their disdain for linking piety to conventional religious rituals. Garrison himself became "more and more hostile to outward forms and ceremonies and observances, as a religious duty," noting on one Thanksgiving the "absurdity" of "this custom of appointing one day in the year to be specially thankful for the good gifts of God."[47] Garrison's alienation from religious forms left him uncertain of his own religious convictions; he claimed that it was Lucretia Mott who had helped him to understand and appreciate scripture so that, "instead of being 'killed by the letter,' he had been 'made alive by the spirit.'"[48] Garrison's acknowledgment of his debt to Mott makes it apparent that in their ability to construct a positive faith as well as to critique orthodox Christianity, these women were looked to as leaders by some who perceived a need for ecclesiastic and doctrinal reform within the Christian Church.

"ACCEPTABLE WORSHIP—THE ACTIVE USE OF ALL OUR GOD-GIVEN POWERS": THE VALUE OF RELIGIOUS ASSOCIATION

Public worship itself became an issue, particularly for the Grimkés, whose experience with it had been the worst. While still in Charleston, Angelina Grimké had held worship meetings for the family and servants. In her gradual conversion to Quakerism, she "mentioned to the servants that I felt the Lord no longer required me to conduct the services and therefore I had given them up—in a very short time I felt that I must not even be present and therefore did not attend."[49] Early in their lecture tour, Sarah Grimké confided in Theodore Weld her relief that she no longer felt obligated to participate in organized religious services.[50] In her later years, she supported church membership mainly as a stepping stone toward further religious enlightenment. She advised Elizabeth Smith Miller to continue attending church "so long as you feel that your soul is benefitted by being there, but whenever the time comes, that you feel as if attendance there belied your inner feelings let it go, it has served its purpose and can now only retard the progress of your soul towards that liberty wherewith Christ maketh his people free."[51]

Despite her ongoing commitment to the Society of Friends, Lucretia Mott was certain that "the worship which is required of us, is the active use of all our God-given powers," not attendance at specified religious services.[52] She told her Irish friend Richard Webb in 1846 that "it is dry work to keep up any form, after the life and power of it have passed away. Our afternoon meetings have long been burdensome, and of late we have ceased attending them." Instead, she and her husband James generally used "that time in visiting the colored people—or some of our poor Irish weavers, who struck some weeks ago for higher wages, and being out of employment much longer than they anticipated were reduced to great poverty and suffering." She added, "Devoting a few hours occasionally in this way, has appeared to us as acceptable worship."[53]

Despite their criticisms, the Grimkés, Mott, and Kelley continued to believe in the principles, if not the practice, of the Society of Friends. That being the case, when the Grimkés were visited by a delegation of Friends and asked to resign their membership, they refused to do so, saying that they

> did not feel at liberty to resign, because we still believed in the great
> principles of the Society, and did not feel as if we could join any other

people, that upon *friends,* and not upon *us* must rest the responsibility of depriving us of the right of membership, and that if they disowned us, we hoped they would remember it was because we acted up to the great fundamental doctrine of the Society, to follow the leadings of the Holy Spirit in the secret of our souls, which duty was more insisted upon in the sermons we heard in our meetings, than any other.[54]

This was the last of their formal associations with an organized religious body, although much later, after years of private devotions and home worship, the Welds participated in a local religious fellowship, which Sarah Grimké referred to in 1869 as a "Christian Fraternity," conducted along Unitarian lines.[55]

Only Lucretia Mott remained a member of any religious body throughout her life. She continued to believe that good could be accomplished within the Society of Friends. Although she carried on a lengthy correspondence with Richard Webb about their mutual dissatisfactions, she was disappointed when he renounced his Quaker membership. She had been aware that he had become increasingly alienated from sect and orthodox doctrine but had hoped that he would not completely cut his ties with the Society of Friends, for "with all our faults, I know of no religious association I would prefer to it. And I would rather hear of R. D. Webb, laboring very faithfully, and in all Christian daring, *in* his Society, than withdrawing from it." On the basis of her observations, Mott believed that it was often easier to bring about reforms from inside the organization; "I have frequently noticed," she continued, "that persons who were once useful in our Society, after withdrawing from it become rather contracted, and selfish; shut themselves out from society at large, and grow censorious." She also felt that such a withdrawal was harmful to the children of such individuals, who, "having no rallying point as they grow older, follow their natural inclination for association, and connect themselves with sects far behind the intelligence and light of their parents."[56]

She noted, "It is often a question and still unsettled with me, whether the various religious organizations, with all their errors, are more productive of good than evil." Still, she felt that "until we can offer something better in their stead, to a people hav[in]g the religious sentiments large and a natural love for association, it requires great care how we shake their faith in existing institutions."[57]

4 ✑
"Let Our Daily Life Be a Prayer"

CHRISTIANITY RE-VISIONED

L UCRETIA MOTT HOPED to replace the formalistic creeds of sectarian Protestantism with a simpler doctrine: "Let our creed be that faith in God which shall inspire us with love one unto another, and having this love let us show our devotion and our worship by our every day duties. Let our daily life be a prayer and our every day actions be worship."[1] She believed that there was a critical distinction between the genuine experience of religion and the artificial constructions of theology. She was adamantly opposed to what she termed a "studied theology and systematized Divinity."[2] Yet, as perusal of her collected sermons and correspondence reveals, she clearly was a consummate theologian herself. Her reflections, along with Sarah Grimké's, form the backbone of what is a clear, assimilable though informal statement of religious principles. The comments of the other women, although generally less extensive, are indicative of their affirmation of these principles.

The theology these women substituted for conventional precepts incorporated elements of Christian theology, along with various unorthodox and non-Christian concepts, including ideas drawn from their own personal experiences. Although they all considered themselves Christians, they also drew freely from other sources: poets, secular thinkers, and movements such as Millerism and spiritualism. Mott, for example, said flatly that it was a mistake for Christians to think that "true religion" started "eighteen hundred years ago." Rather, she claimed, "There have been evidences of it in every age, and even now in all the nations under the sun . . . we find recognitions of the Divine and the Eternal, the Creator of us all, and in some form, ceremony or worship offered unto Him."[3]

They began their theologizing, however, from the standpoint of the liberal Protestantism that developed in the nineteenth century. They believed in the nature of the divine as loving rather than wrathful, in human nature as inherently good not evil, in the ability of individuals to comprehend the divine mandate, and in their freedom to choose to do so. Where they diverged from the mainstream was in their radical assertion of the primacy of individual conscience over all other religious authority, their reassessment of the significance of Christ and the Bible, and their notion of exactly what constituted a righteous life.

"GOD IS LOVE": THE NATURE OF THE DIVINE

The idea of God as a harsh and implacable judge had begun to fade in the nineteenth century to be replaced by an image of a God of love whose ultimate concern was to save souls.[4] The revivalism of the Second Great Awakening brought with it a growing faith that God responds mercifully to the efforts of human beings to live righteous lives. Angelina Grimké did not report attending camp meetings, but her experience was similar to the emotional conversions of many women who did. She claimed that despite her transgressions, "I have ever found my Father willing to receive me back, He has often run whilst I was a *great* way off and thrown his arms around me and kissed me. As soon as I have laid me down at His feet, He has lifted me up and laid me on his bosom."[5] Grimké's extravagant and intimate language was not atypical. Susan Juster, who studied over two hundred accounts of early nineteenth-century religious conversions, found that "the image of God portrayed in the female narratives is most often that of a family member or personal friend" and not uncommonly as "lover." (Men, by contrast, more frequently spoke of God as a sovereign or lawgiver.)[6]

Grimké was particularly impressed by the doctrine of perfectionism as espoused by revivalist Charles Grandison Finney. This doctrine, she claimed, "makes the nature of man and the requirements of God to harmonise and prove that God is not a hard master gathering where he has not sowed, or in other words requiring what man from his very constitution is unable to perform."[7]

Lucretia Mott described the "attributes of Deity" more specifically, stating that they included "a nice sense of justice, a quick perception of love, [and] a keen apprehension of mercy."[8] Abby Kelley echoed these sentiments albeit in a more abstract form. She told her daughter that "when she was a child she used to imagine God looking like a venerable Friend, sitting in a big chair in the garret." As her religious views matured, she came to believe "in a great divine power, the Go(o)d, but not in a God with whom she could hold personal relations as a child does with its parent. . . . Her belief was that the Creator was too great and good for the feeble and imperfect natures of His creatures to comprehend. The truths which he puts into our souls and into nature are the only part of Himself that He allows us to know."[9]

Sarah Grimké's view is the most striking because up to 1836, she most often expressed herself in terms of her fear of God and God's judgment. By 1850, she, who had castigated herself as "unworthy to hold the sacred oil"[10] went so far as to counsel her friends to avoid the suffering caused by a "morbid . . . conscience which magnifies infirmities into crimes, and transforms my blessed father in heaven into a stern judge, who punishes to the uttermost every real, or imaginary departure, from what we apprehend to be his requirements." On the contrary, she became convinced of the truth of the gospel that "Like as a father pityeth his children so doth the Lord pity them that love him."[11] She claimed, echoing the sensual language of Angelina Grimké's earlier remark, "Now my soul is ravished with his love and when I yield to temptation he folds me closer to his heart and inspires me with fresh strength."[12] She also came, as contemporary feminist theologians have done, to envision the deity as having female as well as male attributes. In attempting to encourage a friend, she wrote, "Do you feel as if there were a power on which to lean, to which to appeal, a Father on whose bosom you could recline, a Mother's love on which you could calculate in all emergencies. I say a mother's love, because the power we call God combines the masculine and feminine natures, or it could not, as it does, minister to *all* of our being."[13]

Their ideas of divinity ranged from the Grimkés' faith in God personalized as Father and Mother or, in the tradition of Christian mysticism, as Lover, to Mott's calm acceptance of a God of justice and mercy, to Abby Kelley's conviction of a benevolent and omnipresent reality. The common denominator in their views was their unshakable belief in an ultimate reality that is fundamentally loving in nature.

"THE INNATE PURITY OF MAN": HUMAN NATURE DEFINED

The concept of the fundamental depravity of human nature, or original sin, was another cornerstone of Protestant orthodoxy that was challenged in nineteenth-century America. According to Calvinist tenets, even nonelect infants, although "not moral agents . . . possess a nature not conformable to the law of God: they are depraved, 'children of wrath,' and guilty on account of their own personal depravity." One minister told his congregation that "Hell is paved with the skulls of infants one span long . . . and their parents look down upon them from Heaven, praising God for the justice of their damnation!"[14]

The doctrine of original sin, with its implication of the necessity of infant damnation, became less and less palatable in nineteenth-century America. People increasingly resisted the idea that an infant could be condemned as depraved and consigned to eternal damnation. Even orthodox theologians such as Yale president Timothy Dwight wrestled with this issue and gradually shifted to a more liberal view. For example, while accepting that man was "rebellious, sinful, and odious to his Maker," Dwight nonetheless stipulated that "some parts of human nature remained 'innocent' or imbued with 'natural conscientiousness,' and that these traits explained the ability of even 'natural' man sometimes to obey God."[15] By 1830, according to one historian, most Congregational ministers, regardless of their views on adult culpability, no longer raised the topic of infant damnation either to support or reject it.[16]

Despite the evidence of this liberalizing trend within the culture, the doctrines of original sin and the depravity of human nature remained a strong force in Protestant America. As late as 1850, Lucretia Mott wrote to her Irish friends, Richard and Hannah Webb, that, "I am constantly combating the 'human depravity' doctrine, and preach in its stead, the innate purity of man."[17] Five years later, Sallie Holley wrote to William Lloyd Garrison of her relief when she encountered a soul not burdened by "the awful glooms of Calvin's barbaric theology."[18]

Expanding on the Quaker understanding of the inward light, Mott had faith that humankind "is created innately good," and that all people contain "the heavenly light within them."[19] She believed that there is "a religious instinct in the constitution of man," finding proof of this belief in that "this religious essence [has] grown, and brought forth similar fruits, in every age of the world, among all peoples." This was because "[t]he great principles of justice, love and truth are divinely implanted in the hearts of men." "We may all admit," she claimed, "that if we receive the divine spirit, in its operations in our soul, there will be no mistake; it will be found a reprover of evil."[20]

Sarah Grimké came to a similar conclusion when she embraced spiritualism in her later life. From spiritualist philosophy she accepted the idea that sin was not the natural state of human beings, but the "violat[ion of] the majesty of their own nature." Because of this innate purity, she claimed, "the spirit remains unsullied by the debaucheries of the man."[21]

"LET US NOT HESITATE TO BE THE MESSIAH OF OUR AGE"

Lucretia Mott, however, went a step farther. She not only considered human nature "pure" but spoke in terms of the "divinity of humanity."[22] Describing the results of her own prayers, she claimed that: "when I have risen in the assemblies of the people and with solemn sense of dependence upon a higher power I have asked in humility for his aid to stand by and strengthen and support me, I have been blessed, abundantly blessed. I have felt this divinity rising in my soul."[23]

For Mott, it was not simply a matter of accepting that human beings made in the image of God possess a spark of the divine light. Rather, she believed that individuals are capable of directly receiving and transmitting the will of God to others—just as Jesus did. This led to her heretical view about the nature of Jesus himself. Mott believed that while Christ had a divine mission, he himself was no more divine than any other human being. As she said, "The divinity of Christ was not in mystery or miracle. It was in doing the will of his Father."[24] Further, she deplored what she termed the "superstitious reverence for Jesus" because it resulted in "crying blessed Lord and Saviour instead of doing the works wh[ich] he said."[25]

Mott's view of Jesus as fully human was, although radical, not unique. In his 1841 sermon, "The Transient and Permanent in Christianity," the Unitarian minister Theodore Parker (1810–60) preached that although Jesus had set a great example, "was he not our brother, the son of man, as we are; the Son of God, like ourselves?"[26] This view was not accepted by the majority of Parker's Unitarian peers, most of whom continued to believe in a supernatural Christ, and he was asked to renounce his position as a Unitarian clergyman. He refused to do so, citing Unitarian doctrinal freedom; his colleagues responded by barring him from speaking in their pulpits.

The subject of the nature of Christ was not always a deadly serious topic for Lucretia Mott. On one occasion, she hosted a dinner party that included her spiritual protégé and intellectual sparring partner James Miller McKim,[27] a number of other abolitionists, and Catharine Beecher, the daughter of the renowned clergyman Lyman Beecher. She later wrote to her sister:

> Our subject was the attempt to prove Shakespeare's plays not all written by him—and how sorry they would be to have to believe that we had not *one* Shakespeare. I asked why not more joyful, could it be shewn that there were *ten*—that it came of superstitious idolatry to *make* one fellow being an object of worship. Was it not a reflection on the great Creator, that only one Messiah had come to man—more worthy of Him—that one for every age had appeared—or whenever a necessity as Foxton, my pet, says. Cath. [Beecher] bore the heresy better than I expected. Miller stayed behind as they went to the parlor to laugh, and ask me—or rather congratulate me, on delivering myself of my Messiah hobby.[28]

What underlay Mott's view was her conviction, founded on her belief in the essential divinity of human nature, that all individuals could and should be held up to Christ's example. "Let us," she urged, "aspire to similar purity—to similar glory. It is not too high an aspiration for us, it is only because he has been clothed with kind of God-like robes that people have made him something above imitation. . . . Let us not hesitate to be the messiah of our age."[29]

Sarah Grimké likewise challenged Christ's status as a unique exponent of God's word. Having concluded that nonviolence was one of the highest of spiritual requirements, she once declared that had Jesus preached violence, "I should at once reject Christianity as incons[is]tent with the character and attributes of Jehovah."[30] She also wrote that

> we have no man . . . who gave to the world a purer example . . . yet it seems to me there have been many men and women who have been equally pure, high minded and fearless in promulgating and sustaining the truths of the gospel. . . . I would not abate one jot, or tittle of that homage which is due to the Christ, as the exponent of God to man, but I would reverently bow to Truth wherever and in whomsoever it appeareth.[31]

Grimké numbered the prophets Isaiah and Jeremiah, the apostles Peter and Paul, the Quaker George Fox, and later, Joan of Arc, among this group of hallowed individuals.[32]

Sallie Holley, having declared herself a "Theodore Parker Unitarian," expressed a similar point of view. She spoke of Jesus with reverence, remarking "[w]hat an ever fresh and living interest the life and character of Jesus has!" and referring to him as a "beautiful soul." At the same time, however, she felt his life became "more and more human . . . to me as I live and grow myself."[33] In 1888 she wrote: "Popular theology puts greater emphasis on a *bodily* resurrection than it does on a *spiritual* resurrection. It exalts the physical above the spiritual. Is more anxious to establish the personal rank of Jesus than his character. How *materialistic* it is!"[34]

Abby Kelley expressed equal admiration of Jesus, although she was not specific about his status as either divine or human. Angelina Grimké Weld's stance was more conventional. She described herself as becoming a "*heart* believer in the divinity of Christ" when, under the influence of Millerism and its subsequent discrediting, she reflected on the meaning of the Second Coming. For her this revelation came as a result of her conclusion that Jesus' "body of flesh, was merely 'the form of a servant' which he had taken upon himself for a little while, in order that he might do a particular work for man, which could not be done without this gross instrumentality. I saw too that this *body* was no part of Christ's divinity— that He had existed entirely independent of it, and that when that body died on the Cross, Christ still lived."[35] Grimké Weld's position concerning the divinity of Christ thus differed from the more radical views expressed by her sister, Mott, and Holley. In this she placed herself more in the evangelical tradition of stressing the believer's personal relationship with Jesus Christ as opposed to the others' more transcendentalist view that "all that is personal in [Christianity] is nought. When anyone comes who speaks with better insight into moral nature, he will be the new gospel; miracle or not, inspired or uninspired, he will be the Christ."[36] Yet Grimké Weld concurred with the other women in the standard of perfectionism to which she held human beings. One might say that although these women held varying views as to the exact status of Jesus, they were united in their confidence in human capability to reflect and transmit divine principles.

"ALWAYS THE <u>LISTENING</u> SOUL CAN HEAR THE STILL, SMALL VOICE": INTUITING GOD'S WORD

Like Jesus, these women claimed direct access to divine guidance.[37] They were not the first to do so, of course. That belief was, for example, central to the early Christian mystics. George Fox's concept of the inward light was another manifestation of such a belief. In the nineteenth century it appeared again in the writings of the transcendentalists, who viewed individual intuition of religious truth not only as a possibility but as a necessity. Emerson, for example, in exalting Moral Nature (which was, in his view, the epitome of human religiosity), stated that the discovery of its truth "is guarded by one stern condition; this, namely; it is an intuition. It cannot be received at second hand."[38]

Regarding the authority vested in ecclesiastical institutions, Lucretia Mott preached that "men's teaching, human records, or outward authorities . . . were not to take the place of the higher law inwardly revealed," crediting Elias Hicks for this inspiration. She supported her claim also with reference to the apostle Paul; did not he declare that "those who had known a birth into the gospel, had no more need of the law? that they were under a higher dispensation than were they who were bound by their statutes and ceremonies?"[39] Likewise, Sarah Grimké found that her "inner life" was "sustained by constant communion with the father of spirits." She claimed that God "has brought us out of the legal or Jewish dispensation in which we observed times and seasons and were refreshed by them, and is leading us into that more glorious dispensation where like the Son of God we shall know no intermission of his presence."[40]

It is important to clarify the meaning of the term "intuition" as used by the women studied here. When these women spoke of intuition, they did not mean random flashes of insight, such as we often think of intuition today, but rather guidance and understanding given to them directly by God. Sarah Grimké wrote that, "Whilst I acknowledge that all the books I have read to prove the existence of God have failed to prove it from reasoning, yet it is an intuition of my spirit interwoven with consciousness and existence."[41] Her belief in the possibility of human communication with the divine was reinforced by the example of Jesus and, interestingly enough (given her views on peace and nonresistance), by that of Joan of Arc, whom she claimed was

---

"the most remarkable exhibition of communication between God and man, Jesus excepted, that stands on the records of history."[42]

Lucretia Mott spoke most clearly and directly about the meaning and role of intuition in the believer's life. For Mott, a key aspect of human spirituality was individual intuition of God's presence and commands. Further, "The more our religion is from self-evident conviction, from intuition[,] and to the obedient soul truth is received by intuition, the more we live in accordance with the blessed precepts which truth ever teaches to men, the higher will be the evidence and the more certain the conviction we shall give, that we have fellowship with the Father and the Son."[43] On another occasion, she asserted, "Truth is one in all ages; and always the *listening* soul can hear the still, small voice." "The trouble," she added, "is that we do not listen."[44]

Nor, according to these women, is intuition diametrically opposed to reason; they did not see the need for such a bifurcation. In their worldview, reason as well as intuition was a divine gift. As Sarah Grimké said, "we must never surrender ourselves to any influence, which makes reason and judgment desert the throne where God has placed them, they are the glory and dignity of humanity, allying us with God and Truth, making us but little lower than the angels."[45] They were in accordance with the views of William Ellery Channing, who in his 1820 essay, "Moral Argument Against Calvinism," had stated: "It is an important truth, which we apprehend has not been sufficiently developed, that the ultimate reliance of a human being is and must be on his own mind."[46]

Blanche Hersh considered the relationship of reason and intuition in her study of feminist-abolitionists. Hersh concluded that most of the feminist abolitionists believed in the Quaker principle of the inward light, or what the women here described more generically as intuition. But Hersh also found that her feminist-abolitionists rejected the

> Quaker exaltation of spirit over reason. They were attracted instead to the Unitarian emphasis on human rationality and free will. Reflecting the influence of Enlightenment ideas on liberal religious thought, most feminists believed that God was revealed through natural laws, and that, through knowledge of these rational forces governing the universe, men and women could perfect themselves and their society and do God's will.[47]

The study of these particular women, however, all of whom were included in Hersh's study, shows that they did not accept the primacy of either reason or intuition. Instead they viewed the two as not only compatible but syncretic processes. They rejected the idea that reason and intuition must function antagonistically. This insight was not embraced in their time, but it is one that has been expanded on in the present day by feminist theorists and theologians. Today such thinkers combat what they see as a dualistic mindset, traceable at least to Enlightenment consciousness, that associates masculinity with matter and reason and femininity with spirit and intuition and asserts the superiority of the former over the latter.[48]

"ALL SCRIPTURE GIVEN BY INSPIRATION OF GOD IS PROFITABLE": THE AUTHORITY OF THE WRITTEN WORD

Intuition was also a tool to be used in evaluating the truth of the written word, be it scripture or other text.[49] In regard to the authority of scripture, Lucretia Mott wrote that "no text of Scripture however plain can shake thy belief in a truth which thou perceives by intuition, or make thee believe a thing which is contrary to thy innate sense of right and wrong."[50] On the one hand, here she echoed William Ellery Channing's sentiment, expressed in 1815, that "a Christian minister should beware of offering interpretations of Scripture which are repugnant to any clear discoveries of reason or dictates of conscience. This admonition is founded upon the very obvious principle, that a revelation from God must be adapted to the rational and moral nature which He has conferred on man; that God can never contradict in his word what He has himself written on the human heart."[51] On the other hand, she also agreed with Theodore Parker that "You cannot open this book anywhere, but from between its oldest and newest leaves there issues forth truth."[52]

Mott had a number of reasons for questioning the authority of scripture. She pointed out that "the Bible [is] sought from beginning to end for its isolated passages wherewith to prove the most absurd dogmas that ever were palmed off upon a credulous people."[53] Although she quoted scripture, such as the gospel directive "to bind up the broken hearted, to preach deliverance to the captive" in opposition to slavery, she refused to spend time developing a biblical justification of her antislavery position. "Plenty of Bible," she reportedly said, "will be found in support of Freedom as soon as it becomes a little more popular."[54]

Further, she believed that the Bible contained, along with numerous mistranslations and misinterpretations, many purely historical examples irrelevant to the current age. It could not, therefore, be considered an infallible guide. "The great error in Christendom is, in regarding these scriptures taken as a whole as the plenary inspiration of God, and their authority as supreme."[55] On the contrary, believing that the Bible was of human as well as divine origin, she read and examined it "as I would any other book."[56] As with other texts, it was necessary to apply one's own reason and intuition to "place that which belongs to the history of a more barbarous age where it belongs."[57] Unlike Sarah Grimké in her earlier years, Mott was not burdened by the differences between the Old and New Testaments. To her, this was simply more evidence of the human origin of the Bible: "It is impossible, by any theological ingenuity to reconcile the moral code of the Old and New Testament, as proceeding from Him who is 'without variableness or shadow of turning.' Far safer, therefore is it, to admit man to be fallible than judge God to be changeable."[58]

Finally, just as Mott believed others besides Jesus were capable of divinity equal to his, so too did she believe in the divine inspiration behind many other written works. As others had, she included the books of the Apocrypha in this list of inspired works, but did not stop there. The authors of scripture were "beautifully instructive but ought they to command our veneration more than the divine poetic language of many, very many, since their day, who have uttered truth equally precious?" she asked. "Why not acknowledge the inspiration of many of the poets of succeeding ages. . . . Let us not hesitate to regard the utterance of truth in our age, as of equal value with that which is recorded in the scriptures."[59] In the same vein, during meeting she once quoted from the "scripture of the spiritually minded [William Ellery] Channing," claiming his words to have authority equal to that "of Moses or David, Paul or Peter." In a family letter, she mentioned this incident, adding that she "might have added, 'to say the least'— as respects some of those old writers."[60]

The Grimkés started from a more orthodox position, drawing heavily on scripture to justify their abolitionism and their public roles in the antislavery movement. In defending their identification with women's rights as well as with abolition, Angelina Grimké indignantly declined to justify their speaking in public on the grounds that as Quakers, they were permitted to do so. Rather, she claimed, their right to speak "must be firmly established, not on the ground of Quakerism, but on the only firm basis of human rights the Bible."[61] She also stated in 1836 that "scripture precepts must forever remain *good,* and scripture rules *certain in themselves,* however perverted they may be by the carnal mind of man."[62]

Like Mott, the Grimkés declared that mistranslations and misinterpretations were the cause of many invalid interpretations of scriptural precepts. In the first of her *Letters on the Equality of the Sexes and the Condition of Woman,* Sarah Grimké declared her mind to be "entirely delivered from the superstitious reverence which is attached to the English version of the Bible." Because "King James's translators certainly were not inspired" she claimed the right to interpret scripture for herself, "believ[ing] it to be the solemn duty of every individual to search the Scriptures for themselves, with the aid of the Holy Spirit, and not be governed by the views of any man, or set of men."[63]

There is very little evidence of Angelina Grimké Weld's views on this issue in her later life. Sarah Grimké did undergo a change from her general acceptance of the authority of scripture when properly translated and interpreted. In her embrace of spiritualism in her later years, she nonetheless counseled her friends not to accept unthinkingly the guidance of spirits any more than "Bible believers [should] take for granted that the whole is Inspiration and therefore true."[64] By 1866, she could commend Gerrit Smith on his published work, *The Theologies,* and say in agreement, "The time has fully come when the blasphemies, the monstrosities, the irrationalities of the Bible must be brought face to face with science, reason and common sense."[65]

In the same vein, Sallie Holley was impressed by a sermon she heard in which the preacher explored the historical relativism of scripture. "He began," she wrote, "by a very pertinent allusion to the drought of 1854, and the failure of the harvests. He said it did not avail the farmer or community to remember that three thousand years ago there was corn in Egypt, or that, later, richly laden argosies sailed on the Mediterranean, filled with grain from the ports of countries of fertile fields, to Rome." Putting on "Hebrew spectacles" rather than responding appropriately to the present situation could not resolve the problem. "No, the labor of to-day must satisfy the hunger of to-day." Likewise, rather than concentrate on the specifics of a biblical narrative such as Jonah being swallowed by the whale, it was important today to see how the world is "being swallowed by mammon, bestiality, materialism and hypocrisy." Scripture, according to Holley and the others, was a source more of inspiration, a path to divine truths, than it was an infallible book of rules for particular situations.[66]

"THE HIGHEST EVIDENCE OF A SOUND FAITH": RELIGION AND SOCIAL ACTIVISM

For these women, apprehension of divine truths also necessitated action. Lucretia Mott frequently expressed her distaste for theology, but here as elsewhere she best articulated the theological basis for the link these women perceived between faith and action. Mott continually stressed that "the practical life [is] the highest evidence of a sound faith."[67] After all, she noted, "Jesus did not say, Blessed is the believer in the trinity; blessed is the believer in the popular scheme of salvation; blessed the believer in a mysterious divinity attached to himself. . . . 'Blessed,' he said, 'are the merciful; blessed the pure in heart; blessed the meek.'"[68] Mott found offensive the view that any *belief* could serve as a test of the Christian character or of itself provide any assurance of salvation. Having been handed a religious tract that she summarized as stating that "*Belief* is the condition of salvation," she denounced such an idea as "demoralizing heresy."[69] Neither could the performance of any sectarian ritual aid in achieving salvation. In a sermon delivered in 1849, she asserted:

> the time is come when this undue adherence to outward authorities, or to any forms of baptism or of communion of church or sabbath worship, should give place to more practical goodness among men, more love manifested one unto another in our every day life, doing good and ministering to the wants and interests of our fellow beings the world over. . . . It needs, my friends, in this day that one should go forth saying neither baptism profiteth anything nor non-baptism, but faith which worketh by love, neither the ordinance of the communion table profiteth anything, nor the absence from the same, but faith which worketh by love. . . . Neither your sabbath observance profiteth any thing, nor the non-observance of the day, but faith which worketh by love.[70]

On the contrary, she claimed, "There is now, as there ever has been, but one test—one standard of worship" which, in the words of the prophet Micah was "to do justly, love mercy, and walk humbly."[71]

Abby Kelley was an ardent proponent of the linkage between faith and action. Although the extant correspondence from her earlier years does not support her, she later claimed publicly that before becoming an anti-slavery activist she had been a "doubter, even an atheist, living without God and without hope in the world, with no anchor for her soul." It was only in observing the reform movements of the day, such as temperance and antislavery, that she found she could wholeheartedly embrace "a living Christianity, a Christianity of work." She found these movements to be "inspired by the doctrine of love to God as a Father and love to man as a brother." In these movements she perceived the implementation of the Christian admonitions: "Love thy neighbor as thyself"; "He who loveth not his brother whom he hath seen, how can he love God whom he hath not seen?" and "Whatsoever ye would that men should do unto you, do ye even so unto them." Thereafter, she said, her "life had been devoted to labor for the world's uplifting."[72]

In Kelley's case, her waning faith was reinvigorated by her observation of Christian truths being worked out in practice within the abolition movement. The Grimkés, too, saw their antislavery action as an acceptance of a divine call. When Angelina Grimké wrote her *Appeal to the Christian Women of the South* in 1836, she sent it off to the American Anti-Slavery Society "with fervent prayer that the *Lord* would do just as *He pleases with it.*" "I believed," she added, "he [the Lord] directed and helped me to write it and now it seems as if I had nothing to do but to send it to the AntiSlavery Society, submitting it entirely to their judgment."[73] As she and her sister began their lecture tour, they often stressed that they placed their entire dependence on God. "I am willing to go," wrote Angelina to Jane Smith, "because I believe the Master has sent me out and that He will be near to help and to guide me in every strait and difficulty."[74]

In attributing their antislavery activism to divine mandate, the Grimkés placed themselves within a familiar feminine tradition. Other historians have noted how women who overtly accepted the limitations placed on their sex nonetheless justified various autonomous or public actions by claiming to be "passive" vessels of God's will. The diary of Abigail Abbot Bailey (1746–1815) shows how one eighteenth-century woman was able eventually to free herself from her abusive husband because of her conviction that in so doing, she was acting in accordance with the will of God, her "Heavenly Friend."[75] In the early nineteenth century, female reformers often claimed divine authority for their involvement in political and social issues. Later in the century, female spirit mediums justified their public writings and speech by claiming to be vehicles only for the spirits who spoke through them.[76] The Grimkés, however willful they appeared to others, placed themselves within this framework of passive response to the will of God.[77] Even Abby Kelley, who abandoned any passive language early in her career, said in 1839, "I wait the biddings and leadings of my Heavenly Father, praying that I may not mistake my own will and fancy for the voice of his unerring spirit in the soul."[78]

The relationship between their faith and their activism was a mutually supportive and enhancing one: their religious convictions propelled them into abolitionism and the public arena; their activism contributed to the refinement and expansion of their theologies. As their religious convictions matured, they tended to adopt stronger and sometimes more radical political positions: the result being increasing confidence, creativity, and radicalization in both their thought and actions.

The objections of these women to the state of organized Christianity did not preclude their own profound commitment to a Christianity-based religiosity. On the contrary, their ideas about God and God's plan for the world continued to be primary intellectual concerns and motivators of their actions. Their belief in the benevolence of God, in the purity of human nature, and in the ability of human beings to understand God's directives intuitively and respond to them rationally led them to clarify, and above all, to simplify religious precepts. As Sarah Grimké wrote to Theodore Weld, "For many years I have been inquiring the way to Zion and now I know not but I shall have to surrender all, or many of my long cherished parts of religion and come back to the one simple point, 'Follow after holiness without which no man shall see the Lord.'"[79]

5 ❧

"Abolitionism Is Christianity Applied to Slavery"

AN ACTIVIST FAITH

ESPITE THEIR CONVICTION that they were pursuing a divinely ordained mission, the women we are considering, and others like them, were frequently accused of infidelity to Christianity because of their attacks on the state of Christendom in America. Such accusations came from their fellow abolitionists as well as others. Responding to one such abolitionist critic, Samuel Drummond Porter, Abby Kelley affirmed the common ground upon which she and Porter stood: "I can say from my heart of hearts, with you, abolitionism is Christianity applied to slavery: here is the rock upon which our cause rests, and 'the gates of hell shall not prevail against it.'"[1]

The first and most significant element of these women's action-based theologies was the importance of leading a Christlike life, which they interpreted as working to establish justice within the world. As Sallie Holley said, "I want to do an efficient service for humanity, if possible—I want to be a real child of God."[2]

For these women, the most egregious injustice in their world, and therefore the one most in need of Christian action, was slavery, the bondage of millions of God's children in involuntary servitude. In justifying this interpretation of Christian theology, their first step was to claim that slavery was contrary to God's will and that active resistance was, as Abby Kelley claimed, an inevitable outgrowth of a Christian commitment. They claimed, further, that the abolitionists were the spiritual heirs of the biblical prophets, of Jesus and his apostles, and of the early Christian Church. They did this through biblical exegesis and by appropriating and reinterpreting biblical and ecclesiastical symbols in support of their cause.[3]

The Grimkés' justification of their position is the easiest to trace because unlike the others, they actually published antislavery tracts. In these documents both sisters drew primarily on Christian scripture, with some reference to natural rights principles. In Angelina Grimké's 1836 *Appeal to the Christian Women of the South*, she attempted first to establish a bond between herself and her readers by emphasizing their mutual Christianity, addressing her audience as "Sisters in Christ." She proceeded to construct a biblical exegesis on the subject of slavery, beginning with the book of Genesis. Here she noted that although Adam was given dominion over beasts and fowls and fishes, "he was never told that any of the human species were put *under his feet;* it was only *all things,* and man, who was created in the image of his Maker, *never* can properly be termed a *thing,"*— even, though, she added, "the laws of Slave States do call him a 'chattel personal.'" She denied that the patriarchal servitude described in the Bible could be used to justify American slavery: "Look at Abraham, though so great a man, going to the herd himself and fetching a calf from thence and serving it up with his own hands. . . . Look at Sarah, . . . baking cakes upon the hearth. If the servants they had were like Southern slaves, would they have performed such comparatively menial offices for themselves?" She admitted that "a species of *servitude* was permitted to the Jews," but noted that "the servant was [carefully] guarded from violence, injustice and wrong" by numerous legal codes.[4]

Turning to the New Testament, Grimké took up her opponents' claim that slavery was acceptable because Jesus had never spoken against it. One needed, she wrote, go no farther than Christ's injunction that *"Whatsoever* ye would that men should do to you, do *ye even so to them"* to disprove that argument. Likewise, she defended the Apostle Paul against the charge of actively supporting slavery. Paul's letter to Philemon regarding the return of his runaway servant Onesimus, frequently cited as a defense of slavery, could not, she claimed, legitimately be so construed. Paul asked Philemon to receive Onesimus—a man who had not only run away, but had stolen property from his master—*"not* now as a *servant,* but *above* a servant, a brother beloved": to *"receive him as myself."* "This," Grimké continued, "surely cannot be forced into a justification of the practice of returning runaway slaves back to their masters, to be punished with cruel beatings and scourgings as they often are."[5]

In all Grimké brought forth seven arguments against slavery in her

Appeal, five of which were biblically based. The other two arguments rested on grounds of civil rights: that slavery was contrary to the principle of the Declaration of Independence that *"all* men are created equal" and that the system unfairly "protects the *master* in the most unnatural and unreasonable power, whilst it *throws* [the slave] *out* of the protection of law."[6]

Also in 1836, Sarah Grimké penned *An Epistle to the Clergy of the Southern States.* Like her sister, she immediately identified the common Christian ground she shared with her intended audience: "Brethren Beloved in the Lord," she began, "It is because I feel a portion of that love glowing in my heart towards you, which is infused into every bosom by the cordial reception of the Gospel of Jesus Christ, that I am induced to address you as fellow professors of this holy religion." Like her sister, she also drew a careful distinction between *"men and things,"* noting that under the Jewish Dispensation, "'If a man steal an ox, or a sheep, and kill it, or sell it, he shall restore five oxen for an ox, and four sheep for a sheep.' But 'he that stealeth a man and selleth him or if he be found in his hand, he shall surely be put to death.' If this law were carried into effect now, what must be the inevitable doom of all those who now hold man as property?" She concluded, too, that "Jewish servitude, as permitted by God, was as different from American slavery, as Christianity is from heathenism." Unlike Angelina, who ended by simply setting forth appropriate tasks for her readers, Sarah Grimké warned of the need for repentance and restitution lest the nation face God's judgment and closed with, "Yours in gospel love, Sarah M. Grimké."[7]

Having established to their satisfaction the biblical argument against slavery, the Grimkés proceeded to identify themselves and immediatist abolitionists in general with the Old Testament and the prophets, with Jesus and his disciples, and with the early Christian Church. Angelina Grimké had already done this once before when, in justifying her abandonment of her Presbyterian connections, she had identified herself as experiencing a call similar to that heard by the biblical patriarch Abraham. Later, in the midst of the Grimkés' antislavery lecturing, she claimed more broadly that "those who are engaged in the moral reformation of the day are the *true prophets* of this age. In these Societies (not in the nominal church) is embodied *all the moral power* of our beloved but guilty country."[8] Years later, Lucretia Mott evaluated antislavery organization and came to a similar conclusion, declaring that "the Anti-Slavery

Society, by its advancement of right and justice, has found itself eminently a religious organization."[9]

Grimké also pointedly replied to criticisms from Catharine Beecher in an essay Beecher wrote and directed to Angelina Grimké. Beecher was opposed to slavery in principle, but supported gradualism as the means of its abolition. She believed that gentle moral suasion (as opposed to the abrasive tactics of the immediatist abolitionists) was the most expedient and effective method of abolishing slavery. In her *Essay on Slavery and Abolitionism, with Reference to the Duty of American Females*, Beecher asserted that the "character and measures" of the American Anti-Slavery Society "are not either peaceful or Christian in tendency, but they rather are those which tend to generate party spirit, denunciation, recrimination, and angry passions."[10] Grimké responded that such actions were in fact the heritage of Christ.

> Now I solemnly ask thee, whether the character and measures of our holy Redeemer did not produce exactly the same effects? . . . Listen, too, to his own declaration: "I came not to send peace on earth, but a sword. . . . The rebukes which he uttered against sin were eminently calculated to produce "recriminations and angry passions," in all who were determined to *cleave* to their sins. . . . Why, then, protest against our measures as *unchristian*, because they do not smooth the pillow of the poor sinner, and lull his conscience into fatal security?[11]

Christianity, Grimké added, was simply not the "weak, dependent, puerile creature" Beecher described.

Sarah Grimké responded in a similar vein to the renowned Unitarian minister William Ellery Channing's criticism of the abolitionists as having "acted with great inconsideration" and having been "distinguished by the absence of management, calculation and worldly wisdom." She asked, "Did the prophets and apostles talk of oppression and cruelty smoothly[?]" She added that she had found antislavery meetings to "have usually a solemnity which is rarely found by me even in those congregations assembled for divine worship."[12]

The Grimkés' stand on the religious foundation of the abolitionist cause was endorsed by the first Anti-Slavery Convention of American Women in 1837. The first resolution, introduced by Lydia Maria Child, declared abolition to be the will of God:

Resolved, That a thorough investigation of the anti-slavery cause, in all its various aspects and tendencies, has confirmed us in the belief that it is the cause of God, who created mankind free, and of Christ, who died to redeem them from every yoke. Consequently it is the duty of every human being to labor to preserve, and to restore to all who are deprived of it, God's gift of freedom; thus showing love and gratitude to the Great Redeemer by treading in his steps.[13]

Later, Abby Kelley and Sallie Holley also defended the Christian commitment of the abolitionists. Sallie Holley frequently compared the persecuted abolitionists to the early Christian martyrs of Rome because both were "maligned for speaking the truth."[14] In her response to the letter from Samuel Drummond Porter, mentioned at the beginning of this chapter, Abby Kelley denied Porter's inference that Garrison was "opposed to Christianity," claiming instead that "from my particular acquaintance with him I have evidence that his walk is with God and that Christ has been to him a Savior indeed."

Further, Kelley had little patience with charges that Christian abolitionists ought not to criticize the church or associate with non-Christian abolitionists. She responded that the desperation of the situation left no time for social proprieties.

Abolitionists have faults enough—far too many—may heaven forgive them—but while my brother is under the heels of the plunderer, and my sister in the clutch of the spoiler, I have enough to do to lift up my voice in their behalf, and shall be most happy if persons really infidel, will turn to the rescue, and hold up the priest and Levite, the Scribe and Pharisee to the scorn and indignation of the whole world. I have no time to consult matters of taste at such a crisis.[15]

Likewise, Sallie Holley turned the tables on critics such as those who condemned abolitionist Parker Pillsbury's "bad temper." On one such occasion, she retorted, "Then why don't you mild-tempered people do the work? What do you leave this Christian work to infidels for?"[16]

For herself, she was convinced that abolitionists such as Abby Kelley and Stephen Foster, Parker Pillsbury, and William Lloyd Garrison had a deep religious faith. When asked by a more conservative friend how, "with reverence so large," could Holley "ever lecture with the Garrisonian abolitionists," she replied that, in fact, "it was their deep earnestness of heart and life that irresistibly drew me to them. This may startle you," she added. "It would cause a shudder of horror in some, a smile of utter incredulity in others whom we might name. But, in the sincerity of my soul I repeat it, it was their vital, living confidence in God, in the Eternity of Rights, their practical appreciation of the spirit and principles of Jesus Christ, that won my reverence."[17]

"SECTS HAVE SECTARIAN BUSINESS . . . AND CANNOT ATTEND TO HUMANITY": ABOLITION AND COMEOUTERISM

The abolitionist move toward comeouterism was fueled by the lethargy of the Northern churches on the issue of slavery.[18] Rather than actively oppose the institution, most denominations opted to avoid alienating their slave-owning members, taking the attitude that God's will would eventually be done. Even those that did prohibit slaveowning among their members, such as the Society of Friends, did not, as we have seen, necessarily endorse antislavery activism.

The women lecturers tended to place the blame for this passivity on what they considered to be the mistaken priority placed on assent to creed and traditional expressions of piety at the expense of carrying out Christian principles on earth. As Mott commented,

> Many religionists apparently believe that they are consecrating man to the truth and the right, when they convert him to their creeds—to their scheme of salvation, and plan of redemption. They, therefore, are very zealous for the tradition of their fathers, and for the observance of days; while at the same time . . . they give countenance to war, slavery, and other evils; not because they are wholly reckless of the condition of man, but because such is their sectarian idea. Their great error is in imagining that the highest good is found in their church.[19]

Mott and the others were reacting to sentiments expressed by those such as Lyman Beecher, who considered that some of the main functions of the church were "to prepare believers for Heaven; to protect the purity of the Gospel; to maintain holy order in society, including the protection of the Sabbath and maintenance of public worship of God; to educate the young and the non-believer in true religion; to raise up teachers and ministers of the Gospel; and to aid in the spread of the Gospel by missionaries throughout the country and the world."[20] Beecher's chief concern, as expressed here, was the salvation of souls, which he saw as possible through the propagation of sectarian Christianity.

Mott, by contrast, commented repeatedly over the years, "It is time that Christians were judged more by their likeness to Christ than their notions of Christ."[21] She asked rhetorically,

> And what do we ask now? That slavery shall be held up in every congregation, and before all sects, as a greater sin than erroneous thinking; a greater sin than Sabbath breaking. If any of you are seen on Sabbath day with your thimble on, performing some piece of needlework, the feelings of your neighbors are shocked on beholding the sight; and yet these very people may be indifferent to great sins. . . . To some, the sin of slaveholding is not so horrifying as certain deviations from established observances.[22]

In some churches, reference to the misery of slaves was, if not formally banned, at least a breach of etiquette. A friend of Sallie Holley's told her that he had attended a Wesleyan prayer meeting, and "prompted by a convenient pause and his own ardor" had sung the antislavery song, "Feebly the bondman toiled. Sadly he wept." He reported that "this pious company were so shocked by this rash mention of the Slave, that their devotions, which had before been brightly flaming, instantly died out, and the meeting was abruptly dismissed."[23] Holley herself was chastised for mentioning slavery at a school children's celebration in Cattaraugus County, New York. Having been asked to say a few words, she told her young audience of the slave children "who are not allowed to learn to read or write or spell or commit to memory the multiplication table which they had just repeated so well." In recalling the event, Holley wrote:

> I am very sorry to even seem rude and "fanatical," but know not how to avoid it and be faithful to the cause of the slave. In fact, nothing else is so important and proper for all occasions, to be talked of, as the slave and his cause.

It would be most fitting in every sermon, every oration, every prayer, to remember earnestly the astounding fact, that *Christian* America to-day holds four million men, women, and children in slavery![24]

Indeed, antislavery commitment and action became the fundamental principle by which these women and other immediatists judged Christian churches and individuals. As described earlier, Sallie Holley withdrew her membership in the Unitarian Church because of her belief that the church supported Millard Fillmore. She was still more blunt when she arrived early at a Methodist church at which she was to speak. At their Sunday class meeting, the minister, Holley reported, "asked me 'to express my feelings'"—a request he surely regretted:

> I said, My feelings were that the Methodist Church could not be a Christian church while holding, as she does, many thousands of God's dear children as property,—keeping them on a level with the brute beast. The whole manner of the minister was as much to say, If anybody had such unreasonable feelings as these, it would be more convenient for him if she would keep them to herself. He only said, however, that we had not time to discuss the administration of the church. To which I insisted, "But it is the gospel of Christ."[25]

These women, like other antislavery comeouters, were unsympathetic to arguments that good could be accomplished while working within a proslavery church. At the Second Anti-Slavery Convention of American Women, Lucretia Mott and Abby Kelley are recorded as having spoken in favor of a resolution stating that as "the disciples of Christ are commanded to have no fellowship with the 'unfruitful works of darkness' . . . it is our duty to keep ourselves separate from those churches which receive to their pulpits and their communion tables, those who buy, or sell, or hold as property, the image of the living God."[26]

In 1840, Abby Kelley wrote a letter to the editor of the *Anti-Slavery Standard* condemning the Connecticut Anti-Slavery Society for passing resolutions calling on members not to support pro-slavery politicians but refusing to do the same for clergy. As usual, she did not mince her words: "They must have a set of *politicians* whose hands are clear of the blood of the slave, but those whom they receive as ministers of Christ and *expounders of the* Scriptures, may have hands dripping with the blood of the mangled victim."[27]

Kelley continued to blast any accommodation to the existence of slavery, particularly on the part of elected officials and churches. In 1843 she claimed to be "very industriously circulating the tee-total A[nti]S[lavery] Pledge," which read:

> Believing slavery to be a heinous sin and crime, a "curse to the master and a grievous wrong to the slave," we hereby pledge ourselves never to vote for any candidate for civil office, nor countenance any man as a Christian minister, nor hold connection with any organization as a Christian church, except such as are *practically* pledged to labor with us for its immediate and entire extinction from our country.[28]

Abby Kelley, who was not without her own brand of sectarian loyalty—to the Garrisonian party—added with satisfaction, "This will do up new organization,[29] and destroy the comfort of all who hope to find comfort in political anti-slavery, without ecclesiastical. It succeeds to a charm, whenever I try it. In one place a whole Presbyterian church, minister and all have taken it, and thereby cut their connection—excommunicated the Presbytery."

As is clear from the religious arguments employed by these women, criticism of the churches and even comeouterism did not indicate a lack of religious conviction. Rather, as Ann Braude has said of other nineteenth-century radical reformers, "Their rejection of the churches was a rejection not of religion but rather of the corruption of religion."[30] Neither can it fairly be said that they used reform as a substitute for religion. In no case did any of these women imply that activism was identical to faith, but rather, as Mott stated, the "practical life" was "the highest *evidence* of a sound faith."[31] Abby Kelley referred to abolitionism as Christianity *applied* to slavery, not the sum of Christianity; and claimed that reform movements in general were *inspired by* the doctrine of "love to God" and "love to man."[32]

TURNING THEIR BACKS ON PREJUDICE: RACIAL EQUALITY AND ABOLITIONISM

Another way in which these women demonstrated the breadth of their religious vision of antislavery was in their conception of the movement as embracing economic and educational opportunity, and an end to racial discrimination as well as to slavery itself. White abolitionists often did not make a connection between slavery and racial prejudice or between freedom and opportunity.[33] Nor were abolitionists themselves free from prejudice. Sarah Mapps Douglass wrote with gratitude to Abby Kelley, "[I]t rejoices my very soul to meet with an Abolitionist who has turned her back on prejudice."[34] In contrast to many of their peers, the white women lecturers surveyed here grasped the broader implications of the slavery issue. They were able to articulate these connections; through their leadership, issues of prejudice, education, and economic opportunity were addressed and practical solutions advocated at the women's antislavery conventions of the late 1830s.

The link between slavery and racial discrimination was not, of course, a revelation to free African Americans. In 1832 Maria Stewart had argued passionately that the lack of education and economic opportunity for free African Americans left them little better off than had they been enslaved. "Tell us no more of southern slavery" she demanded, "for with few exceptions . . . I consider our condition but little better than that. . . .[M]ethinks there are no chains so galling as those that bind the soul."[35] She called upon white America to repent of its treatment of black Americans or suffer the consequences. God, she claimed, "will not suffer you to quell the proud, fearless and undaunted spirits of the Africans forever; for in his own time, he is able to plead our cause against you, and to pour out upon you the ten plagues of Egypt." But she also challenged black Americans to "become united as one, and cultivate among ourselves the pure principles of piety, morality and virtue." On a more down-to-earth note, she urged free black Americans to establish schools for black young people and to create businesses for themselves.[36] Likewise, Samuel E. Cornish wrote an editorial for the *Colored American* on March 4, 1837, in which he declared that "On *our* conduct [that of free colored Americans], in a great measure, *their* [the slaves'] salvation depends. Let us show that we are worthy to be freemen; it will be the strongest appeal to the judgement and conscience of the slaveholder and his abettors, that can be furnished; and it will be a sure means of our elevation in society, and to the possession of all our rights, as men and citizens."[37]

The conviction that white Americans would embrace black Americans as equals if the latter proved their piety, sobriety, and industry, was far from universal. On the contrary, Sarah Mapps Douglass asserted that at least as far as Quakers went, "in proportion as we become intellectual and respectable, so in proportion does their disgust and prejudice increase."[38] Nonetheless, the prescription of those such as Stewart and Cornish for action on the part of African Americans was widely accepted. Free African Americans could see clearly that antislavery activity extended to the strengthening of the black community economically and politically.[39]

In addition, whereas white abolitionists tended to concentrate on the institution of slavery as the root evil of American society, black Americans saw the problem as something deeper. Lewis Woodson, writing under the pseudonym Augustine, argued that the source of slavery lay in "the *corrupt moral sentiment* of the country." Political means were necessary to abolish slavery "because slavery has been sanctioned and regulated by law, and [these] laws . . . must be repealed" but "the great *primary* means, and as we may see presently, the almost entire means of its abolition, is the correction of this corrupt moral sentiment."[40] Like Maria Stewart, who implored her readers to "prove to the world that there is a reality in religion,"[41] Woodson argued that the first step in improving this moral sentiment was the "reformation of the church."[42]

The female antislavery lecturers agreed that racial prejudice and lack of opportunity were not only contrary to Christian principles but were fundamental social problems. The Grimkés were instrumental in bringing these issues to the attention of the wider body of antislavery women. When Angelina Grimké responded to Elizabeth Pease's request for advice to the women of England, she urged: "Never fail in any addresses you may send us to touch on the subject of *cruel Prejudice.* The North is awfully guilty on this point and ought to be 'sharply rebuked.'"[43]

At the first Anti-Slavery Convention of American Women, Angelina Grimké proposed a resolution,

> That this Convention do firmly believe that the existence of an unnatural prejudice against our colored population, is one of the chief pillars of American slavery . . . and that we deem it a solemn duty for every woman to pray to be delivered from such an unholy feeling, and to act out the principles of Christian equality by associating with them as though the color of the skin was of no more consequence than that of the hair, or the eyes.[44]

This resolution was passed by the convention. The women also commended the institutions of higher learning that admitted people of color, such as Oneida, Western Reserve College, and Oberlin (with Oberlin receiving special commendation for admitting women as well as men). They agreed to work to eliminate segregated seating in their churches and vowed that "as long as our churches are disgraced with side-seats and corners set apart for [black members], we [the white members] will, as much as possible, take our seats with them."[45] They resolved that it was the duty of abolitionists to hire people of color "whenever opportunities offer for so doing." Abolitionists also needed "to establish and maintain day, evening, and Sabbath schools irrespective of color," and to visit schools where colored students were taught to "strengthen" the teachers and "encourage" the pupils.[46]

In contrast, at another convention of Garrisonian abolitionists held later that month, the all-male delegate body took a more bootstrap approach to the problem of racial prejudice. Although they agreed that it was "essential to eradicate from among our white population, and especially from abolitionists themselves, the remains of that irrational, unnatural and unchristian prejudice" against their colored brethren, they "rejoice[d] in the efforts being made by "our free colored brethren, to improve and elevate their intellectual, moral and religious character." They trusted that "while every encouragement and assistance should be given to these exertions, . . . every colored American will feel that a double responsibility is now laid upon him—that upon his conduct depends, not only his own welfare, but in a great degree, that of his race—and that all will, therefore, endeavor, by constant well-doing, to put to silence the voice of prejudice and persecution."[47]

At the Women's Convention of 1838, after some debate concerning whether "a resolution couched in such phraseology, might, by being misapprehended, injure the abolition cause," the delegates passed Sarah Grimké's resolution that it was "the duty of abolitionists to identify themselves with these oppressed Americans, by sitting with them in places of worship, by appearing with them in our streets, by giving them our countenance in steam-boats and stages, by visiting them at their homes and encouraging them to visit us, receiving them as we do our white fellow citizens.[48]

By 1839, although the Grimkés did not attend that year's convention, several resolutions concerning prejudice and discrimination were passed, including the most specific one to date on the importance of education and employment opportunity: "*Resolved*, That henceforth we will increase our efforts to improve the condition of our free colored population, by giving them mechanical, literary, and religious instruction, and assisting to establish them in trades, and such other employments as are now denied them on account of their color."[49]

Also at the 1839 convention, Lucretia Mott described an encounter with the mayor of Philadelphia, who had approached her with a request. He asked that white women "avoid unnecessary walking with colored people" at the convention in order to avoid such a riot as had occurred the previous year, when Pennsylvania Hall (the abolitionists' newly built meeting place) had been burned to the ground. Mott replied that they "should do as we had done before—walk with them as occasion offered; . . . [that] it was a principle with us, which we could not yield, to make no distinction on account of color" and that she personally "was expecting delegates from Boston of that complexion, and should, probably, accompany them to the place of meeting."[50]

The Grimkés and Abby Kelley were particularly severe on the problem of prejudice within the Society of Friends. Angelina Grimké wrote to Abby Kelley, also still a Quaker at that time, with a damning assessment of the Quaker commitment to human rights:

> A colored man of this city in speaking to me on this subject remarked, the Quakers have desired our emancipation, but *not our elevation*. I have thought a good deal of this observation and must confess from my knowledge of the sentiments of Friends, this is a correct statement. . . . I have often wondered why so few of this class ever attended our meetings, when we stood forth to the world as their best friends, but upon investigation, I find that as a Society we never have practically acknowledged their rights as human being[s], never cast off all "respect of persons," never recommended any one of them as ministers, elders, or overseers and several times refused to receive them even as members, when no other reason could be assigned for such rejection but the color of their skins. Yea more, when they have come to our meetings we have been virtually guilty of saying to them "Stand thou there, or sit here under my footstool"—for they well know that it is expected, they should sit separate from the whites, and take the lowest place among us.[51]

Grimké ascribed this contradiction between principle and action to a "feeling of aristocracy among us" that prevented Friends from desiring true equality with "what are contemptuously called the *lower* orders." Sarah Grimké noted as well that Friends, although prohibited from owning slaves, nonetheless profited from the slave trade because "they were engaged in the cotton trade, and that so far from labouring to destroy the system, they were filling their coffers with the unrighteous gains of oppression."[52]

The Grimkés sought to combat this racial prejudice in their personal lives as well as in their public statements. While still members of the Society of Friends, they began to make a point of seating themselves in the "negro seat," the bench designated for the use of black worshippers. They maintained a lifelong friendship and correspondence with Sarah Mapps Douglass. They complained of being hurt when Douglass visited them at their new home in Fort Lee, New Jersey, for one day only and then wrote to them, thanking them for their "christian conduct" in receiving her. Angelina Grimké Weld replied:

> O! how humbling to receive such thanks! What a crowd of reflections throng the mind as we enquire *Why* does her full heart thus overflow with gratitude? Yes, how irresistably are we led to contemplate the woes which iron hearted Prejudice inflicts upon the oppressed of our land—the hidden sorrows they endure, the full cup of bitterness which is wrung out to them by the hands of professed followers of him who is no respecter of persons.[53]

Sarah Grimké turned to Sarah Douglass and her mother, Grace Douglass, when, in response to the request from Elizabeth Pease, she began to compile evidence of racial prejudice within the Society of Friends in the United States. In "Colorphobia exemplified," the Douglasses' experiences of prejudice and discrimination were prominently featured.

Abby Kelley agreed with the Grimkés' assessment of Quaker prejudice. As she "disowned" the Society of Friends, she stated flatly, "[t]hey are, as a body, pro-slavery at heart." She found this particularly reprehensible, for "[s]tanding as the society does, on such high professions, and having had the credit of being anti-slavery, how much more deadly is its influence against abolition than the professed pro-slavery . . ."[54]

The other women here, like the Grimkés, attempted to address the issues of prejudice and economic opportunity in their private lives as well as in their public words. Mott's correspondence often contains casual references to attending (and speaking at) black religious meetings and socializing with African American friends such as the Purvis and Remond families.[55]

Sallie Holley mentioned once that she had been asked if she "would actually associate with blacks. When I said that I had done it for years, the astonishment was extreme."[56] At least once she enjoyed a stay at "the elegant country home of Robert Purvis."[57] In the 1860s she was still adamant about the linkage between prejudice and slavery. In 1862 she wrote, "Even if Emancipation is consummated the coming year, there remains to conquer this atrocious hatred of color—and to explode utterly all idea of colonization as not only a cruel insult to the colored people—but a miserable national policy."[58] In 1870 she opposed the disbanding of the American Anti-Slavery Society, believing that it continued to be needed to advocate for the rights of African Americans.[59]

The question remains as to how these women, unlike so many of their peers, were able to recognize these problems and why they and the other women at the female antislavery conventions were willing to put their ideas into practice. One significant reason for their being able to do so may have been their own experience of the restrictions imposed on them because of their sex.

It has justly been pointed out that however strongly white women claimed to identify with slavery there was still a critical difference between their understanding and that of women such as Sojourner Truth and Harriet Jacobs who had experienced it firsthand. Jean Fagan Yellin argues that "by conflating the oppression of women who were enslaved and the oppression of women who were free . . . white free antislavery feminists obscured the crucial differences between the experience of women who were held as chattel and their own experience."[60] Indeed, the same might be said for free African Americans such as Maria Stewart, who felt their situation to be equivalent to slavery.

On the one hand, this point is well-taken in the context of the co-optation of slavery as a symbol of the condition of white women. On the other hand, this identification of situation also had its advantages, as in the ability of women to see that the elimination of chattel slavery alone would not result in real freedom for African Americans. Their own firsthand experiences of the limitations that could be imposed on "freedom" made them, perhaps, more aware of the needs that free African Americans faced. The frustration that the Grimkés experienced when first beginning their anti-slavery lecturing is captured in Angelina Grimké's plea for understanding from Theodore Weld: "[C]an you not see that women *could* do, and *would* do a hundred times more for the slave if she were not fettered[?]"[61] Given the frequent reminders of the restrictions society imposed, or tried to impose on women, it is not so surprising that Grimké could readily acknowledge discrimination as an issue, or that her introduction of this issue into the agenda of the Anti-Slavery Conventions of American Women would be so well received.

This is not to argue, however, that these women, with their combination of religious conviction and social experience, had entirely clear and unbiased perceptions of their society. Strewn among their correspondence and published remarks are occasional references that draw attention to their own prejudices. One area about which they tended to express little tolerance was African American religious forms. While the Grimkés and Kelley are silent on this point, Holley, and to some degree, Mott, were straightforward about their distaste for the exuberant style of black worship.

Having moved to rural Virginia after the Civil War to help run a school for black children, Holley had ample opportunity to observe black worship and found it reprehensible:

> The religion of these coloured people is very demoralising. It has no connection with moral principle. They have just had a "three days' meeting" in the old stolen schoolhouse, and made night hideous with their horrible singing and prayers, and dancing in a wild, savage way. The noise and shuffling and scraping can be heard in every direction, and our house, though not very near, seems almost shaken by their dancing. It is like the tread of an army in weight and sound. One of our young lady teachers says it reminds her of a heavy sea beating against a rocky beach! They get drunk on tobacco and then in their high excitement go to meeting and keep up till almost morning, in their fearful, exhausting action![62]

On another occasion she defined her objections to this religious style: "The coloured 'protracted meeting' is this week in full blast, making night hideous with terrible noises. All this kind of religion seems to me *worthless.*

It doesn't save from lies and stealing. Nobody's character is elevated or ennobled. Vanity and self-conceit are fostered. People pray and shout and say the Holy Ghost is moving their souls! It is awful."[63]

Lucretia Mott was less vehement but nonetheless clearly believed that religious conviction was more faithfully expressed in quiet reflection than in singing and shouting (although she also cautioned Quakers against thinking that their silent meeting was the epitome of worship). While she accepted that this dynamic style of worship seemed to be presently neces-sary "among the ignorant coloured people of our city [who] . . . seem to require this animal excitement," she believed firmly that "it is not the high-est idea, the most enlightened view of the exercises of spiritual worship of our God."[64]

An additional blind spot shared by all these women was in the area of class. They did recognize some of the difficulties of urban poor and working-class people and, in Holley's case, of poor rural farmers. They could see obvious problems, such as the need for a day of rest for workers, the unfair working conditions of many household servants, and low wages. Abby Kelley, for example, was struck by the plight of an Irish ser-vant girl she met in a home in which she stayed in Chatham, Pennsylvania. The girl, she wrote to Stephen Foster, "labors hard from morning till night for a dollar per week." Mrs. Hobson "does nothing. Not even so much as make her own bed, but keeps this poor girl constantly on her feet." Kelley felt, too, that her plight went beyond her physical labor, commenting on "the slavish manner in which she is regarded. Shut up in her desolate kitchen—outcast—'Tis too much for a heart of flesh to bear—this pro-scription—this oppression—this casting off a fallen immortal." Kelley added, "I think, Stephen, we should be faithful in the families where we go and bear testimony against this great wickedness. I have been negli-gent."[65] Likewise, in the travel diary Lucretia Mott kept while she was in England, she recorded her observations on the condition of laborers in fields and towns as well as her antislavery conversations. It is worthy of note, though, that at one dinner party the very hospitable and egalitarian Motts seated their "carpenter . . . and 4 others" at a table in the kitchen, even though their large dining table was not quite filled.[66]

Both Holley and Kelley were condescending about the less educated people among whom they traveled and worked. In Indiana, Kelley wrote: "The settlers are mainly the poorer classes from North Carolina. Ignorant, filthy, conceited. . . . They are . . . very jealous of the 'Eastern people who pretend to know such a heap and are so proud as to wear 'boughten cloth.'"[67] Holley tended to be condescending toward the poor blacks she taught at the Holley school and scornful of the poor whites, whom she found ignorant. Writing to Elizabeth Miller after one Christmas, she criticized "these poor whites with their blank, lean faces. Too silly or proud to attend, or to allow their little children to attend our *coloured* school!"[68]

While collapsing distinctions of class for the native Virginians, Holley maintained them in regard to herself. She was, for example, grateful for her vacations from the Holley school not only because of her respite from hard work but because she could for a time cease being the "servant of servants."[69] Included among one of the many anecdotes in her letters was an ethnic joke. Reporting that she had been diagnosed as having "torpidity of the liver," she added: "Did you ever hear of the Irishman who, when his physician told him he had torpidity of the liver, understood that he had a torpedo in his liver?"[70] Another comment that seems to reveal her acceptance of the Irish stereotypes common at the time was her praise of Abby Kelley Foster's "reverence for humanity" as "shown by her ways towards the Irish girls who have lived with her during the past summer."[71]

Neither were the Grimkés immune from class prejudice. While still living with her family in South Carolina, Angelina Grimké tried to restrain her brothers from physically abusing their slaves, but while noting this in an early diary entry, she also clarified her position on the validity of class distinctions:

> When I say that all men are *brothers* I am far from desiring to break the walls of separation which exist between different ranks of society, for I believe these distinctions are right, and tend to the happiness and advantage of the human family at large. Experience has abundantly taught me that so far from its being best to abolish these, that a person of high rank cannot put themselves on an equality with one of lower life, without injuring both, and vice versa.[72]

Although in her antislavery work and in her later life, Grimké subscribed to the view that "God is no respecter of persons," she never explicitly retracted her earlier remark or provided another clear statement of her ideas regarding class.

Sarah Grimké's experience with supervising housekeeping help led her to stereotype servants, commenting once that she had found truthfulness to be "a virtue . . . very rare in servants."[73] Like Holley, though, she identified and deplored class prejudice on the part of others. As she wrote: "I mourn over the aristocracy that prevails among our colored brethren. I cherished the hope that suffering had humbled them and prepared them to perform a glorious part in the reformation of our country, but the more I mingle with them the fainter are my hopes. They have as much caste among themselves as we have and despise the poor as much I fear as their pale brethren."[74]

A final example of their lack of perceptiveness shows itself in the kind but condescending way that they tended to relate to the African Americans with whom they associated in the antislavery movement and as friends. This is less true of Mott, and Kelley says little to indicate her views one way or the other, but it is certainly the case with the Grimkés and with Holley.[75] In the otherwise admirable resolutions proposed at the Anti-Slavery Conventions of American Women, it is significant that the *we's* often employed in the language of the resolutions clearly referred to white women, whereas the *theys* were used in conjunction with some reference to African Americans. This was despite the fact that black women attended the conventions as delegates and even served as officers. Sallie Holley's comments about the disbanding of the American Anti-Slavery Society are well taken, but again her language was condescending. She referred to the Society as the "friends and guardians" of the "coloured race," and claimed that "the American Nation is not good enough to be trusted with the care of the black race." Despite her association with activist African Americans such as Robert Purvis and Sojourner Truth, her language in one letter was particularly condescending. She wrote in 1869 that she was still active in the "Great Cause" as "[t]he negro is not yet where I wish to place him." She also revealed both a racial and regional bias in her communications from the Holley School, commenting for example that "[t]his coloured race is improvident and lacks management. It will take generations to make them like Northerners, in industry, economy, and thrift."[76]

The limitations of these women's visions are regrettable. Although their linkage of women's rights, slavery, and racial prejudice under a broad umbrella of Christian responsibility was farsighted, they did not eradicate all vestiges of cultural bias from their thinking. Nonetheless, perhaps their limitations help prove the point made earlier about the importance of experience in perceiving the reality that lies behind conventionally accepted truths. The positions of these women as relatively privileged, well-educated Easterners made them susceptible to biases against less well-off, less educated people, particularly those who were not from the Northeast. Their gender and religious struggles, however, gave them insight into the institutionalization of sex discrimination and into the injustices perpetrated by religious authorities. Their own marginalization propelled them toward the conclusion that not only was Southern slavery an egregious sin, but that Northern racial prejudice was inextricably linked to that sin, and that the complete abolition of the former required the dissolution of the latter as well.

6

"It Is Not the Cause of the Slave Only Which We Plead"

FAITH IN ACTION FOR WOMEN'S RIGHTS

THE ABILITY OF FREE women to identify with the enslaved did more than strengthen their commitment to antislavery action. As Abby Kelley commented, "in striving to strike his [the slave's] irons off we found most surely that we were manacled ourselves."[1] This realization of the constraints in their own lives was especially pronounced for the women who, like the antislavery lecturers, felt called to work in an unconventional and public way.

As the first abolitionist women to lecture on a large scale to groups composed of men as well as women, we have seen that the Grimkés encountered opposition from the clergy and others directed not simply at their message but at them as public speakers. The propriety of their speaking in public was also a topic of conversation at abolitionist gatherings; there, however, Angelina Grimké "found a very general sentiment prevailing that it was time our [women's] fetters were broken." She added,

> I feel as if it is not the cause of the slave only which we plead but the cause of woman as a responsible and moral being, and I am ready to exclaim 'Who is sufficient for these things?' These holy causes must be injured if they are not helped by us. . . . I see not to what point, all these things are leading me, I wonder whether I shall make shipwreck of the faith—I cannot tell—but one thing comforts me, I do feel as tho' the Lord had sent us, and as if I was leaning on the arm of my beloved.[2]

For the Grimkés, the process of identifying themselves publicly as women's rights advocates paralleled their original commitment to antislavery activism. In the face of the injustice that they observed and in their own cases experienced, they determined that divine will dictated their active resistance.

Ironically, it was the opposition to their appearances as antislavery lecturers that motivated the Grimkés to articulate a theory of women's rights. One can hardly help but wonder if the wiser course for their critics might have been simply to ignore their unconventional activities rather than to draw attention to them. Sallie Holley claimed to have experienced the benefits of such attacks when she spoke at a Congregational church in Rochester in 1855. The previous week the pulpit had been filled by a minister from a neighboring town who "read the notice of my lecture, 'by request' as he was particular to say. And expressed his surprise and grief that the church should be allowed for such a purpose, solemnly exhorting the people not to give their attendance. The direct effect of this advice proved to be, like the cry of 'Mad dog!' Everybody rushed out to see if the 'dog' was 'mad' and how a 'mad dog' looked, reckless of the danger."[3]

But this is wisdom in hindsight. At the time, the opponents of women's public political speech no doubt deemed it essential to register their immediate condemnation of such public flaunting of social convention. In so doing, they—many of whom were clergy—seem both to have overestimated the extent of general deference to their authority and to the social mores they championed, and to have underestimated the strength and eloquence of those they criticized and of their supporters.

In accordance with their original invitation from the American Anti-Slavery Society, the Grimkés first expected to give a series of parlor talks for women only. This would be an act pushing the limits of women's sphere because of the politically charged nature of the issue they were to address, but nonetheless would fall more or less within the bounds of propriety. As Sarah Grimké explained to Elizabeth Pease, "When we came in to this state [Massachusetts] in the 5th Month, we had no intention of holding meetings with any but women." The first transgressors of convention were not the Grimkés, but rather men who, curious about these Southern women who dared to speak in public on such a topic, began to insinuate themselves into the Grimkés' meetings. At the second meeting they held in Boston, Grimké noted, "to my surprise . . . about 50 men, foes as well as friends no doubt, took their seats in the back pews."[4]

The earliest, most notable attack on the Grimkés was a Pastoral Letter of the Congregational Churches of Massachusetts issued in response to their 1837 lecture tour. In this missive, the Congregational clergy warned that women who attempted to usurp male roles, as in public speaking, were doomed to failure and disgrace:

> The power of woman is her dependence, flowing from the consciousness of that weakness which God has given her for her protection . . . . But when she assumes the place and tone of man as a public reformer . . . she yields the power which God has given her for protection, and her character becomes unnatural. If the vine, whose strength and beauty is to lean upon the trellis-work, and half conceal its clusters, thinks to assume the independence and the overshadowing nature of the elm, it will not only cease to bear fruit, but fall in shame and dishonor into the dust.[5]

Others also began to question the wisdom of the Grimkés' lecturing. Only a month after he ridiculed the fears of his fellow clergymen, Amos Phelps himself changed his tune. He viewed with alarm the expansion of the Grimkés' audiences to include men as well as women—an ironic development given the common knowledge among abolitionists that Phelps himself had been one of the first men to slip into a meeting house to hear the Grimkés for himself.[6] Phelps wrote to remonstrate with the sisters and suggested that they allow him to publish the information that they *"preferred* having *female* audiences only."[7]

Sarah Grimké replied to Phelps in what Angelina described as an "admirable letter." Like Angelina, her first line of defense was to assert their obedience to God's will, however arbitrary it might seem from a human standpoint. "We are simply doing our duty," she claimed, "and the consequences we must leave to him who has pointed out this path for us to walk in, if in calling us thus publicly to advocate the cause of the down-trodden slave, God has unexpectedly placed us in the fore-front of the battle which is to be waged against the rights and duties and responsibilities of woman, it would ill become us to shrink from such a contest."[8] Although they did not succeed in convincing Phelps and others like him of the merit of their path, they committed themselves to it regardless of the tribulations they might face. Sarah Grimké gently chided Phelps for advising them to go against what they perceived as God's will, saying, "my brother we have planted our feet on the Rock of Ages and our trust is in Him who saith 'Trust in the Lord for in the Lord Jehovah is ever-lasting strength.'"

Members of the clergy were not the only opponents of these women's antislavery lecturing; nor were all their adversaries male. Catharine Beecher led another attack in her *Essay on Slavery and Abolitionism*. She asserted that although women's influence was critical to the proper functioning of the "Divine economy," it was not to be exercised within the public sphere: "Woman is to win every thing by peace and love; by making herself so much respected, esteemed and loved, that to yield to her opinions and to gratify her wishes, will be the free-will offering of the heart. But this is to be all accomplished in the domestic and social circle." Women who joined anti-slavery societies, and especially those who conducted public lectures, were guilty of creating additional strife rather than acting as "peaceful mediators to hush the opposing elements." Beecher hoped to convince them that their course of action was both "unwise and inexpedient."[9]

Beecher's criticism should have rung somewhat hollow, given her own public mission of establishing teacher training seminaries for women. She did not acknowledge any such contradiction, however; nor was that a charge leveled at her by Angelina Grimké in the latter's lengthy rebuttal.

Instead, Grimké dissected the thinking of those who attempted to assign different roles to women and men. In response to the assertion that "woman is to win everything by peace and love," she retorted, "This principle may do as the rule of action to the fashionable belle . . . whose every attitude and smile are designed to win the admiration of others to *herself*; and who enjoys . . . [the] flattery which is offered to *her* vanity, by yielding to *her* opinions, and gratifying her wishes, because they are *hers*." The Christian woman, Grimké claimed, must set herself a higher standard. "It is not *her* opinion or *her* wishes that should be gratified"; rather "it is *truth* which she seeks to recommend to others, *truth* which she wants them to esteem and love, and not herself."[10]

This document, along with Sarah Grimké's extensive *Letters on the Equality of the Sexes*, was a major contribution toward American feminist theory. The Grimkés' insights were not unprecedented. As Lerner notes, one of the sad features of women's history is the extent to which women, largely unaware of the "obscure" thoughts and writings of other women before them, have not had the luxury of building on one another's thoughts, but rather have had to "reinvent the wheel, over and over again, generation after generation."[11] Nonetheless, the writings of the Grimkés and the sermons of Lucretia Mott over many years are insightful analyses and powerful statements of women's rights.

Letters on the Equality of the Sexes was first published as a series in the *New England Spectator* and the *Liberator* in 1837 and 1838. The *Letters* are a wide-ranging examination of the position of women in society, beginning with Grimké's assertion of the biblical basis for equality: as "God created man in his own image . . . male and female created he them . . . there is not one particle of difference intimated as existing between [men and women]. They were both made in the image of God; dominion was given to both over every other creature, but not over each other."[12]

The congruence of the sisters' views is shown in a letter Angelina Grimké wrote in response to a request to explain her views "on the duty of woman to labor in the Temperance and all other moral Reformations." Having warned her correspondent that her beliefs were "so *ultra* that I doubt whether thou wouldst assent to them, much less be willing to make any use of them," she echoed Sarah Grimké's logic: "at the time our first parents were created God said unto *them* 'have dominion over the fish of the sea, and over the fowl of the air, and every living thing that moveth upon the earth.' Even in a state of primeval purity and bliss man was invested with *no* power over woman, but both alike swayed the sceptre of universal dominion standing side by side right under the moral government of Almighty God.[13] Grimké went on to cite as precedent the numbers of women in the Bible, such as Deborah, Esther, Anna, and Huldah, who served God publicly and with divine authority.[14]

Likewise Lucretia Mott, although never basing her own argument solely on scripture, urged women to examine the scriptures for themselves, "and if they will read that book intelligently, not with the eye of the theologian, nor with a blind faith in what their ministers have taught them, but with a reliance upon their own judgment, they will discover that the Scriptures cannot be wielded against us."[15] At a Woman's Convention in Rochester in 1848, Mott commented that people "had all got our notions too much from the clergy, instead of the Bible." She requested a clergyman who was objecting to the idea of women serving as ministers to "read his Bible over again, and see if there was anything there to prohibit woman from being a religious teacher."[16]

Sarah Grimké's criticism of the most widely used English translation of the Bible, the King James Version, was, as we have found, sweeping. Believing that "King James's translators certainly were not inspired," she stated in the first of her *Letters*, "I therefore claim the original as my standard, *believing that to have been inspired*."[17]

Mott gave some examples of mistranslations that reinforced ideas of women's inequality. She noted that "in the phrase in which 'Phebe, the servant of the church,' is mentioned, those who are familiar with the original have found, that the same word, which is, in her case, translated *servant*, is, in the case of men, translated *minister*."[18] In the same way, she said, the scriptural phrase that had been translated as the "wives of deacons" was accurately translated from the original text as "the *female* deacons."[19]

Just as they determined that the Book of Genesis does not discriminate between men and women, so too did they turn to the New Testament and the precepts of Jesus. Mott noted that "[t]he laws given on Mount Sinai for the government of man and woman were equal, the precepts of Jesus make no distinction."[20] Sarah Grimké agreed:

> The Lord Jesus defines the duties of his followers in his Sermon on the Mount . . . without any reference to sex or condition:—"Ye are the light of the world. . . . Let your light so shine before men, that they may see your good works, and glorify your Father which is in Heaven." I follow him through all his precepts, and find him giving the same directions to women as to men, never even referring to the distinction now so strenuously insisted upon between masculine and feminine virtues.

She concluded: "Men and women were CREATED EQUAL; they are both moral and accountable beings, and whatever is *right* for man to do, is *right* for woman." If, therefore, "it is the duty of man to preach the unsearchable riches of Christ, it is the duty also of woman."[21]

Angelina Grimké pointed out that "a woman was the only earthly parent of the Prince of Peace. . . . To a woman too, he first appeared after his resurrection" and added, "If then the Prince of Peace has conferd such high and special tokens of regard upon woman, ought she not to aid in spreading far and wide those principles?"[22] "I recognize no rights but *human* rights," she claimed. "I know nothing of men's rights and women's rights; for in Christ Jesus, there is neither male nor female."[23]

The Apostle Paul was (and is) the biblical authority most often cited to justify women's domestic and subservient roles, and Mott and the Grimkés addressed his message directly. They argued that Paul's admonitions were designed for specific situations only and were not meant to be applied globally. Otherwise, they argued, why would Paul have given instructions elsewhere on how women were to pray and prophecy? Even prior to her own lecturing career Angelina Grimké had argued that

> In the subject of women preaching, I think thou wilt find from an attentive perusal of the 14 of Cor. that the Apostle was correcting the common practice of women getting up in meetings for worship and disputing with their teachers, in this case they were commanded to be silent or to learn at home. This must be the meaning of the passage for the apostle cannot contradict himself and so far from commanding them not to pray or prophecy he gives them express direction how they were to do it.[24]

Further, Lucretia Mott reminded listeners that, in addition to prohibiting women from public speech, Paul had also advised that it was better for men to remain celibate and for widows to refrain from remarrying. On another occasion, in reference to the suffrage question, she noted that the biblical injunction that a wife must obey her husband might sometimes "cut the other way; as in mine, for example, because *my* husband wishes me to vote."[25] To insist on the inerrancy of the Bible would mean to take all those passages literally.

The above are examples of the construction of a primarily scriptural justification for women's public actions. Although scripture was the focus of their arguments, they drew on natural rights doctrines as well. Angelina Grimké, for example, responded to "the popular objection Slavery is a political subject, therefore women should not intermeddle" by arguing that "it was, but [I] endeavored to show that women were citizens and had dutys to perform to their country as well as men."[26] In the end, though, they were served chiefly by their conviction that to "[God] alone is she [woman] accountable for the use of those talents with which Her Heavenly Father has entrusted her."[27]

In one of her *Letters to Catherine Beecher*, Angelina Grimké also considered men's and women's roles from a different angle, critiquing the notion that men's work might necessarily involve them in unseemly and perhaps even immoral acts. "I prize the purity of *his* character as highly as

I do that of hers. As a moral being, *whatever it is morally wrong for her to do, it is morally wrong for him to do.* The fallacious doctrine of male and female virtues has well nigh ruined all that is morally great and lovely in his character: he has been quite as deep a sufferer by it as woman."[28]

In translating their newly articulated philosophies to action, what began as happenstance shortly became a matter of philosophical commitment. By 1838 the Grimkés' position on mixed audiences was so firm that they were no longer willing to address audiences that were specifically limited to women. In March, Sarah Grimké responded to an invitation to speak, saying, "I do not fully understand what you mean by 'addressing your annual meeting;' whether it is expected that we should address a meeting of women only, or whether it will be a meeting of men and women. If the former we must decline your invitation, but we are quite willing to hold a public meeting on the 24th of next month."[29]

Further, having acted in accordance with their individual apprehension of divine will, the Grimkés proceeded to transmit their views to the wider body of antislavery women. At the first Anti-Slavery Convention of American Women, Angelina Grimké offered the following resolution (mentioned briefly in Chapter 2 and reprinted here in full) with her usual forthrightness and eloquence:

> *Resolved,* That as certain rights and duties are common to all moral beings, the time has come for woman to move in that sphere which Providence has assigned her, and no longer remain satisfied in the circumscribed limits with which corrupt custom and a perverted application of Scripture have encircled her; therefore that it is the duty of woman, and the province of woman, to plead the cause of the oppressed in our land, and to do all that she can by her voice, and her pen, and her purse, and the influence of her example, to overthrow the horrible system of American slavery.[30]

This resolution did not meet with unanimous approval; according to the recorder, it "called forth an animated and interesting debate respecting the rights and duties of women." Unfortunately the recorder did not see fit to report the details of that debate, so we know little more than that Lucretia Mott was one of the principal supporters of this resolution, and that eventually it was passed without amendment. The following day, however, Lydia Maria Child moved that the resolution be reconsidered because of the dissenting views of some of those present on "the province of women." A majority, however, continued to support the original resolution, and Child's motion to reconsider was defeated. To register their disagreement with the outcome some delegates went so far as to ask that their names be recorded in the minutes as opposed to the resolution. Despite this evidence of disharmony, the convention as a whole was remarkable for the unity and clarity of purpose expressed by the proposers of resolutions and the delegate body as a whole. Although not all delegates agreed that an expansion of roles for women should be universalized, the work of the Grimkés was not criticized, at least not publicly.

However, in beginning to articulate principles of women's rights, the Grimkés did alienate more of their erstwhile supporters, even some of those who endorsed women's rights in theory. This was despite the fact that the Grimkés did not address the topic on the lecture platform. After Angelina Grimké convinced one of her male hosts that the Bible endorsed women's preaching, he asked her to address this point in her next lecture. During that lecture, she spoke for two hours without mentioning the topic. Later her host asked her why she did not, and in considering the matter she said, "In fact I had entirely forgotten all about it until his enquiry. . . . Now I believe the Lord orders these things so, driving out of my mind what I ought *not* to speak on. If the time ever comes when this will be a part of my public work, then I shall not be able to forget it"[31]

Despite the fact that they did not use the lecture platform as a forum for the women's rights issue, the Grimkés were undeniably associated with the topic. This concerned many abolitionists, who felt that the controversy surrounding women's rights could only detract from the progress of their main cause, abolition. Although the Grimkés were not asked to stop lecturing on antislavery, they were asked to dissociate themselves as far as possible from the women's rights issue. Lewis Tappan had endorsed the Grimkés' lecturing as the parlor talks originally conceived, and although he personally disapproved of "women in general addressing large promiscuous assemblies, or mixing with men in meetings for business," he tolerated their speaking to mixed audiences, considering them a special case. "But," he explained, "when the public mind became diverted from the Anti-Slavery question to discussing 'woman's right,' it appeared to me unwise for anti-slavery women to persevere in a course of action which, though not sinful, was attended with apparent injury to the abolition cause."[32]

One of their mentors, the abolitionist poet John Greenleaf Whittier, urged the Grimkés to accept that their mere appearances upon lecture platforms were "practical and powerful assertions of the right and the duty of woman to labor side by side with her brother for the welfare and redemption of the world." He applauded that witness, but opposed any more active exposition of women's rights. The position of slaves was so much worse than the "paltry grievance" of women that any involvement by an abolitionist in women's rights could only be taken as selfishness.

> Does it not *look*, dear sisters, like abandoning in some degree the cause of the poor and miserable slave, sighing from the cotton plantation of the Mississippi, and whose cries and groans are forever sounding in our ears, for the purpose of arguing and disputing about some trifling oppression, political or social, which we may ourselves suffer? . . . Oh let us try to forget everything but our duty to God and our fellow beings.[33]

Theodore Weld pressed the additional point that, having been personally acquainted with slavery, the Grimké sisters were ideally suited to press for its abolition, while "[a]ny women of your powers will produce as much effect as you on the north in advocating the rights of *free* women." "Now can't you," he asked, "leave the *lesser* work to others who can do it *better* than you, and devote, consecrate your whole bodies, souls and spirits to the *greater* work which you can do far better and to far better purpose than any body else."[34]

Weld and others believed that

> the abolition question is most powerfully preparative and introductory to the *other* question. By pushing the former with all our might we are most effectually advancing the latter. . . . Let us all *first* wake up the nation to lift millions of slaves of both sexes from the dust, and turn them into MEN and then when we all have our hand in, it will be an easy matter to take millions of females from their knees and set them on their feet, or in other words transform them from *babies* into *women*.[35]

Women's rights, he claimed, was a principle derivative from human rights. Abolitionists were learning gradually to support the rights of women as well as of black Americans, but to attempt to push them along would be disastrous. "Your womans rights!" he scolded them. "You put the cart before the horse; you drag the tree by the top in attempting to push your *womans* rights, until human rights have gone ahead and broken the *path.*"[36]

The criticisms of Weld and others were reflected in the sisters' own doubts about the correctness of their path. As Angelina wrote, "I cannot help feeling some regret that this sh'ld have come up *before* the Anti Slavery question was settled, so fearful am I that it may injure that blessed cause." She went on, however, without pause, and added, "and then again I think this must be the Lord's time and therefore the *best* time, for it seems to have been brought about by a concatenation of circumstances over which we had no control.[37]

The Grimkés were increasingly of the opinion that it was both inadvisable and impossible to separate the reforms of the day. Sarah Grimké responded to one of their critics, writing that it was a "pity that we have got Christianity parcelled off in lots, so that we fancy that what is designed to be one beautiful and harmonious whole will be injured by the parts coming in contact."[38] Angelina Grimké continued this theme, declaring that woman's rights are "a part of the great doctrine of Human rights and can no more be separated from Emancipation than the light from the heat of the sun; the rights of the slave and of women blend like the colors of the rainbow."[39] Again, she asserted their primary justification, that they were fulfilling God's will, and that it was the "Anti Slavery men . . . [who were] trying very hard to separate what God hath joined together." "I fully believe," she added, "that so far from keeping different moral reformations entirely distinct that no such attempt can ever be successful. They are bound together in a circle like the sciences, they blend with each other like the colors of the rainbow—they are the parts only of our glorious whole and that whole is Christianity, pure practical Christianity."[40]

Though the Grimkés were criticized by many, others shared their views on the necessary linkage of reforms. In 1837, Abby Kelley wrote to congratulate William Lloyd Garrison for continuing to speak up in the face of persecution and expressed her hope that he would continue to advocate many reforms:

I trust the time is now *fully* come, when thou wilt take a decided stand for *all truth,* under the conviction that the whole are necessary to the permanent establishment of any *single one;* for, altho' some or rather many of our Abolitionists are fearful of the result of such a course, it appears to me that such have never yet comprehended the *nature of truth.* And yet, how perfectly simple and easy to be understood it is, to the unsophisticated child of nature.[41]

Several of the female antislavery societies wrote to express their support. The Buckingham [Pennsylvania?] Female Anti-Slavery Society spoke most eloquently on this issue of the expediency of addressing women's rights along with slavery. This group of women confessed that they had had "some misgivings as to the *expediency* of having this subject [women's rights] agitated at present lest it might retard the AntiSlavery cause." In considering the matter, however, they concluded that as

the command has gone forth sanctioned by divine authority, to "let the oppressed go free and to break *every* yoke, it seems to us that [to] endeavour to set bounds to it and say thus far shalt thou go and no farther would be like [at]tempting to limit the Holy One. We would therefore say hold fast the form of sound words and keep to our first position that whatever is right must be expedient, for what can be more expedient than to do right. Let then, the right be done tho' all the associations of men be dissolved, and their glory laid low in the dust.

The Society unanimously passed a resolution to "address a letter to our friends S. M. and A. E. Grimké, expressive of our unity with them in their views of woman's rights and responsibilities, and our desire to cooperate with them and encourage them to persevere in this labor of love to the human family."[42]

Interestingly, although the Grimkés were steadfast in pursuing their course, they were not always consistent in the belief that "Truth cannot hurt Truth and to assert the rights of woman in our conduct cannot hurt the cause we are advocating with our tongues."[43] In a situation that paralleled the Grimkés' assertion of their right to appear as speakers on the lecture platform, Lucretia Mott and other women accepted their selection as delegates of various antislavery societies to the 1840 World's Anti-Slavery

Convention in London. This was controversial, given the recent schism in the American antislavery movement over the issue of women in positions of authority, and the British sponsors of the convention were more sympathetic to the non-Garrisonians. Instead of supporting Mott and the other American women, Sarah Grimké commented that "[we] hope the Lord will preserve them from presenting themselves there in the character of delegates, it would we apprehend be . . . any thing but a help. . . . [I]t is desirable and indeed all important that nothing should be done to divert the attention of the meeting from the great subject of human liberty which has called them together."[44]

Much later, Abby Kelley Foster made a similar decision to set women's rights aside in her decision to support suffrage for black men at the cost of suffrage for women. She was strongly chastised for her position by Lucy Stone, now a leader in the woman's suffrage movement. Stone accused Kelley Foster of being "smitten by a strange blindness [to] believe that the nation's peril can be averted if it can be induced to accept the poor half loaf of justice for the negro which is poisoned by its lack of justice for women." Kelley Foster's response was sharp: "I should look on myself as a monster of selfishness if, while I see my neighbor's daughter held and treated as a beast—as thousands still are all over the rural districts of the South, and who are in an unspeakably worse condition than if 'drowning'—I should turn from helping them to secure to my daughter political equality."[45]

In contrast, although the tensions between African American and women's rights were very apparent in the suffrage movement, Sallie Holley's life also shows how the work of her predecessors made her path considerably smoother. By the 1850s, when Holley began speaking, it was still unusual for a woman to give a public lecture, but it no longer met with such overwhelming condemnation. Holley did not establish any new theoretical points and tended to assume that her belief in women's rights went without saying. Abby Kelley Foster in fact once accused Holley of a lack of interest in women's rights. Holley's response indicated how much she felt her support could be taken for granted: "I think you do me injustice when you affirm that I do not appreciate the woman's Rights cause. For proof to the contrary I have only to refer you to the *Liberator* of December 19, 1852!"[46] The article to which she seems to have been referring was, however, no treatise on women's rights, but simply a letter to the editor from another individual suggesting Holley and three other women as possible Lyceum speakers.

Holley was more exclusively devoted to abolition and to African American rights than any of the others, but she also attended women's rights conventions in Rochester, Albany, and Boston in the early 1850s.[47] In 1865 she described an Oberlin College class reunion that she had attended. Asked to describe her activities over the past fourteen years,

> I said I was afraid they wouldn't care to hear how I had been holding anti-slavery meetings all these years and still "spoke in public." Mr. Cooper asked what I lectured upon now. "Oh!" I said, "Black folks must vote all through the country." Helen Finney, who was present with her husband, General Cox, said she thought I wanted women to vote. "Oh, yes!" I said, "that's inevitable," whereupon there was "immense sensation," as the newspapers say.[48]

The issue of the compatibility of reforms was always (and continues to be in the present) a heated one. Those who did not admit to a connection between antislavery and other reforms were exemplified by the correspondent to the *Liberator* who referred stingingly to "the tempting array of philanthropic 'nick-nacks' which have been served up so *piously* for our accommodation." He went on to ask rhetorically, "But what have the no-government theories, non-resistance, woman's rights, hostility to the Ministry, the Church, and Sabbath, to do with sound abolitionism? Just as much as we have with men in the moon—just nothing at all."[49] And clearly, even those who held to the position that such reforms were both desirable and related shifted their own ground from time to time, as issues of expediency and practicality arose. Yet it appears that these women, aided by their awareness of facing limitations of their own because of their sex, were more inclined to believe that reforms did not need to be compartmentalized. On the contrary, Lucretia Mott once wrote approvingly of Susan B. Anthony's lecturing on "agricultural and other subjects," which she felt would prevent her from "becom[ing] of one idea."[50] Mott also declared, after attending women's rights conventions in Seneca Falls and Rochester: "All these subjects of reform are kindred in their nature; and giving to each its proper consideration, will tend to strengthen and nerve the mind for all—so that the abolitionist will not wax weaker in his advocacy of immediate emancipation. He will not love the slave less, in loving universal humanity more."[51]

7

Embracing the Cause of Woman and Humanity

THE "PRIVATE YEARS" OF THE GRIMKÉS

A FTER 1838, THE Grimkés rarely spoke in public. In 1853, Henry Blackwell visited the Grimké/Welds to chastise them for their retreat from public life. In the course of conversation he asked them to explain their withdrawal. Angelina's husband, Theodore Weld, responded that he had had a personal revelation:

> He had been laboring to destroy evil in the same spirit as his antago-
> nists. He suddenly felt that fighting was not the best way to annihilate
> error, and that he could no longer act as he had been doing. . . .
>
> . . .That for him it was no longer possible nor proper to continue
> combating. He had done so manfully, and when his work in that way
> was ended, he was obliged to resign it to others, while he himself
> entered into a higher sphere of experience. So, since then, he has
> thought, and worked, and taught his children, and occasionally lec-
> tured, and helped all whom he has met who needed help. . . .

Angelina Grimké Weld was in accord with her husband. When Blackwell "tried to argue the duty of fighting error so long as it existed," he reported that both the Welds "simply say, 'There is a fighting era in everyone's life. While you feel it so, fight on; it is your duty, and the best thing you can pos-sibly do. But when your work in that line is done, you will reach another and a higher view.'"[1]

Of the women studied here, the Grimkés' change from their earlier style of activism is the most striking. This shift has been reflected in their treatment by their biographers and editors. The two most significant biographies of the Grimkés, Lerner's and Birney's, concentrate attention on the lives of these women up to Angelina's marriage to Theodore Weld.[2] Likewise, the edited collections of their letters and writings are equally focused on this period of political activism. Larry Ceplair's work, *The Public Years of Sarah and Angelina Grimké: Selected Writings 1835–1839*, does so explicitly. Barnes and Dumond's book, *Letters of Theodore Dwight Weld, Angelina Grimké, and Sarah Grimké*, covers more years, but the authors note that the letters they chose were "those which had biographical significance to the life of Weld and those which threw light upon the antislavery agitation."[3] Whether or not this has been the intention of the authors, the effect of these treatments is to convey the impression that after 1840, the Grimkés were no longer significant figures and their lives thereafter dwindled into anticlimax.

This is not the case. Although the Grimkés engaged in different sorts of behavior, they continued to be political activists. This is particularly true in the broader sense of the term, when "political" is defined as activities that have an impact on societal structures and relationships but that do not necessarily pertain to electoral politics, legislative action, or mass political movements.[4] Beyond the acknowledgment of their ongoing activism, however, is the point that emphasizing one short period as the epitome of their lives ignores the richness and complexity of their thoughts and actions throughout their entire lives. It is most appropriate to view them as women with religious convictions that called them at various times to various sorts of political action, rather than as political activists whose convictions brought them briefly into the public arena but whose activism was soon crowded out of their lives by domestic exigencies.

After the Grimké/Weld marriage, the newlyweds plus Sarah Grimké "retired" to their new home in Fort Lee, New Jersey. They plunged into their domestic responsibilities, learning to cook and take care of their house: unfamiliar tasks for both of them, given their aristocratic upbringing. From the start they insisted that these responsibilities were as politically and socially significant as their lecture tour had been. Prior to her marriage, Angelina Grimké wrote to Jane Smith, telling her they had decided to do without servants in their new household. She asked her friend to visit after the wedding and "spend a few weeks so as to teach me how to get along, to make bread and puddings, boil vegetables etc. . . . By putting out our washing and with thy instruction I am sure with the Lord's help I can do better *without* than with a girl, and will be enabled to bear a testimony which will help the cause of woman and of Christianity."[5] In their minds it was no small matter to prove that they were capable of fulfilling domestic responsibilities. Grimké Weld claimed, in fact, that "I do verily believe that we are *thus* doing *as much* for the cause of woman as we did by public speaking. For it is absolutely necessary that we should show that we are *not* ruined as domestic characters, but so far from it, *as soon* as duty calls us home, we can and do rejoice in the release from public service, and are as anxious to make good bread as we ever were to deliver a good lecture."[6] Although this was a disappointment to those who hoped the Grimkés would soon return to their lecturing careers—and also perhaps to some contemporary feminists—it was generally understandable to their peers. Even Abby Kelley, who delayed her own marriage because "my domestic feelings are strong, but my moral organization is stronger and far more active," was also determined "to disprove the assertion that a 'strong-minded' woman would of course neglect her house and family."[7] In fact, Sarah Grimké wrote to Abby Kelley shortly after Angelina's wedding, suggesting that their critics were really opponents of woman's rights who feared "that the woman question will gain ground too rapidly, if it is discovered that the same woman, who can hold an audience in profound attention as an A[nti] S[lavery] lecturer can retire from the sound of public applause and quietly and unobtrusively perform the duties of a housekeeper and a wife."[8]

Neither were the Grimkés inactive even in more traditionally political terms. Although they were not given credit as authors, they performed much of the massive research behind the collection of accounts of slavery published in Theodore Weld's name as *American Slavery as It Is*.[9] Each sister also contributed a personal essay to that volume. In their first year in Fort Lee, they canvassed their area, collecting signatures on antislavery petitions. If we consider the Welds and Sarah Grimké as a unit, the sisters also did their part for the cause by staying home and managing the household while Theodore assisted the abolitionist members of Congress in Washington, D.C., during the legislative sessions of 1841, 1842, and 1843. During this time, their domestic responsibilities increased as Angelina gave birth to two sons, in 1839 and 1841. Her health was also impaired by difficult pregnancies, including one miscarriage. Nonetheless, she wrote to Theodore in February 1842, "we are very anxious that nothing thou canst do for the slave, should be left undone."[10]

It is at this point that Lerner concludes that although the Grimkés had not intended to retire from public life,

> ill health, poverty and domestic problems became the kind of personal obstacles they have always been in the way of active social participation of women. . . . They were no longer sheltered by wealth, privilege or spinsterhood from the basic problem that was to haunt the average woman for the next century: how to have enough energy left over after a day of cooking, housework and childcare to concern herself with issues outside of the home or to do anything about them, even if she cared. . . . The Grimké sisters, at long last, were no longer debating it [the theory of woman's sphere]—they were living the full and common lives of ordinary women.[11]

It is true that the Grimkés had originally expected to be more active politically and also that they sometimes felt themselves bound to domestic chores at the expense of intellectual and social activity. Prior to her marriage, Angelina Grimké wrote that "we hope to spend our time in mutual improvement and in writing for the A[nti]S[lavery] cause, and as way opens we can occasionally go out and lecture."[12] These goals were not achieved to their satisfaction. In the years after the Grimké/Weld marriage, their correspondence includes references to their "retirement," their "hibernating," and their "secluded life" which by the 1850s had made Angelina "shrink indiscribably [sic] from coming before the public."[13] In 1848 Sarah Grimké poignantly described some of the intellectual frustrations of her life:

> I have been very busy cleaning house, and feel almost too tired— "Hope" says the poet "springs eternal in the human breast; Man always is, but never to be blest"—So I hope on, year after year, that there will be less occasion to overexert our physical powers, and year after year, comes disappointment, and with it the blessing of contentment, and hope to brighten the future; indeed, *I have, we have* so much to make us happy, in each other's love, and in our delightful home, that it would be inexcusable to be dissatisfied—Still the spiritual and intellectual natures aspire after nobler, higher pursuits, and feel as if they were not fulfilling their vocation, or ripening for another sphere, while they are so perpetually engaged in providing for the necessities of the

lower nature—Here is a great problem to my mind—Souls panting after better things, yet bound by duty, to think most of earth and earthly things—to provide for the body, while the intellect is starving.[14]

In the face of comments such as these, one cannot deny that the Grimkés considered themselves retired in some sense, or that they found their later lives unfulfilling at times. But this conclusion does not prove that they felt that their public speaking had been the pinnacle of their lives. In the letter of March 1838, although Angelina Grimké noted that she expected to write and lecture again, she added that "we are fully convinced that we never ought to labor so unremittingly in this way as we have done."[15]

Beyond the overtly political acts already detailed, the sisters were active in less public ways. Sarah Grimké spent considerable time in 1839 compiling the instances of racial discrimination within the American Society of Friends that she eventually sent to Elizabeth Pease as "Colorphobia exemplified: Letter on the Subject of Prejudice Against Colour amongst the Society of Friends in the United States." The sisters worked hard to convince their mother to free her slaves—for the good of her soul as well as for the good of those she claimed to own.[16] They stayed abreast of current events and continued to correspond with their friends at home and abroad, reflecting on and responding to the challenges confronting causes such as abolition and women's rights. As noted earlier, other reformers often sought their insights.

One issue in which they took an active interest was whether to form a national society for women's rights, as opposed to continuing the more informal system of ad hoc conventions and local associations. The Grimkés were against the idea of a formal organization. Angelina Grimké Weld composed a letter to the National Woman's Rights Convention in Syracuse in 1852 explaining her views. One of her main points was the distinction she drew between "natural" and "artificial" organizations, the former being of divine origin, the latter human. The difference between the two was not, as one might think, that divinely ordained organizations were inherently more pure. It was rather that these "[n]atural organizations are based on the principle of progression; the eternal law of change," whereas "human or artificial organizations are built upon the principle of crystallization; they *fix* the conditions of society; they seek to daguerrotype themselves, not on the present age only, but on future generations; hence, they fetter and distort the expanding mind." So, her letter continued:

It is not to organization that I object, but to an *artificial society* that must prove a burden, a clog, an incumbrance, rather than a help. Such an organization as now actually exists among the women of America I hail with heartfelt joy. We are bound together by the natural ties of spiritual affinity; we are drawn to each other because we are attracted toward one common center—the good of humanity. We need no external bonds to bind us together, no cumbrous machinery to keep our minds and hearts in unity of purpose and effort; we are not the lifeless staves of a barrel which can be held together only by the iron hoops of an artificial organization.[17]

It seems fairly clear here that her perspective on organizations in general was informed by her experience with religious bureaucracy. This becomes even more apparent in her comment that the main problem with artificial organizations was "their tendency . . . to sink the individual in the mass, to sacrifice his rights, and immolate him on the altar of some fancied good."[18] There is, she said,

a period in moral development when it seems necessary to sacrifice some individual freedom in order to attain strength in our feebleness but that period is passed. . . . Mind must be left perfect by fire; each to develop in its own way and to follow out its own inborn idiosincracies [sic]. Organisations always trammel more or less. If they do not bind the head between boards, they put Chinese shoes upon our feet, or corset the very heart and lungs of our moral being.[19]

This sounds nearly identical to her revelation, nearly twenty-five years earlier, that she had been "called out" of the church; that as "an infant in Jesus" she needed to be taught by "outward instruments" but the time had come to put away childish things for now "the outward preaching often disturbed the inward voice."[20]

Angelina Grimké Weld's letter was read at the convention and others echoed her sentiments. Lucy Stone was one: she commented that she "had had enough of thumb-screws and soul screws never to wish to be placed under them again."[21] In the view of Stone and others, there was a clear distinction between an informal network of women working more or less in concert and responding freely to various calls for national and regional conventions and a formal organization that would by necessity limit the independent action of its members. As Angelina Grimké had said years earlier, such an abdication of individual responsibility was inexcusable; it was "sinful to be so influenced by any human authority as to forget our individual responsibility to Him whose we are and whom we ought to serve, independent of the opinion of man."[22]

The Grimkés did not only communicate by letter. They visited in Philadelphia, New York, and Boston, often reporting having met other reformers, such as Lucretia Mott, at social occasions. They mentored younger activists such as Abby Kelley, Henry Blackwell, Elizabeth Cady Stanton, Elizabeth Smith Miller, and later, Sallie Holley. Finally, and perhaps most significantly, they imparted their values and convictions to the younger generation in the schools they operated, beginning in 1851 in Belleville, New Jersey, then at the Eagleswood School at Ruritan Bay Union, a communal society established in 1854. When Ruritan Bay failed in 1856, the Grimké/Welds continued their school privately. Quite a few of the noted abolitionists of the day sent their children to Belleville or Eagleswood, including Henry and Elizabeth Cady Stanton, Gerrit Smith, and James Birney; three of Lucretia Mott's nieces and nephews attended the Eagleswood School.[23] Sallie Holley used some of the money she managed to save from her small lecturing salary to send one of her nephews to the school; the Grimké/Welds charged her a reduced rate for his tuition.[24] While Theodore Weld served as the headmaster of the school, both sisters taught classes. Angelina apparently enjoyed teaching; Sarah found it less pleasant in part because she was overwhelmed by the importance of the work. Prior to the beginning of the school year in 1852, she wrote: "I tremble as the time approaches to receive again the charge of beings who are to mark the age in which they live, who will shed around them influences for good or for evil to the human race, and who must feel and breathe the atmosphere of my spirit. Grant my heavenly father that I may not do them any evil."[25] Their teaching was, in effect, an extension of their lecturing; in both activities they were attempting to mold the understanding and convictions of others.

All these efforts were considerably less public than their earlier lecturing, but they were significant nonetheless. The Grimkés should not, then, be judged to have forsaken the political realm. They should rather be understood as having left one aspect of it for another. With the emergence of social history as a field, it has become generally accepted that history is not comprised solely of political and military events; studying the Grimkés' later lives is a reminder that the political itself embraces more than the traditional acts of demonstrating, campaigning, and voting. In fact, in abandoning their more overtly political acts, they remained more faithful to Garrison and the Garrisonian perspective than some of their Garrisonian colleagues, for the activities in which they were involved had more to do with moral suasion, albeit on a smaller scale, than the politicking that went on within the antislavery movement after its schism in 1840.

In any event, demonstrating their political commitment was always less important to the Grimkés than was their fundamental dedication to increasing their understanding of God and God's will for them and for the world. Although they viewed social action, and abolition in particular, as part of God's plan, they did not believe it to be the whole of the plan, as the previous chapters have demonstrated. When faithfulness to God's will is placed appropriately as their ultimate goal, then their later lives show a congruity of purpose with their earlier lives—despite the fact that they themselves sometimes found their lives frustrating.

When they absorbed themselves in domestic responsibilities after the Grimké/Weld marriage, they did so believing that they were serving both political and Christian purposes. Sarah Grimké was invited by the Philadelphia Female Anti-Slavery Society to continue her public labors. Grimké responded that she had "spread [this matter] before my Heavenly Father" but that

> His providences clearly indicate that my post of duty is for the present at home. When I went out before, it was at *his* bidding, and *therefore* with his blessing. When I suspended for a season my labors as a public lecturer in 1838, it was with the confident expectation that He who first called me to that field would speedily summon me to it again; that summons I have not received; to go without it would be worse than in vain. If called to resume the same labor by that great voice which summoned me at first to bear up the hands of my precious sister, I shall go forth with joy—till then, I must perform such antislavery labors as from day to day my hands find to do. Let us leave the choice of instrumentalities, with the times and the modes of their operation, to God.[26]

So, too, did her sister believe that her divinely ordained sphere of

This photograph of Sarah Moore Grimké is undated, but was clearly taken after she abandoned her adherence to plain Quaker dress. *Courtesy Library of Congress.*

activity had shifted. Angelina Grimké had bravely and confidently confronted representatives of three different sects in her various religious transitions. She had faced the general hostility of the Northern public, the clergy, and the press. Now she was overwhelmed by self-doubt and felt inadequate to meet another challenge that she was equally sure came from God: the task of raising her own children. Her letters to her husband during the 1840s are filled with reflections on this theme. She accepted the idea that "God establishes families . . . that they might be *nurseries for heaven*." She added, "Shall *ours* be so is a solemn query—shall our children be heirs of God and *joint* heirs with Christ—overwhelming thought! When I look at the family relation in *this light*—I feel as tho' I never had anything to do in my life of half the importance, as tending my babes; and yet there are many other times when I am weary of the unceasing care they require." She went on to reflect on "the dealings of the Lord" with her:

> I have remembered all the way he has led my soul—how one dispensation after another has been meted out to me, each designed to develop my character, to show me what was in my heart. Now I can say my cup of earthly bliss is running over, he seems most emphatically to be trying to see what effect a dispensation of almost unmingled goodness and mercy will produce upon my unthankful heart—he has given me husband, children, a sister more than a mother to me and to them. . . . And yet I turn even blessings into curses by the feelings I have about minding my little ones. I sometimes feel so weary of my work.

For the first time, Angelina Grimké was confronted with a challenge she felt to be divinely inspired, but at which she could make only slow progress. "The fact is," she confided in the same letter, "it has been *very* VERY hard for me to see myself as I really am—my self justifying spirit *always* found excuse for my fretfulness, ingratitude and unloveliness of spirit." Her despair at this point led her to question her own Christian commitment; she could not "consistently entertain any hope that I am a follower of Jesus."[27]

Angelina Grimké Weld felt at this point that her lesson was to learn to subdue her own will. Prior to this time her inclination and her sense of divine purpose had coincided. Now, however, she came to a new truth: "Religion," she declared, "is the subjugation of the *will*. As long as our wills are not in conformity with God's will, we cannot serve him." In her own case, she concluded, "I plainly saw it was the Lord's will I should take care of the children he had given me. . . .With the help and strength of the Lord Almighty, I then determined to subdue my will and bring it into oneness with His, and dearest Jesus has helped me just so far as I have been willing to help myself." Having acted upon this revelation, she continued proudly, "The care of my babes is *now* my pleasure, and instead of little Charley continually calling out . . . [for his Aunt Sarah] he will not seem to remember her more than two or three times in the morning and never cries after her."[28]

Whereas Angelina Grimké Weld's impatience with some aspects of childrearing and her guilt for feeling so may strike a chord with some readers, her religious interpretation of her struggles is less common. But religion was basic to her worldview and she had come to believe that God was calling her to reform herself as much as to reform the world. The fact that modern feminists may be uncomfortable with her interpretation of her life purpose cannot be allowed to diminish its importance in her own eyes. Her field of action shifted; her commitment to doing what she perceived as God's will remained constant.

Further, despite her complaints of being intellectually starved in the 1840s,[29] she found the time and intellectual energy to embrace a new religious movement, Millerism. She had already devoted considerable thought to the possible Second Coming of Christ. As early as 1832, she had asked her brother Thomas, "Dost thou believe in the *personal* appearance of our Adorable Redeemer on Earth during the Millennium[?]"[30] At that time she was simply reflecting on the topic. After her marriage, however, she became increasingly convinced by the Millerite view. She moved from the postmillennialist understanding that the Kingdom of God would be established on earth prior to the Second Coming of Christ to the premillennialist view that God would destroy the world before the return of the Messiah. The optimistic tone that had prevailed in her earlier writing disappeared; she now declared that she was "entirely prepared to give up the old idea of a Millennium and to embrace the opinion that the destruction of the world will *precede* it."[31]

Grimké Weld's Millerism caused some consternation at home and abroad. In her immediate circle, both her husband and her sister, along with her closest friend, Jane Smith, were alarmed about her adoption of a view many regarded as implausible, if not completely ludicrous. She defended her views to her family and friends privately, and in a recapitulation of her former confident style, did not hesitate also to declare them in public. During a visit to Philadelphia in 1842, she attended a gathering at which

> some allusion was made to Miller views—evidently showing that he was regarded as a wild and ignorant fanatic. I felt that it was duty calmly to state my solemn conviction that he had a mass of evidence, from the Bible and History to sustain him in his theory that no other writer on prophecy ever had. They seemed utterly amazed I should think so and asked if it was possible I believed him. I told them I did— that the more I examined the subject the more fully I was persuaded he was right.[32]

In fact, she became so convinced of the Millerite view that in February of 1843 she wrote to Theodore, "I feel entirely willing to leave all arrangements and propositions about the farm, for really I find my mind is becoming so much more convinced of the truth of Miller's views, that it appears perfectly useless to lay any plans for the future."[33]

It is all too easy in hindsight to dismiss Angelina Grimké Weld's enthusiasm for Millerism. Lerner does so, attributing her "religious fanaticism" to "an emotional response to a profound crisis" in her life, that of experiencing a miscarriage in early 1843 during one of her husband's absences, followed almost immediately by another pregnancy, along with her ongoing difficulties in raising her two sons. In addition to characterizing Angelina's interest in Millerism as fanaticism, Lerner asserts that it was simply a result of anxiety and despondence and was a view "from which, in a more active period of her life, her common-sense practicality would have recoiled."[34]

Lerner's dismissal of Grimké Weld's interest in Millerism is not surprising given her view that "theological problems could not long absorb her [Angelina's] interest."[35] It is, however, quite difficult to accept this conclusion in light of the repeated evidence in Grimké's diary and correspondence that religious issues, including theology, were of extreme importance to her. Angelina Grimké Weld's adoption of Millerism was really quite consistent with the progression of her own views on the state of the world, the power and immanence of God, and the necessity of revolutionary change in social institutions and in the hearts and minds of people. Her championship of the cause despite the skepticism it evoked in others was equally consistent.

Often in her earlier correspondence Angelina Grimké Weld had leaned toward the possibility and perhaps the necessity of cataclysmic change. In 1836, toward the end of her self-imposed exile from abolitionism, she wrote to her sister Sarah:

> Dearest dost thou not feel that the Church (not our S[ociet]y only) is approaching a great conflict—the mighty battle between light and darkness, right and wrong—and I believe the saints will find their bitterest enemys among the high professors of religion. It will be a conflict between the form and the substance of religion—sectarian feeling and pure christianity, and the governments of this world will be shaken to pieces in this war of opposing moral elements.[36]

This does not sound so very different from her comment in March of 1843, at the beginning of the period William Miller had predicted would see the destruction of the world.[37] "I do *feel* in my soul," she wrote, "that the Lord has been for some years preparing his way in the hearts of the people and that a great and mighty revolution is at hand, that the present prevailing form of godliness in church organisation will be superseded by the power of religion and the simplicity of the teaching of Jesus and his apostles."[38]

The year 1843 came and went without the expected cataclysmic destruction; nor did the Millerites' revised timetable for the world's end in October 1844 prove accurate. Angelina Grimké Weld continued, however, to ponder the meaning of the prophecy and eventually gave it her own interpretation. In January 1845 she wrote a long letter to "Sarah," revealing her conclusions. In her reflections she had been aided by her earlier view that the destruction to come was not so much material as spiritual. She had studied the Bible and found evidence that convinced her that although "[o]nce I was a believer in the Second personal advent of Christ, . . . now I see that his second coming is to be in the hearts of the people." "I do not now," she added, "believe in the destruction of the world by material fire. . . .The heavens rolled together as a scroll, I believe to be a symbol, denoting the vanishing away of all the mere *externals* of Religion— all forms and ceremonies, sacred places, times and seasons." Indeed, she asserted, "The coming out from the nominal Church is, I believe, the separation of the wheat from the tares, spoken of by our Lord, as taking place at the end of the world—for the end of the world is the *end of the age* marked by the running out of the great prophetic periods."[39]

Like many other abolitionists, Grimké Weld also viewed the approach of the Civil War as God's judgment upon an unrighteous and unrepentant nation. Despite their earlier commitment to nonresistance, both sisters supported the war, interpreting it as a war against slavery. Angelina Grimké Weld wrote to her son Theodore that since she had given up all hope of abolition "except thro' blood and insurrection, I feel willing it should come in my day, for the longer it is put off, the worse it will be."[40]

Turning from Angelina to Sarah Grimké, we find a parallel development in terms of her commitment to discovering the nature of God and of divine purpose. She took a different approach, however, becoming a convert to spiritualism. For her, spiritualism was much more than an amusing fad, or a means of communicating with departed loved ones, or, as many used it, a source of information about health (although she did employ spiritualism in all of these ways as well).[41] Instead, Sarah Grimké found spiritualism appealing mainly because it opened up new spiritual truths that she had not found in Christian doctrine. After a friend died, she wrote: "The blessed truths of Spiritualism had entered into his soul, not as an amusing phenomenon, a speculative theory, but as a new manifestation of the divine."[42] Toward the end of her life she wrote to Gerrit Smith that

> The new gospel of Spiritualism has brought to light one truth, out of many, which has been a great benefaction to my soul and has in some measure given me a victory which I have struggled and agonized in vain to achieve by the light of the gospel. This is the doctrine that what we call sin is the result of ignorance, not of wilful disobedience to the divine within us, and hence that those who do wrong, who violate the majesty of their own nature are to be pitied not to be blamed. . . . Now that I see that the spirit remains unsullied by the debaucheries of the man, I view human beings with a reverence, mingled with compassion, which enables me to forgive my enemies.[43]

As evil must therefore be only "undeveloped good," she now saw clearly the importance of educating souls. She found this idea to be "an infinite comfort." More than any Christian doctrine, it enabled her "to practicalize the love of Jesus to the human family."[44] The idea of demonstrating love of God by service to humankind had been fundamental in her spirituality; spiritualism, however, gave it a more concrete rationalization than she had had before.

Spiritualism, symbolized by the rappings of the Fox sisters, is most often dismissed as spiritual quackery. Sarah Grimké's adoption of it is, in that view, an example of her gullibility rather than evidence of her sincere and scrupulous search for spiritual truth. But as Ann Braude has noted, spiritualist religious ideas embraced the goodness of human nature, individual apprehension of the divine, and the uselessness of ritual and dogma, ideas held by many nonspiritualist radical reformers as well.[45] For Sarah Grimké, the doctrines of spiritualism clarified certain confusing elements of human existence, such as the complete dissimilarity of some children to their parents. At one spiritualist meeting she attended, "The query was asked whether the inhabitants of this sphere had previously lived on any other planet—Yes, was the reply." This possibility addressed issues that had been "great marvels" to her: "If spirits come into this sphere with the knowledge acquired in a previous state of existence, there is not mystery in the gigantic intellect and great moral power, exhibited by certain individuals."[46]

But while crediting spiritualism for a great deal of her own theological enlightenment, Sarah Grimké did not surrender her spiritual autonomy to spiritualist mediums or theories. She continued to maintain the necessity of examining all ideas before adopting any. She wrote to a male medium who had become a friend, that the "privilege" of being "surrounded by an angel band, ready to minister to our necessities and guide us by their larger experience and higher wisdom" must not blind one to the necessity of exercising one's own judgment.[47] Further, she cautioned her friends that there was no purpose to spirit communications unless "they have an influence over us to mellow our hearts and produce in us a likeness to God." She added, "The danger is, that we mistake intercourse with spirits for spirituality and deem ourselves on the high road to perfection, when we are only adding *ideas* to our stock of knowledge, about spiritual things."[48]

Sarah Grimké became increasingly confident about her spiritual views, and she credited a great deal of this to spiritualist doctrine and her own encounters with spirits and spirit mediums. She claimed that her new understanding of the nature of God had radically altered her previous anxious and self-denigrating state. She counseled her young friend Sarah Wattles to avoid her mistakes: "You live too much my Sarah in the slough of despondency and thus deprive yourself of half the joys of life. Once like you I walked through the furnace but having changed my views of the character of God, my whole life is changed and a calm sweet peace reigns within."[49] Such a statement is in great contrast to her earlier spiritual angst. If their available correspondence is an accurate reflection of the reality, the sisters seem, in fact, to have traded roles in their later thinking and pursuits. As Sarah grew more confident and outgoing, Angelina withdrew more and more into herself, becoming convinced of her unworthiness and fearing now that all her past service to God had been legalistic rather then truly gospel-inspired.[50]

Sarah Grimké's spiritual peace of mind was not always reflected in other aspects of her life. She frequently felt herself at loose ends. She had devoted herself to the Weld children, saying that "I know not what would have become of me if it hast not been for Angelina's children, they have strewed my solitary path with flowers and gemmed my sky with stars."[51] But as the children grew older, and also as Angelina grew resentful of her sister's place within the Weld family, Sarah looked around for some other occupation. As she did not enjoy teaching and was not attracted to the communitarian life of Raritan Bay Union, she considered other possibilities, such as becoming an advocate for children's rights, or training for law or medicine.[52] But when the Weld family left to join Raritan Bay, she abandoned her own tentative career plans to follow them. When her friend Harriot Kezia Hunt questioned that decision, Grimké responded in a way that shows, perhaps, both her inability to act decisively on her own and her dependence on a clear sign from God to determine her course of action:

> Why dear I am here, simply because those are here who are dearer than aught beside, and no other place opened that my God and my conscience seemed to indicate, to wrench myself violently from ties which I have ever believed were of my fathers [forming?], without an assurance that He required it would have been senseless and wicked—Yet, as you know, my repugnance to associated life was so great that I held myself in readiness to enter upon any path of duty if opened for me by Providence from the time that T. and A. decided to come here until our actual removal—As nothing offered *naturally*, nothing came to me with a "Thus saith the Lord" stamped upon it I was shut up to the necessity of believing that it was his will for me to remain where I was.

She was not surprised or displeased when Ruritan Bay failed, having strongly disliked many aspects of communitarian life, including the "hotel life at the table" and the "terrible privation of family meals."[53]

Toward the end of their lives, the sphere of the sisters became more public again. Sarah Grimké gave an address to a national woman's rights convention in 1858. Unfortunately, this speech suffered from flaws reminiscent of her earlier years—although departing from Quaker form, she had written it out in advance. Martha Coffin Wright described the occasion to her sister, Lucretia Mott, lamenting,

> But oh! Aunt Sa! Such a ream of prose as she brought forth and deliberately set about reading. I thought I had heard you say she was a speaker. Why it was dreadful—sheet after sheet, closely written and monotonously read till all who were awake were out of all patience. Such hopeless looks as passed round the platform, and nobody could wound the poor old lady with hinting that everybody was half dead. So low and monotonous her tones that she could not be heard 10 feet from the platform—at last—the audience gave way and there came that dreadful measured thump thump of mock applause which she took all for genuine and looked pleased and said "I can raise my voice if I am not heard" and then they applauded more and more. . . . It was an excellent address if they would listen. "Cant hear" said somebody, and she went up a semitone, and took up another sheet and another and another. You never saw anything like it. I was so afraid the poor soul would perceive the smiles and be mortified at last by open uproar, but they stood it and at last there came a sheet with a blank half page, suggestive of a "[ ] and finally brethren." She has lived out of the world so long that she has forgotten what the world can bear.[54]

Mott responded: "I wish we old folks could ever be admonished that our day is over. She was a good speaker, a generation ago . . . [although] [s]he was never equal to Angelina as a lecturer." She added, "I had that self-same essay, I presume, on hand, for weeks, to read and criticise at her request. I ventured to suggest the omission of a part, but it was 'no go.'"[55]

In Sarah Grimké's late seventies, she was again canvassing the countryside, circulating a petition for woman's suffrage in 1870 and collecting clothes for the freed people in Florida in 1871. Like Angelina, she had also written letters to various woman's rights conventions over the years. In 1857, according to Sarah, Angelina wrote "a long and admirable communication" to a Dress Reform Convention. Containing "many interesting and new views on the great subject of woman," it was to be published as a tract.[56] At the same time Sarah had written an essay on the issue of women's suffrage that she was considering having published. In 1863 Angelina gave her first public address in twenty-five years at the convention establishing the Women's Loyal National League.[57] Perhaps the most moving of their final public actions was their suffrage demonstration in 1870. Serving as officers of the Massachusetts Woman Suffrage Association, they decided that a public demonstration was needed to publicize their cause. They led a procession of women to the polling place in Hyde Park (outside Boston) in order to deposit their ballots in a symbolic ballot box. As Catherine Birney recorded it,

> There was a great crowd inside the hall, eager to see the joke of women voting, and many were ready to jeer and hiss. But when, through the door, the women filed, led by Sarah Grimké and Angelina Weld, the laugh was checked, the intended jeer unuttered, and deafening applause was given instead. The crowd fell back respectfully, nearly every man removing his hat and remaining uncovered while the women passed freely down the hall, deposited their votes, and departed.[58]

Sarah Grimké died in 1873 at the age of eighty-one. Angelina Grimké Weld was paralyzed by strokes the last few years of her life; she died at age seventy-four in 1879.

Viewed by any standard, the "public years" of the Grimkés did not end in 1839. Moreover, they were engaged in other activities, such as housekeeping, childrearing, and teaching, which they also believed were acts of significance to the world. Most importantly, the evidence indicates that the lives of these two women were not organized around politics, but around religious conviction. Their political activity was an outgrowth of their religious conviction—an effect not a cause.

8 ❧

"A Great While Growing to Be Sixty"

HOLLEY, KELLEY, AND MOTT

WHAT OF THE OTHER three women whose lives we have been considering? How did their philosophies and actions evolve in their later years? How were they affected by changes in family responsibilities, health, and other life circumstances? Let us consider each woman in turn, examining in particular the evolution of her religious views, her fields of action, and her relationship to the wider reform community.[1]

SALLIE HOLLEY: AN "UNFALTERING FAITH IN IMMORTALITY"

Unlike the Grimkés, Sallie Holley did not have childrearing responsibilities, nor did she suffer from poor health. Perhaps her continuing good health may be attributed in part to her own preventive care. Although she continued to lecture on slavery and African American rights until the dissolution of the American Anti-Slavery Society in 1870, she set a moderate schedule for herself, speaking no more than two or three times per week.[2] This of course is still an impressive undertaking considering the difficulties of transportation and the nonexistence of public address systems in her day. She was solicitous of her health, taking time out periodically from lecturing to make long visits to friends and to take the water cure at Elmira, New York. She developed a close friendship with the proprietors, Dr. Silas Gleason and Mrs. Rachel Brooks Gleason, who apparently offered her the use of their facilities without charge. Holley "[tried] to show my grateful acknowledgment of [their] generous and open-hearted hospitality" by showing newcomers around, reading aloud to Mrs. Gleason, to the children, and to guests, and lecturing in the parlor in the evenings.[3]

The relationship between Sallie Holley and Caroline Putnam continued to be intimate. In 1858 Holley described the depth of her dismay about the change in editors in one of the antislavery newspapers, saying, "I should not have felt worse to have waked up some morning and found Putty's large blue eyes changed into little squinting ones, hopelessly black!"[4]

Letters to the *Liberator* time and time again report positive reactions to Holley and her lectures. Sarah Clay, of Lowell, Massachusetts, wished that it was in her power "to send her to every town in the State, yes, into every State. I know the common people would follow her, and the multitudes flock to hear her—not for 'the loaves and the fishes,' but for 'the *gracious words* which proceed out of her mouth." Her acceptability seems to have stemmed both from her pleasant and sincere manner and from what another correspondent referred to as her overt appeals to the "religious element" in people's nature. This individual claimed that some abolitionists believed that "such Christian appeals [were] wholly unnecessary . . . [because] 'Every body knows slavery is wrong, a great wrong, without going to Christian principles to prove it.'" Still another correspondent detailed his reasons for claiming that "Miss Holley is one of the most effective and successful lecturers now in the field":

> Her Christian gentleness, evident sincerity, and deep earnestness, joined to her many attractive qualities as a public speaker—fine voice and manner, high mental culture, and excellent elocution—familiarity with the Scriptures, in fact, her whole Christian handling and application of her theme—all these brought to bear upon, and consecrated to, such a subject, which, in its turn, consecrates them, are admirably calculated to disarm prejudice, win confidence, and produce conviction, and combine to make her, it seems to me *unique* in her department.[5]

Holley did not invariably please, however. In 1860, H. W. Carter, a local antislavery organizer in Athol, Massachusetts, wrote an outraged letter to Samuel May, Jr., the regional organizer. He complained bitterly that Holley had disregarded his efforts, had only with difficulty been persuaded to speak to the small audience assembled one evening, and then had flatly refused to speak again the following evening. According to Carter, Holley "talked and acted, as if no preparation had been made for her reception; and even after she had been brought face to face with fifty people who had come together, through wind and snow, to hear her, could, with difficulty, be persuaded to fulfill her part of the arrangement." When

James Miller McKim wrote to May asking whether Holley would be a good traveling companion for Anna Dickinson, a young woman just entering the antislavery lecturing field, May replied that Susan B. Anthony (who lectured on antislavery as well as women's rights) would be a better choice than "Miss Holley, who is very particular and somewhat exigeante."[6]

In late 1860, Holley took an extended leave from the lecturing field, spending time with friends and relatives and at the water cure in Elmira. Aside from a three-month lecturing stint in 1863, she lived in semiretirement until 1865. During that time she purchased a home for her mother and she and Caroline Putnam spent a summer "engrossed with builders, carpenters, painters, masons, etc." During an extended stay at the home of Caroline Putnam's mother and stepfather in Farmersville, Holley and Putnam led a successful local temperance campaign. They also taught Sunday School and Bible classes. Holley reported feeling satisfaction with these efforts: "It is affecting to hear these women say they never before got interested in the Bible, always thought it hard, dry reading. Now they love to come, and tell me they find it solid gain." Caroline Putnam was undoubtedly a good part of the reason the two stayed so long in Farmersville. Like the Grimkés, Putnam was convinced of the significance of efforts confined to a narrower region; in addition to her interest in moral and religious reform in Farmersville, she believed that her presence at home kept her mother from demanding the return of her daughter Eunice from her studies at Oberlin College.[7]

Abby Kelley Foster was concerned about Holley's withdrawal from the lecture circuit and in 1862 wrote to ask why Holley had been "so quiet anti-slavery wise the past year." Holley responded that it was not because she felt her work was over or because she was not in demand as a lecturer but that "ten years of field life . . . have left me a good deal worn and exhausted." She assured Kelley that she meant "to gather up my strength for more work as soon as possible."[8]

From Farmersville, Holley continued her correspondence with Kelley Foster and others and followed national events closely. She was not impressed by Lincoln's initial steps toward freeing slaves. "How cold the President's Proclamation is—graceless, coming from a sinner at the head of a nation of sinners. Of course," she added in this letter to Abby Kelley Foster, "such pride must be humbled before God."[9] She remained active in the antislavery cause in other ways as well. In January of 1863 she wrote that she had been traveling over the countryside "begging warm, woollen clothing for the 'contrabands' from these farmers, and have had the satisfaction of sending a large box to those destitute ones of God's poor."[10]

In 1865 Holley returned to lecturing and continued speaking on behalf of African American rights even after the abolition of slavery. In 1862 she had written that "even if Emancipation is consummated the coming year, there remains to conquer this atrocious hatred of color—and to explode utterly all idea of colonization as not only a cruel insult to the colored people—but a miserable national policy."[11] In addition to lecturing, she increasingly took on more responsibilities for the *National Anti-Slavery Standard,* the major antislavery newspaper after William Lloyd Garrison stopped publishing the *Liberator* at the end of 1865. She and Caroline Putnam contributed articles on various topics, accounts of their travels, and excerpts from their correspondence (meeting with objections from some who were not pleased to find themselves in print without their permission). They also worked hard to bolster subscriptions to the paper. In one letter Holley boasted to Putnam, "Yesterday Farmer Covert and I drove sixteen miles for a subscriber, and I got him."[12]

Nor, five years later in 1870, was she in favor of disbanding the American Anti-Slavery Society. "It seems to me," she wrote to Caroline Putnam,

> a sad mistake to discontinue the organisation of the Anti-Slavery Society or the [*Anti-Slavery*] *Standard.* . . . The blacks still need their long-tried and faithful friends of the American Anti-Slavery Society, which is a very different individual from the Nation. To discontinue our earnest defence and guard will be the signal for a volley of abuse and scorn let loose upon their defenceless heads, which Mr. Phillips should still cover with his strong and loving wing.[13]

Holley regretted the dissolution of the Society for more than altruistic reasons. She had thoroughly enjoyed her years as an antislavery agent and was reluctant to have them end. "Never more to have any New England Conventions!" she mourned. "Perhaps I shall never come to Boston again. Anti-Slavery meetings all over with! It seems too soon to give them up!"[14]

The excitement, congenial company, and intellectual stimulation of that period proved to be a painful contrast to her experience over the next twenty years. Caroline Putnam, along with Emily Howland, had in 1868 established a school in Lottsburgh, Virginia, a small rural community at the mouth of the Potomac.[15] The school was open to all, although it was mainly for the benefit of African Americans. Holley assisted in its opening and promoted it among her abolitionist friends during its first year of operation. Visiting in March of 1869, Holley offered to buy land upon which Putnam could build a house. Putnam eagerly agreed, and also insisted that the school was henceforth to be known as the Holley School.

After February 1870, Holley took up residence in Lottsburgh. In addition to their work with the school, Holley and Putnam had campaigned unsuccessfully for the election of Radical Republicans in Virginia. The election of officials hostile to the aims of the Holley School jeopardized its existence. After some years of maintaining a precarious hold on rented land, the school was evicted in 1874. Putnam and Holley decided, however, to build again on the two-acre site Holley had purchased for the home they had built. It was by all accounts not a prepossessing site; Holley described their property as "a two-acre strip of . . . desolate land, exhausted a hundred years ago with miserable tobacco raising."[16] Neither did Holley find her neighbors congenial. As noted earlier, she found both the white and black residents ignorant; the only redeeming aspect was that the African Americans wanted to improve themselves.

The magnitude of need Holley and Putnam encountered was discouraging. In August of 1870, Holley wrote that "our work here seems to me like the twelve labours of Hercules. These coloured people are awfully poor and destitute. Every want of life is theirs, from a lump of sugar for the sick baby to an acre of land for a homestead." She added that the federal government was much to blame for not having redistributed land to the ex-slaves "who had worked all their life-time without wages."[17] Their work gradually evolved into much more than teaching; they began to spend a substantial amount of time petitioning their Northern friends for clothing and supplies and distributing them to their neighbors.

Holley found these conditions as difficult to bear as Angelina Grimké Weld had found her childrearing. "This life in its awful isolation has been exile and martyrdom to me," she wrote in 1887, after seventeen years of labor at the Holley School.[18] Her consolations were her correspondence and her visits to the North and abroad. She generally went to New York City for the winter, staying in Dr. Miller's Hotel on 36th Street. These respites

Sallie Holley, 1891. Around this time she summarized a typical morning as follows: "To draw water from our well, fifty feet deep, light my fire, boil potatoes, make tea, pick peaches from the garden, breakfast, wash up the dishes, make my bed, sweep, etc., consumes the time until half-past eight, when I put on dry clothes and take myself down to the schoolhouse to tend the mail" (to Elizabeth Smith Miller, c. 1888, Holley, *A Life for Liberty*, 270).

Holley School, date unknown. In November of 1888, Holley wrote that "this month our school counts seventy scholars and the Sunday school adds a score or two more. . . . We now have two young ladies from Massachusetts, who are mobilising this little army of students after the pattern of Boston" (letter to Robert Morville, 19 Nov. 1888, Holley, *A Life for Liberty*, 257–58).

made the rest of her life bearable. Prior to one visit she wrote, "No Peri ever more longed to enter the gate of Paradise than I to escape all this grinding toil and incessant work,—and enter New York City, and taste of its ease and happiness."[19] Life as an itinerant lecturer had also been physically demanding, but the isolation of her present life was painful for one who throve on "society, friendship, and love."[20]

Although Holley often looked on her work as an unpleasant duty, unlike Grimké Weld, she did not chastise herself for her failings as a Christian in doing so. She made no apologies for complaining about her life in her correspondence, which in her Virginia years mainly concerned the practical aspects of her life and particularly the needs of the Holley School.

Religiosity continued to be a fundamental element of her life. During her lecturing years, she wrote to William Lloyd Garrison that "He who would successfully confront this monster American Slavery must be inspired with the sublimest virtue—

'Tis God's all-animating voice
That calls us from on high.'"

Further, Holley claimed over and over again that her belief in the immortality of the human soul was the foundation of her spiritual life. She valued that
belief "as the brightest that ever dawned upon the human mind, next to that
of the existence of a God and his superintending providence." Moreover, she
shared her conviction with her friends, who were often less certain than she.
In 1875 she explained her faith in a letter to Elizabeth Smith Miller:

> It has been the habit of my whole life,—as it was my father's before
> me—to cherish an unfaltering faith in immortality. In the highest and
> most real experiences of my spirit, I always see it the clearest and most
> distinctly. In the deepest griefs and most trying trouble, the assurance
> comes to me—like a voice from heaven. In the human soul I see proofs.
> How can death have power over the great affections,—the noble mind,
> the rich character, the high hopes, the long, patient, self-denying efforts
> after growth and improvement, the sublime trust in hours of test? Why
> should we ever have this exalted faith and purifying hope unless it be
> eternally vital? Why should we be subject to such great and joyful
> attraction unless our destiny is proportioned?[21]

Holley was not above entertaining other points of view, however. She
recounted with some amusement an encounter with Ernestine Rose, an
atheist who disavowed any belief in an afterlife. Holley wrote that she had
talked with Rose about eternal life and had said to Rose, "But I think I shall
meet you in a life beyond and above this." She enjoyed Rose's direct
response: "Then you will say to me, 'I told you so,' and I shall reply, 'How
very stupid I was!'"[22]

Her faith in the workings of the divine spirit and in immortality did
not ebb during her years at the Holley School. For example, upon the occasion of Angelina Grimké Weld's death in 1879, she wrote to Theodore
Weld: "More than ever do I believe in immortal life—quite above and
independent of flesh and blood. Mrs. Weld is among angels and glorified
spirits." And then, as she felt her own health declining in the late 1880s,
she wrote that "my old elasticity and vigour of body are declining" but

that "I look forward with intense joy to an interminable existence, independent of flesh and blood."[23]

Holley used her visits in New York to pursue her intellectual and spiritual interests. Chadwick commented that throughout her life she maintained this interest, both in orthodox ways, such as Bible study, and in unorthodox ways, following the religious movements of the day and being particularly interested in Mental Science and Christian Science. She attended a course of parlor talks by Mrs. H. M. Poole on "mental science" and found them to be "of irresistable power and beauty." There again, what she particularly appreciated was that they dealt with the topics of spirituality and immortality; "You know," she reiterated to Miller, how "I incline with all my being, to the spiritual and immortal side of life."[24] In another visit in 1892, she wrote, again to Miller, "Next week I join a class in *The Soul's Progress in God*, a book written by one of the saints of the middle ages—Professor Davidson's lectures in Dr. Newton's All Souls' Chantry. I wish it were possible for you to join me every Saturday in this rare feast of thought. Every Sunday morning I am a joyful partaker of Felix Adler's spiritual banquets at Chickering Hall."[25] Holley was also a member of Sorosis, a women's club, and attended meetings on woman's suffrage.

Despite the hardships of her life, Holley was proud of what she and Caroline Putnam had accomplished.

> Twenty years ago this very month, out of pity, commiseration, and sorrow for the poverty and ignorance of these people, I came down to Virginia to lighten their burdens and kindle their souls to a better life. To-day I cannot but believe this school and its influences have accomplished a solid and enduring blessing, good for time and good for eternity. We have taught hundreds and hundreds to read and write and cipher, besides some knowledge of geography, history—especially that of the United States. . . .
>
> Some of our old pupils are now teaching public coloured schools in this part of the state, earning, every month, twenty-five dollars. Many of our boys and girls are in service in Baltimore and New York. A few of the older scholars have married here and are now in homes of their own.[26]

Holley died in January 1893, after contracting pneumonia on one of her visits to New York City. While she had made no secret of the fact that she found her final years difficult in many ways, she also found them rewarding, and continued her work up to her death. In 1890, at age seventy-one, she summed up her later years in a way that evoked her old optimism:

> We have a continual struggle to keep up the school and this mission in Virginia. We have to pinch and scrimp all the time. But this work is more and more of a success every year, and I want to persevere a few years longer. Then I shall be worn out in body and shall have to give it up,—though I think old age is the loveliest part of human life, infinitely beyond any youth I ever saw or knew.[27]

ABBY KELLEY FOSTER: A "LIFE OF LABOR"

Abby Kelley proved to be one of the most dedicated of all the antislavery lecturers, female or male, spending the better part of thirty years on the lecture circuit. She lectured all over the Northeast, but was also one of the most diligent antislavery agents in the Old Northwest, particularly in Ohio, Indiana, and Michigan.

Kelley believed that it was essential to build antislavery sentiment in this region. Ohio was her first target; writing from Cleveland in 1846, she stated, "We think Ohio is to the West what Mass[achusetts] is to N[orth] E[ast] in point of influence."[28] By 1854, Indiana was a focus of her attention. She spent two months there in the spring, writing that "Did my strength permit, I should remain in Indiana during the entire summer, and lecture in the villages during the busy season and the short evenings. I have never been in any new field where there was a more candid spirit of inquiry than here." She was impressed by the eagerness of the inhabitants to explore the issue and also by their generosity toward the cause, despite the fact that it was "a newly settled section, and therefore possessed of little wealth."[29]

Kelley did not allow the demands of domesticity to circumvent her antislavery mission. She and Stephen Foster declared their love for each other in 1843, but she refused to marry until she felt sure it would not interfere with her antislavery work. The two were finally married on 21 December 1845. Foster was also a radical reformer, an antislavery activist, and a comeouter, but he wanted to establish a home and family and was somewhat reluctant to assent to his wife's confident assertion that "both of us are willing to lay house, friends, all on the altar for our interest in the establishment of the great principles which lie at the foundation of the world's renovation."[30]

In 1847 Kelley Foster was surprised to find herself pregnant, having confided to Lucy Stone that "[i]f I am not mistaken in physiological facts, I never can be a mother while I work so hard in this cause."[31] She decided to wean her daughter at nine months and resume the lecture circuit, despite acknowledging that Alla had "so thoroughly entwined herself about me that I fear it would rend me in pieces to take her away."[32] But unlike the Grimkés, she remained convinced that her primary duty lay with the slaves. Responding to the criticism of a friend who said that her example would reinforce the "too prevalent custom" of leaving children in the care of "[a]unts and sisters and kind nurses who cannot have for them the feelings of a parent," Kelley Foster took the high ground and replied that what she was doing was "for the sake of the mothers who are robbed of all their children."[33]

Kelley Foster was much less solicitous of her own health than Holley was of hers. In late 1855 Kelley Foster's friends urged her to take a leave of absence from her lecturing and recoup her health. She finally agreed to do so and spent much of the next two years working on the Foster farm in Tatnuck. The Fosters did not abandon the cause, however; Stephen Foster took Abby's place in Ohio the following fall. She then returned to her antislavery work, combining it with participation in the women's rights movement, but was halted again in 1858 and 1859 when Alla was diagnosed with a severe spinal curvature that made her an invalid for a year. During that time, Kelley Foster devoted herself almost exclusively to her daughter.

Much of the time, however, Kelley Foster was single-minded and relatively merciless in the pursuit of her goals, the primary one of which was to establish Garrisonian abolitionism in the North to the exclusion of any other antislavery faction. She did not hesitate to use harsh language to characterize those people and ideas that she opposed. As noted previously, her energy and unstinting dedication to her cause won her numerous admirers; she was disliked by many others.[34] Sarah Pugh, a Philadelphia abolitionist, once wrote to Maria Chapman that "very many here who are ready for strong meat would turn away in disgust if it were set before them in its raw state by A. Kelley."[35] And according to Sarah Hallowell Willis,

Abby Kelley Foster, c. late 1850s, a time when Kelley Foster was absorbed both
with the difficuties of fund-raising for the antislavery cause and with the health
of her daughter Alla. *Courtesy American Antiquarian Society.*

who was accompanying Sallie Holley on one of her tours, Holley sometimes found churches closed to her "because the people are shocked at the Fosters infidelity and impolite manners."[36] Kelley herself contrasted her speaking style with that of the popular Holley: "She speaks beautifully and effectively on general principles and [sets home?] convictions with great force on the heart and conscience, tho' she has so much poetry intermingled in her addresses the sword is very much covered." "Still," Kelley added kindly, "this is her way and I want she should pursue it."[37] Kelley, in contrast, never minced her words. She told Wendell Phillips that "[m]y constant prayer is to be preserved in the full flower of fanaticism and saved from the beginnings of popularity among a people who participate tho' ever so remotely in holding slaves."[38]

While frequently criticizing the motives and actions of others, Kelley strongly resented any imputation of wrongdoing of her own. She did not display the soul-searching and the openness to criticism of the Grimkés and Holley nor the more gentle but penetrating insights of Mott. She refused to defend herself from criticism passed on by Maria Weston Chapman in 1843, saying—somewhat surprisingly from one whose career was in public speaking—"When it comes to be needful for me to defend my position by word I will give up all claim to honesty. My life is a constant definition."[39] She was livid about accusations of heresy from the Oberlin College faculty in 1846 and their decision that she would not be welcome to return to Oberlin. Kelley refused to acknowledge any justice in their position, even though Lucy Stone, one of her most fervent admirers, told her that the complaint was largely due to the Fosters having circulated a book discussing the Sabbath in a way that even Stone, another religious radical, felt was very unsound.[40] Unbending in her wrath, the following year she told her husband she was surprised to hear he was going to Oberlin as she could not imagine that he would "again attempt to cast pearls before such dirty swine."[41] Years later, in 1859, she again reacted violently to criticism, this time from William Lloyd Garrison, who stated publicly that he believed she was being inconsistent in seeking funds from leading Republicans while at the same time denouncing their party "as the worst and most dangerous [obstacle] in our path." Denying any inconsistency, she rejected the efforts of Wendell Phillips and others to conciliate her, refused repeated invitations to sit on the Board of Managers of the American Anti-Slavery Society, said that she no longer felt that she could go west in the fall to help the Western Anti-Slavery Society, and after an unsatisfactory correspondence with Garrison himself on the subject, cut off her association with him for nearly ten years.[42]

Kelley, more than any of the others surveyed here, was political in the most narrow sense of engrossing herself in the machinations of antislavery politics. The letters of the other women in this study embrace a wide range of social, intellectual, and theological issues; after 1841, Kelley's are confined mainly to the business of abolitionism. She wrote mainly of strategies and tactics rather than of philosophies. She not only preached antislavery, but also opposition to the New Organization, the non-Garrisonian wing of the abolition movement. She was an implacable foe, mocking Gerrit Smith, a representative of the New Organization, even as he made an effort to reconcile himself with her, and vigorously opposing David L. Child's tenure as editor of the *Anti-Slavery Standard*.[43] Her letters frequently leave the impression that her efforts were concentrated more on debunking the New Organization and the Liberty Party than in promoting antislavery sentiment. When she was challenged for the language she used in one speech, she claimed she had been misinterpreted: she had only called the Liberty Party "dirty"; she didn't say it was the "*dirtiest*" of all three parties.[44] After a week of meetings in New Ipswich, she proudly told Stephen Foster: "We have done up the satisfactory work of fixing in the minds of the true, the idea that Liberty Party is the guardian of Slavery in the Church, and hence their final and greatest foe."[45]

Kelley Foster's avowed lack of interest in theoretical issues and her absorption in antislavery politics stand in sharp contrast to the interests of the other women here, who were more overtly dedicated to the pursuit of philosophical truth as well as social justice. In this respect, Abby Kelley comes the closest to Hersh's description of antislavery feminists as women who substituted reform for religion. Dorothy Sterling, while asserting Kelley's ongoing religiosity, does not dwell upon it. In a more recent essay, Keith Melder finds that Kelley, even in the midst of the religious reflection that led her into her lecturing career, did not fit the "stereotype" of an individual who engages in religious meditation, because, he says, "although she sought divine guidance and inspiration, her aim was to throw off religious authority, not surrender to it." He concludes that Kelley was successful in her efforts, and by the end of 1841, had "emerged a fully liberated person."[46]

It must be acknowledged that after her initial declaration of a divinely sanctioned mission, Kelley comes closer than any of the others to having replaced religion with reform. Yet it is not fair to dismiss Kelley as having "liberated" herself from religion. Her primary interest in this regard was to free herself from *human* religious authority, which, like the other women in this study, she found incompatible with faithfulness to divine authority.

Kelley's letters, first of all, may not be wholly reliable indicators of her thoughts; she once confided in her future husband that:

> I never write a letter without a *little* impatience and at times a *great deal*. I have not the temperament for writing. I would much rather talk even on a subject that does not interest me, four hours, than write on it for one. I presume one reason for my distaste of writing is, that I have not the power of condensing my ideas like some, and therefore, when a large sheet is covered I find but few of the many things I wished to place upon it.[47]

Her actions and spoken words may thus be more revealing of her state of mind. While lecturing, she claimed that she had no time to indulge in intellectual pursuits. She confided in Sallie Holley, though, that she hoped to find her "longing desires for time for mental cultivation and social enjoyment" fulfilled "on the other side of Jordan" as "as a reward for [her] unceasing labors here."[48]

After Kelley Foster was no longer active as a lecturer, and despite her declining health, she began to attend meetings of the Radical Club and the Free Religious Association in Boston. The latter was founded in 1867 "to unite all honest searchers after the essentials of the universal, in religion and in life," and held annual conventions as well as publishing a newspaper.[49] The Radical Club was a loosely affiliated group mainly of older transcendentalists and reformers that began meeting in 1867 on the first Monday of every month at the home of John and Mary Sargent in Boston. According to Mary Sargent the purpose of the club was to "meet a demand for the freest investigation of all forms of religious thought and inquiry."[50] Kelley Foster was an active participant in those discussions. Mary Elizabeth Sargent records Kelley Foster as having asserted, for example, that the way to understand God's attributes was to do God's will. In her usual practical manner, somewhat belied by her attendance at such a meeting, she claimed that "whoever went about among men, entirely devoted and self-consecrated to the work of doing them good, seeking the poor, the tempted, and the sorrowing, as Jesus did, would be more sure of growing into sympathy with God's heart and coming to an understanding of his will than by any other process."[51] On the basis of this evidence of her thinking in her later years, when she was no longer so completely absorbed in her antislavery work, it seems most likely that while Kelley Foster should be taken at her word in her general disinterest in theologizing, it would be presumptuous to deny her religiosity. It seems clear that she believed herself to be living out her religious principles in her antislavery work—though, unlike the other women here, she did not feel the need to continually reevaluate her theological views, at least not in communications that survive today. Her reassertion of religious interest in her later years supports the view that religion continued to provide the foundation for her world view.

Abby Kelley Foster died 14 January 1887, the last day of her seventy-fifth year. Her daughter Alla attested to Kelley Foster's faith in a continued existence, which, she said, "gave a calmness and peace to her later life which enabled her to live or die with equal resignation." Abby Kelley Foster did not, however, look for eternal rest in death any more than she did in life. According to Alla, she expected that the afterlife would consist of a "life of labor, not of rest, for she believed that only by struggle could spiritual and intellectual powers be developed."[52]

LUCRETIA MOTT: "HERETIC OF HERETICS"

In comparison to the others', Lucretia Mott's life was one of remarkable consistency. She was publicly active in reform movements for almost the whole of her long life. Antislavery and women's rights were her two major reform interests, but she was also involved in many other issues, including nonresistance and temperance as well as Free Produce, antisabbatarianism, Native American rights, and opposition to capital punishment. She rarely let herself be halted by her various physical ailments, which included a chronic and quite painful dyspepsia.[53]

Her sister Martha frequently urged her to slow her pace. In 1856, receiving one such plea, Mott responded, "As to 'taking a long breath,' it is what I have not done since the Convention of 1833—rather since the Separation or 'Split' in 1827—indeed to speak the truth, since I was born—

Lucretia Mott in a photograph taken in the late 1860s or early 1870s. Although her aging is apparent, her pose and demeanor are remarkably similar to those of the 1841 portrait shown in chapter 1. *Courtesy Friends Historical Library of Swarthmore College, Swarthmore, Pennsylvania.*

except in days of yore, when I could sit and sew carpet rags in some obscure corner of your house."[54] Although this might have been unwarranted boasting for some, it was the simple truth for Mott, who set an unparalleled example in her attention both to great causes and to household details. She traveled and preached; she hosted frequent social events; she maintained a regular and wide-ranging correspondence with family and friends. In 1848 she wrote to Richard Webb that: "With all this travel[in]g and reading and writing I find time to darn lots of stockings and attend somewhat to a family numbering from 10 to 20 every day—for though all our children, save Martha the youngest, are married and have left us, yet they and their children, 9 grandchildren in all, are coming constantly."[55] Some visitors Mott seldom mentioned in any of her correspondence were the fugitive slaves she and her husband sheltered. As far back as 1835 she wrote, "We have now under our care a poor runaway with her infant not yet a month old."[56] They performed this service throughout the years as a matter of course. In an 1857 letter to her sister, Mott sandwiched the simple comment, "We have fugitives by the dozen coming almost every week" between a reference to the national financial crisis and a comment about having had some friends over for tea.[57]

That same year the Motts sold their large Philadelphia home and moved to Roadside, a smaller house between Philadelphia and New York City. Although this was supposedly to reduce the physical demands on them, they continued to entertain on a large scale; in one undated letter she mentions that two guests could not come "so our long table was not quite filled."[58]

Like Angelina Grimké Weld, Mott was interested in the debate over the formation of an equal rights society. She, too, was skeptical about the value of institutions and organizations. She based her reservations on her distrust of any group that relied in any way on coercion. She saw this reliance as a primary flaw of state institutions and claimed that she had little interest in "the various shiftings of opinions" in politics, for "while their base is physical force, the structure must be evil."[59] Mott also noted that in all religious associations, and presumably others as well, there was a tendency toward, as she put it, "retrogression." An original desire to affiliate might be the result of a genuine move toward reform and enlightenment, but "there is a disposition . . . to go back again to the weak and beggarly elements and to desire, and be willing, to be brought into bondage again."[60]

The weapon with which to combat the evils of organization and coercive power was nothing more than "true religion, the religion of Jesus." This faith would "lead into laying the axe at the root of the corrupt tree of arbitrary power which has been produced by the assumption of false claims of man over his fellow-man."[61]

Unlike all the others', Mott's religious commitment has been accepted as a matter of course. Indeed, the danger her biographers have faced has been not that of minimizing her religious conviction but of avoiding hagiography.[62] But although Mott's religiosity is not questioned today—as it was in her own day—her religious radicalism has not been fully appreciated. She expressed the most extreme theological views of any of these women, not hesitating to challenge the standing of the Bible as the infallible word of God and of Jesus as Messiah. Also unusual was her insistence on granting divine status to secular works, such as some poetry, and to the words and actions of other human beings.

Although she had a preference for the Quaker style of worship, she, like the others, believed that faith was best expressed through everyday actions and attempts to improve the condition of the world. The majority of her sermons and speeches were given to Quaker audiences, but she mingled with people from a variety of religious traditions, including Unitarians, black church groups, and spiritualists. One of her favorite religious writers was the Spanish ex-priest Blanco White, who had left the Catholic Church for Anglicanism, then went through a period of atheism, and eventually embraced Unitarianism. She spoke highly of the atheist Ernestine Rose, appreciating "her honest, out-spoken radicalism, her discerning and discriminating mind, and her enlarged charity and forbearance toward the ignorant criminal and wrongdoer—as well as wrong *thinker*." Mott added, "Her lectures always attracted me—so rare is candor in unpopular heterodoxy."[63] Like Abby Kelley Foster, she attended meetings of the Free Religious Association, although she refused to join the group until its mission was redefined from calling for the "scientific study of theology" to the "scientific study of the religious nature of human beings."[64] She addressed the Annual Meeting of the Free Religious Association every year from 1870 to 1873 and again in 1875 and was, like Kelley Foster, an active participant in the discussions at the Radical Club.

Mott was open to a variety of forms of religious expression, although, as noted previously, she found rituals of any kind generally unhelpful. On the basis of this view, her comment that the dances and strawberry festivals of some Native American tribes had as much "reasonableness and rational worship in [them] as in passing around the little bread and wine" is probably less an endorsement of the former than a disparagement of the latter.[65] She appreciated spiritualism for having assisted in tearing down various orthodox doctrines, but when an enthusiastic visitor came to inquire if she herself was a devotee, she "let him know quickly that Garrison called [her] 'Thomas surnamed Didymus.'"[66]

Mott appears rather more conventional than she was for a number of reasons. She was generally mild-mannered, putting "the silken snapper on her whiplash" in order to deliver "the gentlest and yet most cutting rebuke."[67] She was not interested in self-aggrandizement, preferring that others take the lead whenever they were willing and able to do so. Especially in her later years, she was happy to pass on the torch of women's rights advocacy to younger women so that "some of us older warriors may begin to retire from the field and give place to them."[68]

Just as the severing of connections from organized religion makes the others appear less religious, in Mott's case, her lifelong membership in the Society of Friends has made her appear more orthodox. Having chosen to affiliate with the Hicksites in the schism of 1827, later she did not even join the Progressive Friends, a group whose views were ideologically closer to her own. Apparently, though, her decision was based less on personal inclination than on practicality. As she somewhat wistfully noted, "Our young people have little interest in these reorganizations and without their cooperation they must die out."[69] By the end of her life, when her Society had come closer to adopting her own viewpoints, Mott was rehabilitated as a respected figure, and certainly Quakers today want to claim her as their own. It is clearly easier to overlook the religious radicalism of a woman who chose to remain affiliated with a religious body than it is to overlook that of women like the Grimkés or Abby Kelley. Nonetheless, when asked to clarify her religious convictions, Mott once replied: "Put me down as heretic of the heretics, radical of the radicals, and, although I am not an infidel, I am also not an orthodox, and would as lief be thought one as the other."[70] Even her longtime but somewhat more conservative friend, James Miller McKim, once accused her of having lost her faith. Her response to him was simple: "Thee hasn't listened to me preach if thee believes that."[71]

Suffering from poor health throughout many of her later years,

Lucretia Mott nonetheless outlived many of her contemporaries, dying in 1880 at the age of eighty-eight. With her death the reform community lost one of its most dedicated members and one of its most articulate and insightful voices. The magnitude of that loss was reflected in the tribute she was accorded at her graveside. After an initial eulogy, silence fell. When the rest of the company was invited to speak, one only replied: "Who can speak? The preacher is dead."[72]

❦

Conclusion

"THE GOSPEL OF TRUTH AND FREEDOM"

W E HAVE SEEN how a sense of mission led the Grimkés, Kelley, Holley, and Mott to embrace antislavery lecturing, and how their self-identification as lecturers led to the formation of a particular reform community. In that community these women acknowledged special ties to one another as well as to the wider community that in turn granted them a unique status.[1]

In their later years, each of these women found their convictions evolving and their activism modified by various demands and concerns. This occurred on the personal level, in response to health, family obligations, and their own aging and maturing. It was spurred on by outside events, such as the expanding women's rights movement, the controversies within the antislavery movement, the Civil War, and emancipation. The changes in their personal lives and their individual responses to national events make it appear that by the end of their lives, the community that linked them in their earlier antislavery days had evaporated. The Grimkés retired to a quiet life of farming and teaching; Kelley became absorbed in abolition infighting; Holley interspersed her lecturing with rest cures and eventually spent most of her last twenty-three years in rural Virginia; Mott wrestled with ill health and the demands of the various causes in which she was involved.

The paths of these women in their later lives were not, however, as widely divergent as one might think. They continued to encounter one another throughout their lives. The Grimkés and Abby Kelley Foster corresponded with Sallie Holley, who regarded all three as mentors. Holley was an occasional guest at both the Grimké/Weld and Foster homes. After a week with the Grimké/Welds, Holley and Putnam found the sisters as admirable as Holley had years before: "She [Angelina] and her sister, Sarah

Grimké, give the impression of radiant youth, they are kept so fresh and bright with the life of thought and principle." For her part, during the same visit Sallie Holley gave a lecture that Angelina Grimké Weld attended. Afterwards Grimké Weld declared that Holley's talk had made her feel like "going out herself again in this great crisis to plead for the black man's right of suffrage."[2] Lucretia Mott, too, was grateful for Sallie Holley's entry into the lecturing field. Mott also appreciated Abby Kelley Foster's talents despite the differences in their styles. After they concluded their antislavery lecturing, Kelley Foster and Mott both participated in meetings of the Free Religious Association and the Radical Club in Boston. Both the Grimké/Welds and the Fosters contributed supplies to the Holley School.

The wider reform community continued to defer to these women. Sarah Grimké often advised Elizabeth Smith Miller, and Lucretia Mott continued to correspond with Elizabeth Cady Stanton. Susan B. Anthony visited the Motts. Sarah Parker Remond wrote to Abby Kelley Foster that she probably would not have attempted any lecturing "but for the words of encouragement I received from you."[3] The *Boston Sunday Herald* reported that Lucretia Mott "had a hand in the making of Anna E. Dickinson,"[4] a young woman who took up lecturing in the 1860s (see Appendix). Their names were used on calls to antislavery fairs and women's rights conventions. All of them but Holley either spoke or addressed public letters to women's rights conventions. Kelley Foster was asked to serve on the board of managers of the American Anti-Slavery Society in 1859. All five women obviously continued to be regarded as leaders within the reform community.

From the perspective of their philosophic and religious ideals, one finds an internal consistency in their thinking, and a roughly parallel evolution of conviction that, while manifesting itself in various ways, continued to reflect the faithfulness of the women to underlying principles. Not only did these women maintain social contacts with one another, but their interests developed along parallel lines. One of their primary concerns was the position of the newly freed slaves, and that of African Americans in general. Kelley Foster supported black male suffrage even when it came at the cost of the vote for women. Holley, like some other abolitionists, devoted herself to educating ex-slaves. Sarah Grimké collected clothing for freed men and women. Both sisters, but Angelina Grimké Weld in particular, advised and supported two nephews they did not discover until 1868—offspring of a long-standing relationship between their brother and one of the enslaved women on his estate.[5] In Philadelphia, Lucretia Mott worked to secure equal access to streetcars for African Americans. The Foster home as well as the Motts' was a station on the Underground Railroad.[6]

The issue of woman's rights was another shared concern of their later years. As in the issue of race relations, they not only campaigned for their issues, they articulated theoretical justifications for their views and actions. All of them agreed that women had an important role to play in the "regeneration" of the world. They disagreed, though, as do modern feminists, as to whether the qualities that made women's role important were innate or learned, and whether they made women men's equals or their superiors.

Both Sarah Grimké and Abby Kelley Foster claimed a special role for women, although they disagreed about its origin. According to Kelley Foster, women could

> do more than men for the extension of righteousness. Not that they are naturally better or wiser but because they have not, from the customs of society, been so much perverted. The temptations, the tolerated tricks and falsehoods of trade and politicks into which the boy is baptized and in which the heart when it comes to manhood becomes petrified more than half and in some instances entirely unfits it for the work of purifying the world. Women are not so situated as to be so entirely corrupted and hence their moral perception is much clearer.[7]

Women, then, were morally superior to men only because their sphere had not exposed them to the hazards that confronted men. Sarah Grimké's claim was more extensive. She wrote:

> I am well satisfied from observation that boys have not generally as much of the love element as girls and it is true brothers seldom pay as much attention to sisters as they receive from them; it is our part to soften the masculine nature and try by patient and unwearied tenderness to cherish and fructify the seeds of affection. Woman's love nature is her crowning blessing, it is through this she is destined to regenerate the world.[8]

Men were in a sense handicapped for they could generally claim only "physical power" and "intellectual effort" in attempting their goals, attributes that were not sufficient for the task at hand. It was, therefore, woman's responsibility to "live out the life of love, if ever she is instrumental in bringing man out of the pit of moral degradation into which the exercise of irresponsible power has cast him." Men would then eventually come to realize the sinfulness of such institutions as slavery and abolish them.[9]

Grimké did not, however, believe women's potential for moral superiority was realized in current practice. In 1853 she was very severe upon woman's "love of admiration, her vanity, her littleness, her want of moral courage, her devotion to fashion." She also claimed (obviously prior to her suffrage work) that she "should lament the right of suffrage being granted us because there are so few of us worthy of being the arbiters of a nation's faith."[10]

Mott disagreed with the view of women's natural superiority, even in the more moderate way proposed by Kelley Foster. She preferred to think of women as "efficient co-workers," whose abilities and interests should not be stifled by social prejudices about gender roles.[11] Indeed, she cautioned women at the 1853 Woman's Rights Convention in Cleveland:

> It has sometimes been said that if women were associated with men in
> their efforts, there would be not as much immorality as now exists in
> Congress, for instance, and other places. But we ought, I think to claim
> no more for woman than for man; we ought to put woman on a par
> with man, not invest her with power, or call for her superiority over
> her brother. If we do, she is just as likely to become a tyrant as man is
> as with Catherine the Second.[12]

In contrast, if women and men were truly coworkers, one could "be sure there would be a better rule than now; the elements which belong to woman as such and to man as such, would be beautifully and harmoniously blended." As a result of this blending of natural traits, Mott hoped that there would be "less war, injustice, and intolerance in the world than now."[13]

Religious concerns occupied these women in many ways. Angelina Grimké Weld gave considerable thought to the idea of the Second Coming of Christ. The Welds participated in their local, unaffiliated religious assembly. Their daughter Sarah married the minister of the group, a Mr. Hamilton, who, said Sarah Grimké, had "bravely fought his way from grim, benighted orthodoxy to radical Unitarianism."[14] Sarah Grimké embraced spiritualism. Abby Kelley Foster and Lucretia Mott met with others to debate the meaning and relevance of religion in a world that was becoming more self-consciously scientific. Sallie Holley continued to combine her commitment to biblical studies with her interest in new approaches to spirituality. Regardless of their different paths, they all continued to adhere to the principles to which they had subscribed much earlier: of a benevolent God; of the goodness of human nature; of the ability of individuals to understand directly the will of God; of God's desire for justice in the world—which included racial and gender equality among other things; and of human responsibility to bring God's plan into existence.

There is one final link between these women, related both to their sense of divine mission and to their characters. That link is their passionate commitment to truth; truth conceived of in religious terms, based on the ability of individuals to perceive and act upon divine principle. As Lucretia Mott stated in one sermon, "Are not the aspirations for truth, proof that we have a present God with us?"[15] Back in 1837, Abby Kelley had written that she supported "tak[ing] a decided stand for *all truth*."[16] Ten years later she consoled her husband, who was questioning the value of the reformers' efforts, by saying,

> I trust our children's children shall see a clear sun-rise. Let us toil and faint not, if so be we can add but one ray to that better day, if it be only for their sakes. I would not have another generation enveloped in so deep a gloom as that which enshrouds us. But altho' my conviction, founded on fact, is that the scale of humanity is rising, if it were not so, I should still deem it our duty, not only to live well, but to live truly, and we could not do so, if, having the ability to use our voices for the utterance of truth we should keep silence.

She added her belief that "The *preaching* of truth does do good. I see, and if I did not see, I should believe ours has done good—for the necessary tendency of proclaiming the truth is to make it loved and embraced the more."[17]

Their commitment to discovering truth was the lens by which these women surveyed themselves and the world, and it was the measure of their actions as well. As Abby Kelley stated in her letter resigning her membership in the Society of Friends, "it is my constant desire and prayer to Him, in whose hands are all hearts, that he would turn and overturn, till truth shall cover the earth as the waters do the great deep."[18] Sallie Holley complained that many people "never dream that religion has anything to do with honesty or truth."[19]

Sarah Grimké, in proposing religious authorities other than Jesus, had proclaimed, "I would reverently bow to Truth wherever and in whomsoever it appeareth."[20] Their conviction that in attempting to apply that truth to their world they were being faithful to divine will sustained these women throughout many hardships. They were generally willing, with the occasional abstention of Abby Kelley, to open their hearts to new truths and to expose their own fallibility. While defending her opinion on women's roles to one of their most vocal abolitionist critics, Angelina Grimké had commented, "I am glad thou hast thrown out thy objections to my ultra doctrine. I want to have it thoroughly sifted, for I think Truth is *more precious* to me than any thing else."[21] Her commitment to this ideal never faltered, as was evident in her analysis of her shortcomings in later years.

Their shared sense of mission is perhaps best summarized by the preacher, Lucretia Mott: "All we can do, one for another, is to bring each to know the light of truth in the soul. It is pure, holy, unmistakable. . . . And we should come to recognize the great principles of justice, humanity, and kindness, holiness in all its parts, in the full belief that the establishing of the dominion of these in the earth is the divine purpose of the Eternal."[22]

Appendix

OTHER FEMALE ABOLITIONIST LECTURERS

SARAH AND ANGELINA GRIMKÉ, Sallie Holley, Abby Kelley, and Lucretia Mott were not the only women who lectured against slavery. A few major figures, such as Maria Stewart, Lucy Stone, and Sojourner Truth, were not included in this study, along with numerous others who are less well known.

A few words on the logic of the selection of the subjects of this book may be useful. My first criterion was to include only those women who were identified, or who self-identified primarily as abolitionists. By this criterion, Lucretia Mott was included, despite her significant involvement with many other causes, but Lucy Stone, who identified more strongly with woman's rights, was excluded. I also included only women whose speaking engagements had taken them away from their homes and placed them on a lecture circuit. These were the women who were most in the public eye, most likely to have encountered challenges from clergy and others, and most likely to have articulated a response to those challenges in their correspondence and their recorded remarks. This criterion (along with the final one) ruled out a woman like Maria Stewart. Most significantly, and perhaps most controversially, I chose not to include women for whom little primary source material, correspondence in particular, exists. For the purposes of this work, I felt I needed to hear my women "talk"; that is, I had to have access to their voices, both public and private. What I most regretted was that this excluded most of the African American women who lectured, such as Sojourner Truth and Sarah Parker Remond.

This appendix may assist those who wish to know more about other women who became antislavery lecturers. This is not a comprehensive list. As I have done the research for this book, names of other lecturers continue to appear, women who did not achieve the national prominence of the

Grimkés or Truth and who have not achieved the place in history to which their activism might have entitled them.

This selection also goes somewhat beyond the bounds of antislavery lecturers, strictly defined, because it includes some women, mainly African Americans, whose lecturing focus was more on the uplift of the black community than on the abolition of slavery per se. However, as the Peases (among others) have pointed out, the line between slavery and freedom was less clearly demarcated for "free" African Americans than it was for white Americans. As the subjects of the foregoing study also understood, prejudice and discrimination are also forms of enslavement, albeit on a less severe scale. Nonetheless, it is clear that African Americans such as Maria Stewart and Mary Ann Shadd Cary saw their advocacy of moral uplift and black self-reliance as directly linked to the fight against slavery.

For the basic biographical information provided here, I am indebted in most instances to two sources. In the case of the Euro-American women, I have relied heavily on the classic three-volume biographical dictionary, *Notable American Women,* edited by Edward T. James and Janet Wilson James. For African American women, I have turned to the excellent and more recent two-volume encyclopedia, *Black Women in America,* edited by Darlene Clark Hine, Elsa Barkley Brown, and Rosalyn Terborg-Penn, as well as to *Notable American Women.*

Following the discussion of each woman in this appendix, I have noted the sources of the information provided. Both the dictionary and the encyclopedia include a detailed bibliography for each of their entries. In the source documentation that follows each discussion below, I have noted instances in which additional sources are available that are not listed in the dictionary or encyclopedia bibliographies. A list of abbreviations used appears in the Notes section that follows this appendix.

MARY ANN SHADD CARY (1823–93)

Mary Ann Shadd was the oldest of thirteen children born to Abraham and Harriet Shadd, a well-to-do African American family in Wilmington, Delaware. Abraham Shadd was a prominent abolitionist. Mary Ann Shadd attended a Quaker school for free black children in West Chester, Pennsylvania, and taught school herself in Delaware, Pennsylvania, and New York.

In 1849, Shadd published a pamphlet entitled *Hints to the Colored People of the North*, advising free blacks to refrain from imitating the materialism of whites and to take political action to improve their situation. Moving to Canada in 1851, she helped found the *Provincial Freeman*, a weekly newspaper serving the interests of people of color in Canada. Shadd traveled on behalf of the paper, raising funds through a lecture tour in the United States. Her focus was on developing black self-reliance. She was a firm supporter of integration and left the African Methodist Episcopal Church in Canada because of its racial separatism to join a Methodist church.

Shadd married Thomas F. Cary in 1856. During the Civil War she recruited black soldiers for the Union Army in Indiana, Ohio, Michigan, and Pennsylvania. Widowed by 1869, she moved with her daughter to Washington, D.C., where she taught in public schools for fifteen years. She also successfully completed studies at Howard Law School, opening a law office in Washington after her graduation. In addition to this work, she was active in women's rights issues. She died in Washington, D.C. and was buried in Harmony Cemetery.

[*BWA*, 1:224–26; *NAW*, 1:300–301; also Silverman, "Mary Ann Shadd" 87–100.]

LUCY NEWHALL DANFORTH COLMAN (1817–1906)

Lucy Newhall was raised in Massachusetts. Her mother died when she was six. Newhall was not attracted to the evangelical religion that swept through New England in her early years; instead she embraced Universalism. She married at the age of eighteen and moved with her husband to Boston. Her husband died of consumption six years later.

In 1826, she married again and had a daughter two years later. At some point the Colmans moved to Rochester, New York, where Mr. Colman worked as a railroad engineer. He was killed in an accident in 1835. Colman noted in her memoirs that his funeral service was conducted by the spiritualist Andrew Jackson Davis. She herself had become a spiritualist after having "given up the Church, more because of its complicity with slavery than from a full understanding of the foolishness of its creed."[1] (Colman later became an adamant opponent of spiritualism.)

After her husband's death, Lucy Colman tried to get a job to support herself and her daughter, but was rejected when she applied at the railroad company, the post office, and a print shop. She eventually secured a teaching position, but at less than half the salary paid to the previous teacher, a man. Dissatisfied with this position, she considered becoming an antislavery lecturer. Her good friend in Rochester, the abolitionist Amy Post, supported her in this mission, setting up meetings for her and accompanying her. The two traveled to Michigan for an annual convention of the Western Anti-Slavery Society, and Colman was appointed an agent of that society. Initially she had to pay her own expenses and earn her own salary, but after three successful months in Michigan, the American Anti-Slavery Society agreed to pay her a salary and her expenses. Colman traveled and lectured extensively in Michigan, Ohio, Indiana, and Illinois.

In 1862, Colman's daughter died suddenly and Colman lost interest in her work. A friend persuaded her to accept the position of matron in the National Colored Orphan Asylum in Washington, D.C. Colman found the children so badly treated by the teacher in charge that she rediscovered an interest in life and worked to improve the facility. Later she was named a superintendent of schools in Washington, D.C. Colman is the white woman who escorted Sojourner Truth on Truth's visit to President Abraham Lincoln. (Colman was not impressed by Lincoln, disliking his patronizing treatment of Truth and his refusal to identify himself as an abolitionist.)

After the war, Colman worked on behalf of the freed men and women. Her memoirs were published in 1891; I have not found any accounts detailing her activities for the remainder of her life.

[Lucy Colman, *Reminiscences* (Buffalo, New York: H. L. Green, 1891). Her dates of birth and death are taken from the Library of Congress catalog record of her book.]

ELLEN CRAFT (1826–91? 97?)[2]

Ellen Craft was born in Clinton, Georgia, the daughter of an enslaved mother and a white cotton planter. She met her future husband, William Craft, in Macon, Georgia. In 1848 they succeeded in escaping from slavery: Ellen Craft disguised herself as a white gentleman; William Craft as the gentleman's body servant.

Once in the North, they lived in Boston for two years, becoming active participants in the antislavery movement and popular speakers on the lecture platform. After Georgia slave catchers traced them to Boston, they left the United States and traveled to Great Britain, where they were also quite successful speakers. They returned to the United States in the late 1860s. Ellen Craft spent the last years of her life with her daughter in Charleston, South Carolina.

[*BWA*, 1:290; *NAW*, 1:396–98]

HANNAH CONANT TRACY CUTLER (1815–96)

Born in Becket, Massachusetts, Hannah Conant attended the local day school, but studied rhetoric, philosophy, and Latin on her own initiative. Her family moved to Rochester, Ohio, in 1831. Conant wished to study at Oberlin College, but her father vetoed the idea. At the age of eighteen, she married John Martin Tracy, a man who became an antislavery lecturer. Ten years after their marriage her husband died. In order to support her children, she began to write for Ohio newspapers and taught school.

She became an advocate of women's rights and peace issues, traveling to England and lecturing there in 1851. After her second marriage in 1852, she moved to Dwight, Illinois, and worked on the family farm. In 1859 she began lecturing again, first in New York, then in Illinois. Although her primary focus was women's rights, she addressed antislavery issues as well.

Cutler attended a school for homeopathic medicine in Cleveland and received her M.D. in 1869. She practiced medicine in Ohio and Illinois. She served as the president of Lucy Stone's American Woman Suffrage Association in 1870–71. She was sporadically active in the women's rights movement after her husband's death in 1873. She died at age eighty in her daughter's home in Mississippi.

[*NAW*, 1:426–27. See also her 1862 letters to the editor of the *Liberator* (23 May, 30 May, 13 June, 4 July).]

ANNA DICKINSON (1842–1932)

Anna Dickinson was the youngest of five children in a Philadelphia Quaker family headed by John and Mary Dickinson. Her father died when she was two, and the family had to work hard to remain solvent. Dickinson worked as a copyist and a teacher and in 1861 took a job with the U.S. Mint.

While in her teens she became interested in women's rights and abolition. In 1860 she attended the Annual Meeting of the Pennsylvania Anti-Slavery Society and gave an impressive impromptu speech. She was encouraged by abolitionists such as Lucretia Mott to launch a speaking career, which she did, becoming immensely popular. She addressed various issues, including abolition, woman's rights, and equal rights for all citizens regardless of color. She also campaigned on behalf of the Republican Party during the Civil War. After the war, she continued her talks on the Lyceum circuit; her biographer, Giraud Chester, claimed that she grossed $23,000 from her speaking engagements in 1872.

Becoming less able to draw crowds to her talks, she attempted to write and star in two plays, both of which failed. Despite a lecture tour on behalf of the Republican Party in 1888, she was never able to regain her popularity as a public speaker. Exhibiting signs of mental illness, she was involuntarily committed to the Danville (Pennsylvania) State Hospital for the Insane in 1891. She succeeded in getting released and eventually won a lawsuit against those who had had her committed. She remained poor, however, and was disgruntled about her inability to achieve success on the lecture platform or stage. She lived quietly with friends in New York for the last forty years of her life.

[*NAW*,1:475–76; Chester, *Embattled Maiden*.]

MARY GREW (1813–96)

Mary Grew was born in Hartford, Connecticut, where her father, Henry Grew, had served as pastor of the First Baptist Church from 1807 to 1811. She attended Catharine Beecher's Hartford Female Seminary. Eventually the Grew family settled in Philadelphia and Mary Grew became an active member of the Philadelphia Female Anti-Slavery Society. In addition to organizing and writing, she also did some public speaking. She was one of the speakers at the 1838 Anti-Slavery Convention of American Women on the day that Pennsylvania Hall, their meeting place, was attacked by a mob and burned down. She also served as a delegate to the 1840 World's Anti-Slavery Convention in London.

In 1845 Grew was a member of a group that toured Pennsylvania counties bordering the slave states of Delaware, Maryland, and Virginia.

Their intention was "to win new converts to the antislavery cause, to reinvigorate old ones, to cement bonds of union among abolitionists, to circulate antislavery newspapers, tracts, and books, to promote the annual fair, and to advance the antislavery movement any way they could."[3] Her biographer also reports a speaking engagement in October 1858 in West Chester, Pennsylvania, which she performed in company with Lucretia Mott, and additional meetings in 1860.[4]

In addition to her antislavery work, Grew was active in the woman's suffrage movement. She lived in Philadelphia until her death at the age of eighty-three, and was buried in Woodlands Cemetery.

[*NAW*, 2:91–92; Brown, *Mary Grew.*]

JOSEPHINE WHITE GRIFFING (1814–72)

Josephine White Griffing was born and raised in Connecticut. She married Charles Griffing in 1835 and moved to Litchfield, Ohio, in the early 1840s. The Griffings sheltered fugitive slaves in their home. Josephine Griffing served as an officer of the Western Anti-Slavery Society and contributed articles to the *Anti-Slavery Bugle,* an abolitionist newspaper published in Salem, Ohio. In 1850 she agreed to join Abby Kelley Foster on the lecture circuit.[5] Throughout the 1850s and early 1860s, she served as an agent of the Western Anti-Slavery Society, lecturing in Ohio, Indiana, and Michigan. During the Civil War, she joined the Women's Loyal National League and lectured throughout the Northwest to gain support for making the abolition of slavery a necessary condition of a Northern victory.

After the war, Griffing moved with her daughters to Washington, D.C., where she aided the freed men and women by serving as the general agent of the National Freedman's Relief Association of the District of Columbia. She helped lobby for the creation of the National Freedman's Bureau. She was also active on women's rights issues. Griffing contracted a disease diagnosed as consumption and died in Washington at the age of fifty-seven.

[*NAW*, 2:92–94; Sterling, *Ahead of Her Time,* 261; *Liberator,* Letters to the editor, (1860: 24 Feb., 31 Aug.; 1861: 1 Feb., 15 Feb., 12 Apr., 28 June, 26 July). The 24 Feb. 1860 letter is by Marius R. Robinson; all the others are written by Griffing herself.]

FRANCES ELLEN WATKINS HARPER (1825–1911)

Frances Ellen Watkins was born in Baltimore, the only child of free African American parents. She was orphaned before the age of three and raised by her uncle, William Watkins, and his family. She attended the William Watkins Academy for Negro Youth, a school that her uncle had founded. Her first job was as a seamstress in Baltimore. When her uncle moved his family to Canada in 1850, Watkins moved to Ohio and took a job as a sewing teacher at Union Seminary (later to become Wilberforce University). After moving again to take a teaching position in Little York, Pennsylvania, Watkins became more committed to the antislavery cause and moved to Philadelphia, where she lived in the home of William Still, a center of abolitionist and Underground Railroad activity.

In August of 1854, Watkins delivered her first antislavery lecture, "Education and the Elevation of the Colored Race" in New Bedford, Massachusetts. It was received enthusiastically, and the Maine Anti-Slavery Society hired her as an agent. For the next two years she traveled around Maine, delivering antislavery lectures and giving poetry readings from her book *Poems on Miscellaneous Subjects,* published in 1854. (This book sold over ten thousand copies in its first three years and established Watkins' reputation as a poet.)

From 1856 to 1860, Watkins continued to travel and lecture in New England, Canada, Pennsylvania, New Jersey, New York, Ohio, and Michigan. In 1860 she married a widower, Fenton Harper, and settled with him and his three children on a farm near Columbus, Ohio. After his death in 1864, Watkins Harper returned to her lecturing career. She traveled throughout both the North and the South, lecturing on behalf of the freed men and women.

Returning to Philadelphia in 1871, Watkins Harper continued her writing. She was also active in the temperance and women's rights movements and helped to organize the National Association of Colored Women. She was Unitarian but was active in African Methodist Episcopal programs as well. Despite her ill health in her later years, she continued to be an influential voice for reform and education efforts. She died in Philadelphia; funeral services were held at the First Unitarian Church, and she was buried in Eden Cemetery.

[*BWA,* 1:532–37; *NAW,* 2:137–39; Loeweberg and Bogin, *Black Women.*]

LAURA SMITH HAVILAND (1808–98)

Laura Smith Haviland was born into a Quaker family in Canada. Her family moved to Niagara County, New York in 1815 and she was educated at home and at the Union Free School, a Quaker school in Lockport, New York. She married Charles Haviland, Jr., in 1825, and moved with him to Michigan Territory in 1829. They joined with others to establish the first antislavery society in Michigan. The Havilands resigned their memberships in the Society of Friends because of Quaker disapproval of their antislavery activities. Laura Haviland became a minister in the Wesleyan Methodist Church but rejoined the Society of Friends in 1872.

Haviland many times assisted fugitive slaves through the western states into Canada. She delivered public lectures on behalf of various antislavery societies. She was also active in the temperance and woman's suffrage campaigns. She is recorded as having died of apoplexy at the age of eighty-nine at her home in Grand Rapids, Michigan.

[*NAW*,2:159–60.]

JANE ELIZABETH HITCHCOCK JONES (1813–96)

Jane Elizabeth Hitchcock, the youngest of eight children, grew up in the "burned-over district" of New York. She was another convert of Abby Kelley to antislavery lecturing. She began lecturing in New England and eastern Pennsylvania. In 1845, she traveled with Benjamin Smith Jones to Salem, Ohio, where they helped to organize local antislavery societies and coedited the *Anti-Slavery Bugle*. Hitchcock and Jones were married in 1846.

Hitchcock Jones also lectured on behalf of women's rights and health and hygiene. She continued her antislavery lecturing in the 1850s in Ohio, Pennsylvania, and New York. Sometime after her husband's death in 1862, she returned to her family's home in Vernon, New York, and lived there until her death.

[*NAW*,2:285–86.]

SARAH PUGH (1800–84)

Sarah Pugh was born in Alexandria, Virginia, but upon her father's death in 1803, her mother moved the family to Philadelphia, where she opened a dressmaking shop. Sarah Pugh attended a Quaker boarding school in Westtown, Pennsylvania. From 1821 to 1828, she taught at the Twelfth Street Meeting's Friends' School, but resigned her position after the schism within the Society of Friends in 1827. Pugh established her own school in Philadelphia in 1829.

Like Angelina Grimké, Sarah Pugh was profoundly affected by the British abolitionist George Thompson's speeches in 1835 and joined the Philadelphia Female Anti-Slavery Society. She served as president of the society for many years. She traveled with Lucretia Mott to England in 1840 for the World's Anti-Slavery Convention and was the author of the letter protesting the women delegates' exclusion from the convention floor.

The responsibility for caring for her mother limited her antislavery activities in the 1840s and early 1850s. After her mother's death in 1851, Pugh returned to England for seventeen months, during which time she toured the country, giving antislavery lectures and assisting women to organize themselves on behalf of the cause.

Back in the United States, Pugh continued her work within the Philadelphia Female Anti-Slavery Society. After the Civil War, she worked on behalf of the freed men and women. She was also a women's rights advocate. In addition to her other activities, she frequently attended woman's rights meetings as companion to Lucretia Mott. From 1864 until her death, Pugh lived with her brother in Germantown, Pennsylvania.

[*NAW*, 3:104–5; Brown, *Mary Grew*, 52.]

SARAH PARKER REMOND (1826–94)

Sarah Parker Remond was one of eight children born to John and Nancy Remond. She grew up in Salem, Massachusetts, and attended public school there. Her father, a native of the West Indies, became a successful merchant in the United States. Her family members were committed abolitionists; her older brother Charles Lenox Remond was a respected antislavery lecturer.

From 1856 to 1858 Sarah Parker Remond accompanied her brother on antislavery lecture tours through New York, Massachusetts, Ohio, Michigan, and Pennsylvania, speaking along with him on the platform. At the end of 1858, she traveled to England. In the next two years, Remond gave at least forty-five speeches in England, Scotland, and Ireland, describing American slavery and racial prejudice to sympathetic audiences, and urging support for the American antislavery movement. At the same time, she also took classes at the Bedford College for Ladies.

Following the Civil War, Remond stayed in England, lecturing on behalf of the freed men and women. In 1866 she traveled to Florence, Italy, and enrolled as a medical student at the Santa Maria Nuova Hospital. In 1871 she received a diploma entitling her to practice medicine and did so for the next twenty years. She married a Sardinian, Lazarro Pintor, in 1877. Remond died in 1894 and was buried in the Protestant Cemetery in Rome.

[*BWA*, 2:972–74.; *NAW*, 3:136–37.]

MARIA W. STEWART (1803–79)

Maria W. Stewart, née Maria Miller, was born into a free African American family in Hartford, Connecticut. She was orphaned at the age of five, and bound out to a clergy family until she left them at the age of fifteen. She continued to work as a domestic servant until she married James W. Stewart, a Boston outfitter of whaling and fishing ships, in 1826 and changed her middle and last name to conform with his. Her husband died in 1829, however, and unscrupulous white businessmen deprived Maria Stewart of his estate.

Stewart was profoundly impressed by David Walker's *Appeal . . . to the Coloured Citizens of the World*, published in 1829, and by her own religious conversion in 1831. That same year, she took her manuscript, *Religion And The Pure Principles Of Morality, The Sure Foundation On Which We Must Build*, to William Lloyd Garrison, who recognized it as an important contribution to antislavery thought and published it in the *Liberator*.

Although the need to end slavery was a given for Stewart, she focused her public contributions on the need for educational and moral uplift in the African American community. Between September 1832 and September 1833, she gave four lectures in Boston on these themes. Her audiences appear to have been drawn mainly from the African American community, but did include men as well as women. Exactly one year to the day after her first speech, she gave her "Farewell Address," citing the hostility she had received as a woman speaker as her reason for ending her public lecturing.

However, despite having delivered her four public lectures five years in advance of the Grimkés' lecture tour, and having had them reprinted in the *Liberator*, Maria Stewart did not attract the widespread condemnation faced by the Grimkés. Some historians have suggested that the issues in her case were more complicated, noting the more general acceptance within the African American community of women's action in the public sphere.[6] Shirley Yee, author of *Black Women Abolitionists: A Study in Activism, 1828–1860,* has speculated that the resentment incurred by Stewart resulted mainly from her harsh criticisms of African American men.[7] Stewart's language was strong; in one of her lectures, for example, she asked if it was "blindness of mind, or stupidity of soul" that had inhibited older men from speaking out publicly for their race. She issued what could certainly have been received as an insulting challenge: "If you are men, convince them that you possess the spirit of men"[8]

Stewart moved to New York City, where she taught school. She published the texts of her speeches in 1835 as the *Productions of Mrs. Maria W. Stewart.* Her last recorded antislavery act was her attendance as a corresponding member of the First Anti-Slavery Convention of American Women, held in New York City in 1837. In 1852, she moved to the Washington, D.C., area, teaching school in Baltimore and later in Washington itself, and becoming matron of the Freedman's Hospital by the early 1870s. In 1879, she published *Meditations from the Pen of Mrs. Maria W. Stewart,* a reprint of some of her earlier writings and speeches, along with some new writings. Stewart died in December of that year; her funeral services were held in St. Luke's Episcopal Church in Washington, D.C.

[In additon to the references cited above, see *BWA,* 2:1113–14 and *NAW,* 3:377–78.]

LUCY STONE (1818–93)

Lucy Stone was raised on a farm near West Brookfield, Massachusetts, one of seven surviving children born to Francis and Hannah Stone. She began teaching school at the age of sixteen, continuing to study sporadically at local seminaries. In 1843 she enrolled at Oberlin College. Graduating with honors in 1847, she was invited to write a commencement address for her class. She declined to do so because she was not to be allowed to deliver it herself; she would have had to give it to a man to read.

While at Oberlin, Stone was profoundly influenced by a visit from Abby Kelley, appreciating Kelley's radical religious views as well as her advocacy of immediate abolition of slavery. After her graduation, Stone was appointed an agent of the American Anti-Slavery Society. While she was firmly committed to the antislavery position, she devoted more of her energies to the cause of women's rights. She soon reached an agreement with the AASS to lecture for them on weekends, while reserving weekdays for lecturing on women's rights.

Stone married Henry Blackwell in 1855 and was, if not the first, the most prominent American woman of her day to keep her own name. Stone became increasingly involved in women's rights issues, vigorously campaigning for woman's suffrage after the Civil War. She broke with the arm of the movement headed by Elizabeth Cady Stanton and Susan B. Anthony in 1869, founding her own organization, the American Woman Suffrage Association. She was largely responsible for founding and editing the *Woman's Journal*, a weekly newspaper devoted to women's issues. Lucy Stone died of a stomach tumor at the age of seventy-five and was cremated in Boston.

[*NAW*, 3:387–90; also see Lasser and Merrill, eds., *Friends and Sisters*; Kerr, *Lucy Stone*; and Stone, *Loving Warriors*.

SOJOURNER TRUTH (C. 1799–1883)

Sojourner Truth was the name appropriated later in life by an enslaved woman who was given the name Isabella at birth. She grew up in Ulster County, New York, and was married at the age of fourteen. Following a conversion experience, she joined a Methodist church in Kingston, New York. State law freed her in 1827.

Isabella lived in New York City until 1843, working as a domestic servant and, from 1832 to 1835, participating in a utopian religious community under the leadership of a man known as Matthias. Years after the collapse of that community, she joined another group, the Northampton Association, and was profoundly influenced by the antislavery and women's rights convictions that she encountered there. Claiming the name Sojourner Truth in 1843, she became an itinerant preacher. By 1846 she had begun lecturing on behalf of abolition and women's rights. She continued to do so into the 1860s. After the Civil War, Truth was very active in securing assistance for freed men and women. Sojourner Truth died in her home in Battle Creek, Michigan, in 1883.

[*BWA*, 2:1172–76; *NAW*, 3:479–81; see also Painter, *Sojourner Truth*; Mabee, *Sojourner Truth*.]

HARRIET TUBMAN (C. 1821–1913)

Harriet Tubman, daughter of enslaved parents Benjamin and Harriet Greene Ross, grew up on the Eastern Shore of Maryland. She performed domestic chores as a child and became a field hand when older. She married John Tubman in 1844. Fearing that she and her family would be dispersed and sold down South, she succeeded in escaping to Philadelphia.

After her escape, she returned to the South many times to assist others to escape. She succeeded in rescuing, among some two hundred others, her parents, and her sister and two brothers and their families. Achieving fame for her work, Tubman was a popular speaker at antislavery conventions.

During the Civil War Tubman worked in the Carolinas and Florida as a Union spy and strategist, and a nurse. After the war she founded a home for elderly former slaves in Auburn, New York. Prior to her death in 1913, Tubman succeeded in obtaining a $20-per-month pension from the U.S. government for her military service.

[*BWA*, 2:1176–80; *NAW*, 3:481–83.]

Notes

ABBREVIATIONS

AAS	American Antiquarian Society
APS	American Philosophical Society
B&D	Barnes and Dumond, *Letters of Theodore Dwight Weld, Angelina Grimké Weld, and Sarah Grimké*
BWA	*Black Women in America*
CLMT	William L. Clements Library, University of Michigan
CRNL	Cornell University
FHL	Friends Historical Library, Swarthmore College
HVFD	Haverford College
LC	Library of Congress
MHS	Massachusetts Historical Society
MOOR	Moorland-Spingarn Research Center, Howard University
NAWSA	National American Woman Suffrage Association
NAW	*Notable American Women*
OBRLN	Oberlin College
RBD/BPL	Rare Books Department, Boston Public Library
SCHL	Schlesinger Library, Radcliffe College
SMTH	Smith College
UMASS	University of Massachusetts at Amherst
UR	University of Rochester
UT	University of Texas at Austin
WHM	Worcester Historical Museum

INTRODUCTION

1. Samuel J. May, *Some Recollections of Our Antislavery Conflict* (1869; reprint, New York: Arno Press, 1968), 233, 236. May was referring to the Parable of the Talents, as it appears in Luke 19:12–26 of the King James Version of the Bible. In this parable, a master rewards those servants who made a profit with the pound he left with each of them before setting out on a journey; but he chastises the servant who did no more than return the original pound to him, saying "Lord, behold, here is thy pound, which I have kept laid up in a napkin."

2. Angelina Grimké to Theodore Weld, 18 May 1837, Grimké-Weld papers, William L. Clements Library, University of Michigan Ann Arbor.

3. Maria Stewart is generally given credit for having been the first American woman to lecture in public. I am grateful to Alfred Young, who is working on a biography of Deborah Sampson Gannett, for bringing her lecturing career to my attention. See the appendix for more information on Stewart and a more complex consideration of the factors involved in her retreat from lecturing.

4. See Nancy Hewitt's book, *Women's Activism and Social Change: Rochester, New York, 1822–1872* (Ithaca: Cornell Univ. Press, 1984) and Lori Ginzberg's work, *Women and the Work of Benevolence: Morality, Politics, and Class in the Nineteenth-Century United States,* (New Haven: Yale Univ. Press, 1990), both of which call into question the premise that the ideology of separate spheres reflected practice. As Ginzberg notes in her introduction, she found that "the reality of women's lives was quite different from the ideology which they themselves used." (3, n. 5). In her 1989 University of California at Berkeley Ph.D. dissertation, "Transcending the Public/Private Divide: The Local Dimension of Laborers' Lives, 1810–1860," Karen Hansen proposed one interesting solution to the gap between ideology and reality. She introduced a third sphere, the social, which encompassed behaviors such as visiting, churchgoing, and meeting attendance, and which mediated between the public and private spheres.

5. Ashbel Green, "The Christian Duty of Christian Women. A Discourse, Delivered in the Church of Princeton, New Jersey, August 23d, 1825, before the Princeton Female Society, for the Support of a Female School in India," *Christian Advocate* 4 (1828), in Rosemary Radford Ruether and Rosemary Skinner Keller eds., *Women and Religion in America,* Vol. 1, *The Nineteenth Century* (San Francisco: Harper and Row, 1981), 35.

6. Lucretia Mott, "I Am Not Here as a Representative of Any Sect," Remarks delivered at a Meeting held in Boston, 30 May 1867, in Dana Greene, ed., *Lucretia Mott: Her Complete Speeches and Sermons* (New York: Edward Mellen Press, 1980), 295.

7. Gerda Lerner, *The Grimké Sisters from South Carolina: Pioneers for Woman's Rights and Abolition* (New York: Schocken Books, 1971), 257; Katherine Herbig, "Friends for Freedom: The Lives and Careers of Sallie Holley and Caroline Putnam" (Ph.D. diss., Claremont Graduate School, 1977), 124; Keith Melder, "Abby Kelley and the Process of Liberation," in *The Abolitionist Sisterhood: Women's Political Culture in Antebellum America,* ed. Jean Fagan Yellin and John C. Van Horne (Ithaca: Cornell Univ. Press, 1994), 239, 245; Dorothy Sterling, *Ahead of Her Time: Abby Kelley and the Politics of Antislavery* (New York: W. W. Norton, 1991).

8. Lerner, *Grimké Sisters,* 257; Blanche G. Hersh, *The Slavery of Sex: Feminist-Abolitionists in America* (Urbana: Univ. of Illinois Press, 1978). Hersh includes all five of the women examined here as part of her study. Alma Lutz also wrote a book dealing with abolitionist women, *Crusade for Freedom: Women of the Antislavery Movement* (Boston: Beacon Press, 1968). This book focuses on short individual biographies rather than on analysis of antislavery women as a group.

9. Hersh, *Slavery of Sex,* 136–52; 253. In 1985, Hersh expanded somewhat on her views in an essay, "To Make the World Better: Protestant Women in the Abolitionist Movement," in *Triumph over Silence: Women in Protestant History,* ed. Richard L. Greaves

(Westport, Conn.: Greenwood Press, 1985). In this essay, Hersh continues to speak of the abolitionist women as making "efforts to cleanse their society of sin [which] became, in effect, their religion" (174). Although her account of the content of that religion continues to be vague, she did add that "they drew from diverse other protestant strains—Evangelical, Unitarian, Quaker—to create an eclectic, working religion of reform" (198).

10. For scholarly works on popular religion, see, for example: Jon Butler, *Awash in a Sea of Faith: Christianizing the American People* (Cambridge: Harvard Univ. Press, 1990); David D. Hall, *Worlds of Wonder, Days of Judgment: Popular Religious Belief in Early New England* (Cambridge: Harvard Univ. Press, 1990); Peter Williams, *Popular Religion in America: Symbolic Change and the Modernization Process in Historical Perspective* (Chicago: Univ. of Illinois, 1989).

11. Ann Douglas, *The Feminization of American Culture* (New York: Avon Books, 1977).

12. Ann Braude, *Radical Spirits: Spiritualism and Women's Rights in Nineteenth-Century America* (Boston: Beacon Press, 1989), 201, 62.

13. Robert H. Abzug, *Cosmos Crumbling: American Reform and the Religious Imagination* (New York: Oxford Univ. Press, 1994); Gilbert Hobbs Barnes, *The Anti-Slavery Impulse 1830–1844* (1933; reprint, Gloucester, Mass.: Peter Smith, 1957), 58.

14. In raising these broad issues, I am indebted to other scholars, particularly Nancy Isenberg and Maureen Fitzgerald, for their work in documenting the neglect of religion in women's history. In her impressive master's thesis, "Religion and Feminism in Elizabeth Cady Stanton's Life and Thought" (University of Wisconsin-Madison, 1985), Fitzgerald analyzed religion as a factor in the life of Elizabeth Cady Stanton. Like many other radical reformers, Cady Stanton has been viewed primarily as a secular figure; as Fitzgerald notes, when her religious ideas have been examined it has been primarily "in the context of her anti-church and anti-clerical emphasis" (2). Yet, Fitzgerald makes a convincing case that "the fact is that Cady Stanton continued throughout her life to perceive herself as a religious person, to identify her goals and theory in essentially moral and religious terms, and to assert her belief in God" (5). In Nancy Isenberg's Ph.D. dissertation, "'Co-Equality of the Sexes': The Feminist Discourse of the Antebellum Women's Rights Movement in America" (University of Wisconsin-Madison, 1990), she analyzes some of the basic texts on nineteenth-century women's history—Eleanor Flexner's *Century of Struggle,* Ann and Andrew Scott's *One Half the People,* and Ellen DuBois' *Feminism and Suffrage*—and demonstrates how these authors systematically minimized the importance of religion in the early women's movement. She shows, for example, how the Scotts, in discussing the Declaration of Sentiments at Seneca Falls in 1848, referred only to the secular appeal for suffrage, the "*inalienable* right to the elective franchise," rather than the religious phrase also used, the "*sacred* right to the elective franchise" (29).

15. James G. Moseley, *A Cultural History of Religion in America* (Westport, Conn.: Greenwood Press, 1981), 53, 65.

16. Stephen L. Carter, *The Culture of Disbelief: How American Law and Politics Trivialize Religious Devotion* (New York: Basic Books, 1993), 6–7.

17. Gerda Lerner, preface to *The Creation of Feminist Consciousness* (New York: Oxford Univ. Press, 1993), vii–viii.

18. Although Lerner discusses the religious affiliations of the sisters, she generally ignores their wide-ranging theological explorations, except in the limited ways she perceives those views affecting their choices regarding social and political action. She uses the contents of their journals, which are primarily spiritual accounts each sister kept over a number of years (Angelina Grimké for five years and Sarah Grimké for seventeen), mainly to document their activities and discontents with their lives, and does not analyze the content or significance of their religious speculations. At one point, she dismisses Angelina Grimké's theological reflections simply as attempts to persuade her sister Sarah to support her in her budding abolitionism (*Grimké Sisters*, 135–36). Later in the book Lerner attributes Angelina Grimké Weld's consistent and well-documented Millerite convictions to ill health and emotional strain (306–8). Lerner also concludes that family, health, and financial considerations were the factors that kept the sisters from returning to their public careers after Angelina's marriage, without reference to what my reading of the sources indicates was a major shift in their understanding about the nature of God's purpose for them on earth.

19. Nell Irvin Painter, *Sojourner Truth: A Life, A Symbol* (New York: W. W. Norton, 1996), 261. See also "Coda: The Triumph of a Symbol," 281–87.

20. Lawrence J. Friedman, *Gregarious Saints: Self and Community in American Abolitionism, 1830–1870* (New York: Cambridge Univ. Press, 1982).

21. Carroll Smith-Rosenberg, "The Female World of Love and Ritual," in *Disorderly Conduct: Visions of Gender in Victorian America* (New York: Oxford Univ. Press, 1986), 76.

22. Nancy F. Cott, *The Bonds of Womanhood: "Woman's Sphere" in New England, 1780–1835* (New Haven: Yale Univ. Press, 1977), 194. Cott notes as well, however, that this same group consciousness also resulted in an acceptance of the "different but equal" doctrine that accepted women's domesticity but gave it importance equivalent to men's public roles in business and politics.

23. Sarah and Angelina Grimké are the two exceptions, as they are almost never considered independently of each other—an approach that has its own problems. Generally, however, these women, who have obviously made unique and individual contributions to American history, have been studied independently of one another, as the number of biographies and other scholarly works about each of them attests. In addition to Blanche Hersh's and Alma Lutz's works, Jean Fagan Yellin highlights a few significant individuals, including Angelina Grimké, in her book, *Women and Sisters: The Antislavery Feminists in American Culture* (New Haven: Yale Univ. Press, 1989), a study of the discourse and culture of the antislavery feminists.

24. See, for example: Wendy Hamand Venet, *Neither Ballots nor Bullets: Women Abolitionists and the Civil War* (Charlottesville: Univ. Press of Virginia, 1991); Shirley Yee, *Black Women Abolitionists: A Study in Activism, 1828–1860,* (Knoxville: Univ. of Tennessee Press, 1992); Yellin and Van Horne's, *Abolitionist Sisterhood.* Jean R. Soderlund's unpublished paper, "The Philadelphia Female Anti-Slavery Society: Priorities and Power," presented at the 1991 Annual Meeting of the Organization of American Historians, is another excellent source on women's antislavery activism.

25. In quoting from nineteenth-century documents, I have generally retained the original spelling, except where idiosyncracies might confuse the reader. Punctuation (such as the substitution of periods for dashes and the insertion or deletion of commas) has occasionally been edited for clarity and ease of reading. The symbol "&", frequently used in correspondence, has been replaced by the word "and." Words that are italicized in this text were originally underscored by their authors. In referring to efforts on behalf of women, I have left intact original references to "woman's rights." In general usage I have used the current expression, "women's rights."

1. "A HEART TO WORK A TONGUE TO SPEAK": THE CALL TO MISSION

1. Angelina Grimké to Jane Smith, 29 May to 5 June 1837, CLMT.

2. Catherine H. Birney, *The Grimké Sisters: Sarah and Angelina Grimké, The First American Women Advocates of Abolition and Women's Rights* (1885; reprint, Westport: Greenwood Press, 1969), 8. Birney's is an interesting account by a younger contemporary of the Grimkés, who clearly had access to diaries and letters although she did not provide specific references in her book. Other biographical information is supplied by Lerner, *Grimké Sisters*, chap. 2.

3. Sarah Grimke, "Account of Religious Development," 3 June 1827, CLMT. (The title given here is that supplied by the archive, the original document is untitled.)

4. A very interesting article exploring nineteenth-century conversions, and particularly the difference between men's and women's experiences, is Susan Juster's "'In a Different Voice': Male and Female Narratives of Religious Conversion in Post-Revolutionary America" *American Quarterly* 41, no. 1 (Mar. 1989): 34–62.

5. Sarah Grimké, "Account of Religious Development."

6. The American Quaker John Woolman (1720–1772) is best known for his essays against slavery. He published *Some Considerations on the Keeping of Negroes* in 1754 and *Considerations on Keeping Negroes: Part Second* in 1762. His journal, a classic American spiritual autobiography, was published posthumously in 1774.

7. Sarah Grimké, "Account of Religious Development."

8. Sarah Grimké, Diary, 15 May 1821, CLMT.

9. Abigail Barker to Sarah Grimké, 8 Dec. 1835, CLMT.

10. Diary, 26 Oct. [1822 or 1823]; 12 Oct. 1834.

11. Diary, 3 July 1832; 16 Sept. 1830.

12. Diary, 25 May 1831; 31 Aug. 1831; 8 June 1833; 14 Feb. 1836.

13. Diary, 3 Aug. 1836.

14. Sarah Grimké to Joseph Talcot, 25 Oct. 1837, Talcot Family papers, Quaker Collection, Haverford College Library.

15. Angelina Grimké to Jane Smith, [26] June 1837, CLMT.

16. The quote appearing in the section title is an excerpt, dated 23 October to 30 October 1827, from a series of Angelina Grimké's religious reflections. She wrote: "When I first put on the gospel harness I rushed forward expecting to bear down all before me. This was like

the wind and storm, the earthquake and fire in which the Lord was not. I think I have learned that I can effect more by the still small voice of example than in any other way" (23 Oct. 1827, CLMT). This passage is ironic given her explosion into antislavery prominence in 1836, but sheds some light on her actions in her later life, as discussed in chapter 7.

17. Angelina Grimké, autobiographical manuscript, c. June-July 1828, CLMT.

18. Ibid. This passage is also noteworthy for the distinction Angelina Grimké draws here between Gospel truth and mere "moral discourse." She does not explain herself explicitly but it appears from these and other comments that she is distinguishing between the coolness of a faith she perceived as intellectualized and detached versus the intimacy and passion of a more evangelical style.

19. Angelina Grimké to Anna G. Frost, 17 Mar. [1828], CLMT.

20. Angelina Grimké, Diary, 2 Feb. 1828, CLMT.

21. Diary, 10 Jan. 1828.

22. Autobiographical manuscript, 1828.

23. Ibid.

24. Ibid.

25. Angelina Grimké to Elizabeth Bascom, 18 Apr. 1828, CLMT.

26. Quoted in J. William Frost, ed., *The Quaker Origins of Antislavery* (Norwood, Penn.: Norwood Editions, 1980), 2.

27. Angelina Grimké to Elizabeth Bascom, 18 Apr. 1828. Lerner's account of Angelina Grimké's life makes slavery the central issue in her decision to leave the Presbyterian Church (see *Grimké Sisters*, 70–71). I believe this is to misread the evidence in Grimké's diary and correspondence, which focuses on the more purely theological aspects of her conflict with the church. Although she had become increasingly opposed to slavery, her absorption in that issue came later.

28. Ibid.

29. Diary, 19 Dec. 1828.

30. Sarah Grimké to Jane Bettle, 20 Feb. 1825, UT.

31. Diary, 5 Oct. 1829.

32. See numerous diary entries from February to October 1829, especially 10–17 Apr., 31 May, 12 June, 22 July, 24 July, and 2 Aug.

33. Diary, Feb. 1829.

34. Diary, 23 Apr. 1829.

35. Diary, 24 June 1829.

36. Diary, 13 Aug. and 15 Aug. 1829.

37. Angelina Grimké, quoted in Birney, *The Grimké Sisters*, 89.

38. In 1827, the American branch of the Society of Friends split into two factions, both of which claimed to be the more faithful representation of Quaker principles. The Grimkés, probably owing to the affiliation of Sarah's original acquaintances, were allied with the more conservative orthodox branch, although the somewhat more progressive Hicksite branch would likely have been more accommodating of their interests. For a more detailed discussion of the Quaker schism, see H. Larry Ingle, *Quakers in Conflict: The Hicksite Reformation* (Knoxville: Univ. of Tennessee Press, 1986).

39. Angelina Grimké to Thomas S. Grimké, 3 June 1832, CLMT.

40. Diary, 20 Dec. 1829.

41. Lerner, *Grimké Sisters*, 118–20.

42. Angelina Grimké to William Lloyd Garrison, 30 August 1835, reprinted in the *Liberator,* 19 Sept. 1835.

43. Sarah Grimké, Grimké sister history, "Colorphobia exemplified, A Letter on the Subject of Prejudice Against Colour amongst the Society of Friends in the United States," 1839, CLMT. (Another original handwritten version, along with editing marks presumably made by Elizabeth Pease, is held at the Boston Public Library.)

44. Sarah Grimké, Diary, 25 Sept. 1835.

45. Sarah Grimké to "My dear Friend," [Elizabeth Pease], 10 Nov. 1839. Included in "Colorphobia."

46. Angelina Grimké to Sarah Grimké, 19 July 1836, CLMT; *Appeal to the Christian Women of the South* (New York, 1836; reprint, New York: Arno, 1969).

47. Angelina Grimké to Sarah Grimké, 19 July 1836, CLMT.

48. Lerner, *Grimké Sisters*, 227.

49. Theodore Weld, quoted in letter from Angelina Grimké to Jane Smith, 27 Mar. 1838, CLMT.

50. Otelia Cromwell, *Lucretia Mott* (Cambridge: Harvard Univ. Press, 1958) 4.

51. Lucretia Mott, from the *Proceedings, Woman's Rights Convention, October 5,6,7, 1853* (Cleveland, 1854): 169–70. Quoted by Otelia Cromwell, *Lucretia Mott,* 5.

52. See Margaret Bacon, *Valiant Friend: The Life of Lucretia Mott* (New York: Walker, 1980), 18.

53. Cromwell, *Lucretia Mott,* 14–18 (Quotation on page 18).

54. Lucretia Mott, undated reminiscences dictated to Sarah J. Hale, FHL.

55. Cromwell, *Lucretia Mott,* 19 and 22.

56. Cromwell, *Lucretia Mott,* 25; Anna Davis Hallowell, ed., *James and Lucretia Mott: Life and Letters* (Boston: Houghton, Mifflin, 1884), 53–54.

57. Hallowell, *James and Lucretia Mott,* 55.

58. Cromwell, *Lucretia Mott,* 30, 31. Ministry in the Society of Friends was an acknowledgment of one spiritual gift among others, not a paid position set apart from the laity.

59. James Mott, Sr., to Adam and Anne Mott, 15 Oct. 1818, in Hallowell, *James and Lucretia Mott,* 64.

60. Hallowell, *James and Lucretia Mott,* 99.

61. Mott reminiscences.

62. Letter from Lucretia Mott, 15 Dec. 1819, in Hallowell, *James and Lucretia Mott,* 69.

63. Maria Mott (Davis) was born in 1818; a second boy named Thomas in 1823; Elizabeth Mott (Cavender) in 1825; and Martha (Pattie) Mott (Lord) in 1828.

64. Lucretia Mott to James Miller McKim, 8 Apr. 1834, CRNL.

65. Hallowell, *James and Lucretia Mott,* 89.

66. Bacon, *Valiant Friends,* 111.

67. The quotation appearing in the title is from a letter to the Grimké/Welds, 14 Jan. 1839, in which Abby Kelley wrote, "Angelina asks if I feel as though I could lean upon

my heavenly Father in faith? I can say yes, most assuredly; for I have no other support. O! may I not mistake what he requires of me. Though all may look forbidding in the way which may be cast up for me, yet if he sends me into it, I desire to be made willing to walk therein." CLMT; reprinted in Gilbert H. Barnes and Dwight L. Dumond, eds., *Letters of Theodore Dwight Weld, Angelina Grimké Weld and Sarah Grimké 1822–1844* (Gloucester, Mass.: Peter Smith), 2:747.

68. Alla K. Foster (Abby Kelley Foster's daughter), "Reminiscences of Mrs. Abby Kelley Foster," read at the fortieth anniversary of the First National Woman's Rights Convention, reprinted in *The Woman's Journal*, 7 Feb. 1891.

69. Ibid.

70. Sterling, *Ahead of Her Time*, 17–18.

71. Alla Foster, "Reminiscences."

72. Sterling, *Ahead of Her Time*, 32. Kelley claimed in some reminiscences that her abolitionism was sparked by hearing William Lloyd Garrison speak in 1829 or 1830 in Lynn. As she was not in Lynn in those years, Sterling's placement of the event in Worcester seems more likely. See reminiscences by Abby Kelley Foster, written "in response to a request that she write a brief statement of the facts of her career," 26 Jan. 1885, WHM.

73. Abby Kelley to Darlings, 10 Dec. 1837, WHM, quoted in Sterling, *Ahead of Her Time*, 36.

74. Abby Kelley, in letter published in *The Woman's Journal*, 30 Jan. 1886.

75. Abby Kelley to Darlings, 22 July 1838, WHM.

76. Abby Kelley Foster, "Brief Statement of the Facts . . ."

77. Abby Kelley, quoted in Sterling, *Ahead of Her Time*, 64.

78. William Lloyd Garrison to Sarah T. Benson, 19 May 1838, BPL.

79. Abby Kelley Foster, "Brief Statement of the Facts. . ."

80. Alla Foster, "Reminiscences."

81. Ibid.

82. Abby Kelley Foster, "Brief Statement of the Facts . . ."; Sterling, *Ahead of Her Time*, 93.

83. Herbig, 13–14, 21–22; Sallie Holley, *A Life for Liberty: Antislavery and Other Letters of Sallie Holley*, ed. John White Chadwick (1899; reprint, New York: Negro Universities Press, 1969), 20–27, 208.

84. Herbig, "Friends for Freedom," 16–17, 19; Quotation taken from a letter from Sallie Holley to Caroline Putnam, 18 Nov. 1861, Holley, *A Life for Liberty*, 187.

85. Holley, *A Life for Liberty*, 31.

86. Herbig, "Friends for Freedom," 27.

87. Ibid., 31–36.

88. Ibid., 38

89. Ibid., 39.

90. According to Herbig, Holley also continued to receive financial assistance from a number of individuals, including Gerrit Smith ("Friends for Freedom," 39; 54).

91. See Abzug, *Cosmos Crumbling*, for a discussion of the tension between evangelical and radical religion.

92. Text from 2 Corinthians 6:14–17.

93. Sarah Grimké to Augustus Wattles, 22 Jan. 1865, UT.

94. Sallie Holley to Caroline Putnam, 24 Oct. 1852, Holley, *A Life for Liberty*, 97.

95. Female students were subject to restrictions not applied to their male peers. There were different courses of study for men and for women. Antoinette Brown Blackwell, who in 1853 became the first female ordained minister in America, chose to take the male course, but although she completed it successfully, was not granted a degree. For more information, see Carol Lasser and Marlene Deahl Merrill, eds., *Friends and Sisters: Letters Between Lucy Stone and Antoinette Brown Blackwell, 1846–93* (Urbana: Univ. of Illinois Press, 1987) and Elizabeth Cazden, *Antoinette Brown Blackwell: A Biography* (Old Westbury, N. Y.: Feminist Press, 1983).

96. Holley, *A Life for Liberty*, 49. Disagreement over the appropriate role for women in the antislavery movement was the catalyst for the 1840 division of the movement. See Friedman, *Gregarious Saints*, chap. 3, for a discussion of the Tappanite faction.

97. Sallie Holley to Gerrit Smith, 20 May 1863, as quoted in Herbig, "Friends for Freedom," 50.

98. Holley, *A Life for Liberty*, 54, 50. Charles Finney, the best known revivalist of the Second Great Awakening, also served Oberlin as a professor and later president of the college.

99. Ibid., 50 and 55.

100. Sallie Holley to Caroline Putnam, 16 Sept. 1850, Holley, *A Life for Liberty*, 69.

101. Putnam was born in Massachusetts in 1826, the daughter of Eliza Carpenter Putnam and Dr. Putnam. Her father died during her childhood and she and her mother and siblings went to live with her mother's mother, also in Massachusetts. Her mother married Levi Peet in 1840, and they moved to Putnam's stepfather's farm in Farmersville, New York. (Herbig, "Friends for Freedom," 58–60).

102. Caroline Putnam to Samuel May, 22 Jan. 1887, Samuel May Collection, MHS.

103. Herbig, "Friends for Freedom," 73–6.

104. Holley, *A Life for Liberty*, 61.

105. Sallie Holley to Caroline Putnam, 16 Sept. 1850, Holley, *A Life for Liberty*, 69.

106. Sallie Holley to Caroline Putnam, 26 Aug. 1852, Holley, *A Life for Liberty*, 87.

107. Sallie Holley to Porters, 30 Sept. 1851, Holley, *A Life for Liberty*, 80.

2. "A BODYGUARD OF HEARTS": THE ANTISLAVERY LECTURERS AND THE BUILDING OF ABOLITIONIST COMMUNITY

1. Angelina Grimké to Sarah Mapps Douglass, 25 February [1838], CLMT, reprinted in *B&D*, 2:573–74. Emphasis added.

2. Sallie Holley to Porters, 30 Sept. 1851, Holley, A *Life for Liberty*, 81.

3. Holley, *A Life for Liberty*, 74.

4. Maria Mott Davis to Edward Davis, 3 May 1838, Mott papers, Friends Historical Library, Swarthmore College.

5. Sarah Grimké to Elizabeth Smith Miller, [Jan. 1853], CLMT.

6. Abby Kelley to Anna [Anne] Warren Weston, 29 May 1839, Antislavery Collection, RBD/BPL.

7. Sallie Holley to Caroline Putnam, 19 Dec. 1852, Holley, *A Life for Liberty*, 107.

8. Angelina Grimké to Sarah Grimké, 7 Dec. 1828; Angelina Grimké to Jane Smith, 26 Oct. 1837, CLMT.

9. Angelina Grimké Weld to Anne Warren Weston, 15 July [1838], RBD/BPL.

10. Sallie Holley to Caroline Putnam, 24 Oct. 1852, Holley, *A Life for Liberty*, 96. The reason for this disapprobation was a rumor, which Holley declared to be false, that Lucretia Mott had—against Quaker policy—*requested* someone to give a prayer at a woman's rights convention. According to Quaker discipline, prayer and all other remarks had to be the spontaneous act of an individual motivated at that moment by the spirit. Chadwick did note, however, that Lucretia Mott had given him permission to advertise her speaking in his pulpit, telling him, "The Spirit always gives me about twenty-four hours intimation" (96).

11. This is in contrast to Lawrence Friedman's findings in *Gregarious Saints,* in which male abolitionists also shared emotional and physical intimacies, such as private meetings, hand holding, and cheek kissing, but did so secretly (137–38).

12. Abby Kelley to Anna [sic] Warren Weston, 29 May 1839, RBD/BPL.

13. Angelina Grimké Weld to Theodore Weld, 5 June 1839, CLMT.

14. Elizabeth Cady Stanton to Angelina Grimké Weld and Sarah Grimké, 25 June 1840, CLMT, reprinted in *B&D,* 2:847.

15. Angelina Grimké to Abby Kelley, 15 Apr. 1837, Abby Kelley Foster Collection, AAS.

16. Angelina Grimké to Jane Smith, 6 Oct. 1837, CLMT.

17. Sarah Grimké to Abby Kelley, 15 June 1838, AAS.

18. Abby Kelley to Theodore Weld, 14 Jan. 1839, CLMT, reprinted in *B&D,* 2:747.

19. Angelina Grimké Weld to Abby Kelley, 24 Feb. [1839], WHM.

20. Caroline Putnam to Samuel May, 22 Jan. 1887, Samuel May papers, MHS.

21. Caroline Putnam to [Ma?] and Ann, 19 Nov. 1851, Emily Howland Collection, CRNL.

22. Sallie Holley to Abby Kelley Foster, 13 May 1857, AAS.

23. Lucretia Mott to Phebe Post Willis, 12 Feb. 1838, Post Family papers, Department of Rare Books and Special Collections, University of Rochester Library.

24. Angelina Grimké to Queen Victoria, 26 Oct. 1837, BPL. This letter was sent through an intermediary and, for better or for worse, apparently never reached the queen. See Elizabeth Pease to Angelina Grimké, 12 Feb. 1838, CLMT, reprinted in *B&D,* 2:546.

25. Angelina Grimké to George Bancroft, 14 [n.m.] [1837 or 1838], George Bancroft Papers, MHS; Sarah Grimké to William Ellery Channing, 19 June 1837, William E. Channing Papers, MHS.

26. J. R. Johnson to Friend Garrison, 22 Jan. 1856, Putnam, Connecticut, published in *Liberator,* 8 Feb. 1856, p. 22, col. 6.

27. See letter from Putnam to Holley, 28 Nov. [n.y.], in which Putnam signs herself, "Putty." CRNL.

28. Sallie Holley to Caroline Putnam, 18 Nov. 1861, Holley, *A Life for Liberty,* 186–87.

29. Caroline Putnam to Sallie Holley, 21 Nov. 1852, Emily Howland Collection, CRNL.

30. C. F. Putnam to Mr. Garrison, Dryden, New York, 30 November 1856, printed in *Liberator,* 12 Dec. 1856, p. 198, col. 6.

31. Sallie Holley to Abby Kelley Foster, 8 Sept. 1857, AAS.

32. Sarah Grimké to Joseph Talcot, 25 Oct. 1837, HVFD. Of course, this was not universally true of the clergy, some of whom were strong supporters of women's rights as well as being ardent abolitionists. Angelina Grimké reported a pleasant encounter with Joseph Cross, a Massachusetts Congregational minister, who allowed them to preach in his pulpit despite the knowledge that his fellow clergy would be angry with him for having done so. He told her that "he meant to throw down the gauntlet and call upon them to prove that women had no right to preach; when the Apostle said, 'Help those women who labored with me in the gospel,' did he mean they made tea only" (Angelina Grimké to Jane Smith, 26 Aug. 1837, CLMT).

33. Sarah Grimké to Elizabeth Pease, 18 Dec. 1837, BPL.

34. Sarah Grimké to Jane Smith, 6 Oct. 1837, CLMT.

35. Abby Kelley Foster, "Brief Statement of the Facts . . . "

36. Abby Kelley to Hudsons, 12 Apr. 1841 and 6 Aug. 1840, Hudson Collection, UMASS.

37. Daniel Neall, an abolitionist, was the president of the Pennsylvania Hall Association. Rebecca Bunker Neall was a cousin of Lucretia Mott.

38. Hallowell, *James and Lucretia Mott,* 132–33; Lucretia Mott to Maria Weston Chapman, 13 May 1840, BPL.

39. Hallowell, *James and Lucretia Mott,* 294.

40. *New York Commercial Advertiser,* reprinted in the *Liberator,* 2 June 1837, quoted in Sterling, *Ahead of Her Time,* 50.

41. *Pittsburgh Manufacturer,* 9 Mar. 1838, reprinted in Judith Papachristou, *Women Together* (New York: Alfred A. Knopf, 1976), 16.

42. Abby Kelley Foster to Samuel May, 9 Nov. 1853, BPL.

43. Lucy Colman, Letter to the editor, *Liberator,* 20 Nov. 1857, p. 187, col. 1.

44. Amos A. Phelps to Charlotte Phelps, 14 July 1837, RBD/BPL.

45. Sarah [Gould] to Abby Kelley, 15 Nov. 1841, AAS.

46. Lucy Stone to Fosters, 25 Mar. 1846, AAS.

47. Esther Moore to William Lloyd Garrison, 15 Nov. 1840, RBD/BPL.

48. Sarah Mapps Douglass to William Bassett, Dec. 1837, in "Colorphobia."

49. See, for example, letters reprinted in the *Liberator*: Mary Clark to Angelina Grimké, on behalf of the Female Anti-Slavery Society of Concord (25 Feb. 1837, p. 33, col. 1); Angelina Grimké to L. L. Dodge of the Essex County Olive Branch Society (14 Apr. 1837, p. 62, col. 3); Mary S. Parker and Maria Weston Chapman of the Boston Female Anti-Slavery Society to Female Anti-Slavery Societies throughout New England (9 June 1837, p. 95, col. 4); E. T. Loud and Lydia Pratt, of the South Weymouth Female Anti-Slavery Society, to William Lloyd Garrison (27 Oct. 1837, p. 174, col. 5).

50. *Proceedings of the Anti-Slavery Convention of American Women, Held in the City of New York,* May 9th, 10th, 11th, and 12th, 1837 (New York: William S. Dorr, 1837) 7, 9, 13. The substance of these resolutions and others is discussed in more depth in chapters 5 and 6.

51. *Proceedings of the Anti-Slavery Convention of American Women, Held in Philadelphia, May 15th, 16th, 17th, and 18th, 1838* (Philadelphia: Merrihew and Gunn, 1838).

52. *Proceedings of the Third Anti-Slavery Convention of American Women, Held in Philadelphia, May 1st, 2d and 3d, 1839* (Philadelphia: Merrihew and Thompson, 1839).

53. Elizabeth Pease to Angelina Grimké, 27 Dec. 1836, CLMT, reprinted in *B&D,* 1:350.

54. Angelina Grimké, *Appeal to the Christian Women of the South* (New York: n.n., 1836).

55. Angelina Grimké to Elizabeth Pease, 17 Mar. 1837, RBD/BPL.

56. Clare Midgley, *Women Against Slavery: The British Campaigns, 1780–1870* (New York: Routledge, 1992), 145, based on a letter from Elizabeth Pease to Maria Weston Chapman, 23 Apr. 1840, RBD/BPL. The pamphlet that Pease published in England, presumably her edited version of "Colorphobia," was entitled *The Society of Friends, in the United States—their views of the antislavery question and treatment of the people of colour.*

57. Lucretia Mott to Richard Webb, 17 Mar. 1843 and 23 Mar. 1846, RBD/BPL.

58. This is not to say that the lecturers were the only women looked to for leadership. Other frequently mentioned sources of authority included the Boston organizer Maria Weston Chapman, and the writer and editor, Lydia Maria Child. Owing no doubt to their itinerancy, visibility, and widespread public recognition, though, the lecturers seem to have attracted a broader range of adherents.

3. THE "OUTSIDEISMS OF RELIGION": PROBLEMS AND POSSIBILITIES OF THE CHRISTIAN CHURCH

1. Dr. C. B. Judd (Physician) to Rev. A. A. Phelps, 4 Mar. 1846, RBD/BPL.

2. Sallie Holley to Caroline Putnam, 18 Nov. 1861, Holley, *A Life for Liberty,* 187.

3. Sallie Holley to Abby Kelley Foster, 13 May 1857, AAS.

4. Sarah Grimké to Elizabeth Smith Miller, 4 Nov. [1849], CLMT.

5. The quotation in the title of this section is from a letter from Lucretia Mott to Richard and Hannah Webb, 12 Oct. 1840, RBD/BPL.

6. Lucretia Mott to Martha Coffin Wright, 28 Nov. 1841, Hallowell, *James and Lucretia Mott,* 221–22.

7. Sarah Grimké to Elizabeth Smith Miller, 20 Feb. 1850, CLMT. It is interesting to note in these passages that Grimké here denies the efficacy of "scholastic doctrines" intellectually derived, while at the same time she claims to use reason, based on intuition ("the heart") to reject them. It appears that it is not so much the intellect that she deplores as it is the misuse of the intellect. In this she has taken the stance neatly summarized by G. K. Chesterton, "You can only find truth with logic if you have already

found truth without it" (Quoted in *The Little Zen Companion,* ed. David Schiller [New York: Workman Publishing, 1994, 354].

8. Holley, *A Life for Liberty,* 57. Antoinette Brown studied theology at Oberlin and was the first ordained woman minister in the United States. Not many years after assuming the pastorate of a Congregational church, she suffered a crisis of faith and left the pastoral ministry. Later, she described this process in a letter to Theodore Weld, saying that she had believed it necessary that natural and revealed religion ("natural" meaning "moral and intellectual natures" and "revealed" meaning the Bible) agree on all points, and had resigned her pastorate when she decided this was not so. She added that since then "I have found again assurance which seems to me too firm ever to be again shaken, of a personal God, an immortality to men, of an absolute right which is concentrated in that love to God and men which was taught by Jesus and illustrated in his life and in his sublime death. . . . [H]aving formally connected myself with the Unitarian Association, as that most nearly at one with me in religious belief, it is my desire to return again to my early work in the religious ministry" (Antoinette Brown Blackwell to Theodore Weld, June 1879, CLMT).

9. Sallie Holley to Porters, 8 Mar. 1854, Holley, *A Life for Liberty,* 139.

10. Angelina Grimké, autobiographical manuscript, 1828.

11. Abby Kelley Foster, as summarized by Mrs. John T. (Mary Elizabeth) Sargent, *Sketches and Reminiscences of The Radical Club of Chestnut Street* (Boston: James R. Osgood, 1880), 181–82.

12. Lucretia Mott to Richard and Hannah Webb, 2 Apr. 1841, RBD/BPL.

13. Sarah Grimké to Harriot Kezia Hunt, 16 Dec. [1849?], CLMT.

14. Sarah Grimké to Gerrit Smith, 6 July 1851, CLMT. Grimké was quoting Ezekiel 18:4 and John 10:28.

15. Lucretia Mott to Richard and Hannah Webb, 2 Apr. 1841, RBD/BPL.

16. The quotation that appears as the title of this subsection is from a letter from Angelina Grimké to Jane Smith, 5 Jan. 1838, CLMT, in which Grimké complained that Quakers in a town had been warned "against giving any countenance . . . as their doing so would weaken the hands of Phila. Friends in dealing with us. So much for the bitter fruits of sectarianism, thus would it desire that the unprotected stranger should be treated."

17. Angelina Grimké to Jane Smith, 26 Aug. 1837, CLMT.

18. Lucretia Mott, "To Speak Out the Truth," Speech delivered at the Semi-Annual Unitarian Convention, Philadelphia, 20 Oct. 1846, Greene, *Lucretia Mott: Speeches and Sermons,* 54–55.

19. Gilbert Tennent (1703–64), quoted in Winthrop S. Hudson, *Religion in America,* 3rd. ed. (New York: Charles Scribner's Sons, 1981), 81–82.

20. Nathan Hatch, *The Democratization of American Christianity* (New Haven: Yale Univ. Press, 1989), 220.

21. Clifford Olmstead, *History of Religion in the United States* (Englewood Cliffs, N.J.: Prentice-Hall, 1960), 246 and 251. The figures for Presbyterian and Congregationalist membership are from 1850.

22. Sarah Grimké, Grimké Sisters' history, in "Colorphobia."

23. Angelina Grimké to Sarah Grimké, 14 Aug. 1836, CLMT; Angelina Grimké to Jane Smith, 18 Sept. 1836.

24. Bacon, *Valiant Friend*, 106. Mott did not submit meekly to this criticism. According to Bacon's account, after Barker's sermon, Mott delivered an hour-long rebuttal, commenting afterwards: "I did not spare her, stranger though she was. Every stale objection she urged . . . I was favored to meet, as if I had taken notes."

25. *Free Religious Index*, Boston, 25 Nov. 1880.

26. Copy of Abby Kelley's letter of resignation to the Uxbridge Monthly Meeting of Friends attached to a letter addressed to William Lloyd Garrison, 30 Sept. 1841, RBD/BPL.

27. Sallie Holley to the Porters, 9 Dec. 1853, Holley, *A Life for Liberty*, 130. Holley did not identify any particular sects of which Pillsbury might have been speaking.

28. Sarah Hallowell Willis to Amy Kirby Post, 6 Mar. 1852, Post Family papers, UR.

29. Sallie Holley to Caroline Putnam, 20 Mar. 1854, Holley, *A Life for Liberty*, 139–40.

30. Sallie Holley to Abby Kelley Foster, 13 Mar. 1854, AAS.

31. Fragment of letter from Sallie Holley to Abby Kelley Foster, [1858?], AAS. There were nonmembers present at this meeting, and one woman spoke to Holley afterwards, regretting that "'any but the church should hear such censures.' She said, it was all true but the 'impenitent' and 'unconverted' might make a bad use of it etc."

32. Sarah Grimké to Harriot Kezia Hunt, 5 Apr. 1853, CLMT.

33. Lucretia Mott to Richard Webb, 23 Mar. 1846, RBD/BPL.

34. Sarah Grimké to Theodore Weld, 20 Sept. 1837, CLMT, reprinted in *B&D*, 1:447.

35. Angelina Grimké to Jane Smith, 26 Oct. 1837, CLMT.

36. Abby Kelley to E. D. Hudson, 6 Aug. 1840, copy at AAS, source of original unknown.

37. "The Practicability of Suppressing Vice," quoted in Abzug, *Cosmos Crumbling*, 41. Beecher did, however, also include one societal ill, intemperance, in his list of the most dangerous sins.

38. Lucretia Mott, "Worship in Spirit and in Truth," Greene, *Lucretia Mott: Speeches and Sermons*, 272.

39. Lucretia Mott, "The Truth of God . . . The Righteousness of God," Sermon delivered at Marlboro Chapel, Boston, 23 Sept. 1841, Greene, *Lucretia Mott: Speeches and Sermons*, 33.

40. Sallie Holley to Miss Tyler, 14 Oct. 1891, Holley, *A Life for Liberty*, 262.

41. Lucretia Mott, "The Duty of Prayer and its Effects," Sermon delivered at Cherry Street Meeting, Philadelphia, 14 Oct. 1849, Greene, *Lucretia Mott: Speeches and Sermons*, 116.

42. Henry C. Wright, 16 May 1847, quoted in Lewis Perry, *Childhood, Marriage, and Reform: Henry Clarke Wright, 1797–1870* (Chicago: Univ. of Chicago Press, 1980), 149–50.

43. See Lucretia Mott, "Progress of the Religious World," Remarks delivered to the Anti-Sabbath Convention, Boston, 23–24 Mar. 1848, Greene, *Lucretia Mott: Speeches and Sermons*, 64.

44. Sarah Grimké to Gerrit Smith, 27 May [1850s], UT.

45. Lucretia Mott could have been disciplined under this rule, had it been true, as it was rumored, that she asked someone to offer a prayer at a woman's rights convention in Syracuse in 1852. Sallie Holley, who recounted this story, indignantly denied the rumor, saying, "This is entirely untrue. She is particularly careful to avoid violating any of the rules that are laid on Quaker ministers" (Sallie Holley to Caroline Putnam, 24 Oct. 1852, Holley, *A Life for Liberty*, 96).

46. For two different treatments of camp meeting behavior and effects, see Dickson Bruce, *And They All Sang Hallelujah: Plain-Folk Camp-Meeting Religion, 1800–1845* (Knoxville: Univ. of Tennessee Press, 1974) and Hatch, *Democratization of American Christianity*, section 2.

47. William Lloyd Garrison to George W. Benson, 27 Nov. 1835, in Walter Merrill, ed., *The Letters of William Lloyd Garrison*, vol. 1, *I Will Be Heard! 1822–1835*. (Cambridge: Harvard Univ. Press, 1971), 561.

48. From an account of a conversation between William Lloyd Garrison and Lucretia Mott, published in the *Liberator*. Quoted by Hallowell, *James and Lucretia Mott*, 296–7.

49. Angelina Grimké, autobiographical manuscript, 1828.

50. "I almost rejoice in the prospect of a release from the *duty* as it has heretofore seemed to me of attending public worship, for truly it has been a weariness to my soul" (Sarah Grimké to Theodore Weld, 11 June 1837, in *B&D*, 1:402.)

51. Sarah Grimké to Elizabeth Smith Miller, 20 Feb. 1850, CLMT. Her words are a paraphrase of Galatians 5:1.

52. Lucretia Mott, "Worship in Spirit and in Truth," Greene, *Lucretia Mott: Speeches and Sermons*, 271.

53. Lucretia Mott to Richard Webb, 23 Mar. 1846, RBD/BPL.

54. Sarah Grimké, Grimké Sisters' history "Colorphobia." The Grimkés were severe in their criticisms of the Society of Friends, one gains perspective, however, by noting their views on other faith traditions. Catholicism, for example, they viewed not just with distaste but with horror. Sarah Grimké wrote to Gerrit Smith from Boston that, "As I passed the huge cathedral this morning and felt its cold and gloomy shadow fall upon me obstructing the sunshine I queried Is this symbolical of the power which Catholicism is to exercise in this country, so black, so massive. Is there yet to be a fearful struggle between light and darkness[?]" (18 November 1871, UT). She was less critical of Judaism, although in a rather patronizing manner, remarking that she would like to visit a Jewish friend "and see how he keeps his jewish sabbath. . . . I honor him for his conscientiousness. . . . I delight to see every one following out the honest convictions of their souls, such souls grow, *in spite of intellectual errors*" (emphasis added) (Sarah Grimké to Elizabeth [Smith] Miller, 4 Nov. [1849?], CLMT).

55. Sarah Grimké to Preston Day, 19 Jan. 1869, CLMT.

56. Lucretia Mott to Richard and Hannah Webb, 25 Feb. 1842, Hallowell, *James and Lucretia Mott*, 224. By contrast, she confessed that she believed Abby Kelley Foster was "a more efficient laborer, than while she was a member of the Society of Friends" (Lucretia Mott to Richard Webb, 23 Mar. 1846, RBD/BPL) and noted that William Lloyd

Garrison had never joined any sect (Lucretia Mott to Webbs, 25 Feb. 1842, Hallowell, *James and Lucretia Mott,* 224).

57. Lucretia Mott to Richard D. Webb, 21 Feb. 1847, RBD/BPL.

4. "LET OUR DAILY LIFE BE A PRAYER": CHRISTIANITY RE-VISIONED

1. Lucretia Mott, "Keep Yourselves from Idols," Sermon delivered at Cherry Street Meeting, Philadelphia, 17 Mar. 1850, Greene, *Lucretia Mott: Speeches and Sermons,* 178.

2. Lucretia Mott to Martha Coffin Wright, undated, excerpted in Hallowell, *James and Lucretia Mott,* 120.

3. Lucretia Mott, "Worship in Spirit and in Truth," Greene, *Lucretia Mott: Speeches and Sermons,* 275.

4. The quotation in the title of this section is taken from a letter from Sarah Grimké to Elizabeth Smith Miller, 20 Feb. 1850, CLMT.

5. Angelina Grimké, spiritual reflections, 15 May 1827, CLMT.

6. Susan Juster, "'In a Different Voice,'" 40–43.

7. Angelina Grimké Weld to Jane Smith, 15 [March 1843], CLMT.

8. Lucretia Mott, "Sermon to the Medical Students," Delivered at Cherry Street Meeting, Philadelphia, 11 Feb. 1849, Greene, *Lucretia Mott: Speeches and Sermons,* 84.

9. Alla Foster, quoted by Lillie Buffum Chace Wyman in "Reminiscences of Two Abolitionists," *New England Magazine* (Jan. 1903): 538.

10. Sarah Grimké Diary, 7 July 1833.

11. Sarah Grimké to Elizabeth [Smith] Miller, 20 Feb. 1850, CLMT.

12. Sarah Grimké to Sarah Wattles, 4 July [1861?], CLMT.

13. Sarah Grimké to Wattles, 2 Apr. 1854, CLMT.

14. From the *Biblical Repertory and Princeton Review,* quoted in Gilbert Barnes, *The Antislavery Impulse 1830–1844* (1933; reprint, Gloucester, Mass.: Peter Smith, 1957), 203 note. 4; also Barnes, 5.

15. Abzug, *Cosmos Crumbling,* 36.

16. Barnes, *Antislavery Impulse,* 203 note 4.

17. Lucretia Mott to Richard and Hannah Webb, 28 May 1850, RBD/BPL.

18. Sallie Holley to William Lloyd Garrison, 26 Feb. 1855, RBD/BPL.

19. Lucretia Mott, "Sermon to the Medical Students," Greene, *Lucretia Mott: Speeches and Sermons,* 84. Yukio Irie's book, *Emerson and Quakerism* (Tokyo: Kenkyusha, 1967), explores similarities (and differences as well) between Emerson's transcendentalist view of the possibilities of human insight and intuition and the Quaker doctrine of the inner light. In her introduction to *The Spirituality of the American Transcendentalists* (Macon, Ga.: Mercer Univ. Press, 1988), Catherine Albanese points out that faith in intuition extends back to the Puritans as well, who by keeping journals of their spiritual lives, demonstrated their "sensitivity to the God who was immanent as well as transcendent" (3).

20. Lucretia Mott, "Religious Instinct in the Constitution of Man," Sermon deliv-

ered at Yardleyville, Bucks County, Penn., 26 Sept. 1858, Greene, *Lucretia Mott: Speeches and Sermons*, 235, 240, 242.

21. Sarah Grimké to Gerrit Smith, 13 Mar. 1866, CLMT. For more on spiritualism and human nature, see Ann Braude, *Radical Spirits: Spiritualism and Women's Rights in Nineteenth-Century America* (Boston: Beacon Press, 1989), chap. 2.

22. Lucretia Mott, "Keep Yourselves From Idols," Greene, *Lucretia Mott: Speeches and Sermons*, 177.

23. Lucretia Mott, "The Duty of Prayer and Its Effects," Greene, *Lucretia Mott: Speeches and Sermons*, 121.

24. Lucretia Mott, "Sermon to the Medical Students," Greene, *Lucretia Mott: Speeches and Sermons*, 86.

25. Lucretia Mott to Richard Webb, 14 Apr. 1850, RBD/BPL.

26. John White Chadwick, *Theodore Parker: Preacher and Reformer* (1900. Reprint, St. Clair Shores, Mich.: Scholarly Press, Inc., 1971), 96.

27. The Motts had met McKim at the founding of the American Anti-Slavery Society in 1833. At that time, McKim was a young Presbyterian seminarian. He and Lucretia Mott apparently struck up an instant friendship and he confided in her his theological uncertainties, eventually abandoning Presbyterianism and dedicating himself to the antislavery cause. Mott mentioned him as an example of the appeal of "religion when stripped of the appendages of bigoted sectarianism, and gloomy superstition! . . . His [McKim's] mind has at length burst the fetters of Presbyterianism, and, retaining all that is truly 'pious' and valuable, he is walking forth in 'the liberty wherewith Christ makes free'" (Lucretia Mott to Martha Coffin Wright, undated, excerpted in Hallowell, *James and Lucretia Mott*, 120).

28. Lucretia Mott to Martha Coffin Wright, 11 Mar. 1856. Garrison Family Papers, Sophia Smith Collection, SMTH.

29. Lucretia Mott, "Keep Yourselves from Idols," Greene, *Lucretia Mott: Speeches and Sermons*, 178.

30. Sarah Grimké to Gerrit Smith, 16 Feb. 1838, CLMT, reprinted in *B&D*, 2:550.

31. Sarah Grimké to Gerrit Smith, 13 Mar. 1866, CLMT.

32. Grimké found Joan of Arc to be "an example of faith, courage, fortitude and love rarely equalled and never surpassed" (Sarah Grimké to Preston Day, 4 Mar. 1867, CLMT. Her admiration led her to translate Alphonse de Lamartine's book *Jeanne d'Arc* into English. It was subsequently published as Joan of Arc (Boston: Adams, 1867).

33. Sallie Holley to Caroline Putnam, 18 Nov. 1861, Holley, *A Life for Liberty*, 187.

34. Sallie Holley to Miss Tyler, 6 Dec. 1888, Holley, *A Life for Liberty*, 258–59.

35. Angelina Grimké Weld to Sarah, January 1845, Theodore Weld Collection, Library of Congress.

36. Ralph Waldo Emerson, journal entry, 29 December 1834, in Stephen E. Whicher, ed., *Selections from Ralph Waldo Emerson* (Boston: Houghton Mifflin, 1957), 99.

37. The quotation that appears in the section title is from Lucretia Mott, quoted in Sargent, *Sketches*, 158.

38. Ralph Waldo Emerson, "Address to the Senior Class of the Harvard Divinity

School," 15 July 1838, quoted in Whicher, *Selections from Emerson*, 104. Although Emerson is often credited with the introduction of this idea in nineteenth-century America, one of his biographers has noted that this and other of his ideas had been previously expressed by William Ellery Channing (1780–1842), the renowned Unitarian minister, in his ordination speech for Jared Sparks in Baltimore in 1819. See Gay Wilson Allen, *Waldo Emerson: A Biography* (New York: Viking Press, 1981), 316–17.

39. Lucretia Mott, "Likeness to Christ," Sermon delivered at Cherry Street Meeting, Philadelphia, 30 Sept. 1849, Greene, *Lucretia Mott: Speeches and Sermons*, 111–12.

40. Sarah Grimké to Sarah Mapps Douglass, 27 Jan. 1845, CLMT.

41. Sarah Grimké to Sarah Wattles, 23 Dec. [1853], CLMT.

42. Sarah Grimké to Preston Day, 4 Mar. 1867, CLMT.

43. Lucretia Mott, "Keep Yourselves from Idols," Greene, *Lucretia Mott: Speeches and Sermons*, 175.

44. Lucretia Mott, quoted in Sargent, *Sketches*, 159.

45. Sarah Grimké to Preston Day, 19 Jan. 1869, CLMT.

46. William Ellery Channing, "Moral Argument Against Calvinism," *Christian Disciple*, 1820, quoted by Jack Mendelsohn, *Channing: The Reluctant Radical* (Boston: Little, Brown, 1971), 166.

47. Hersh, *Slavery of Sex*, 142.

48. In the first chapter of *Tapestries of Life: Women's Work, Women's Consciousness, and the Meaning of Daily Experience* (Amherst: Univ. of Massachusetts Press, 1989), Bettina Aptheker provides a good summary of modern feminist theory and its resistance to the patriarchal constructs within which theorizing has been expected to operate, such as basing prescriptive theory on artificial intellectual models (such as Marxism and capitalism, for example) which, in addition to other flaws, have consciously or unconsciously assumed the subordination of women. Most relevant to this analysis is her discussion of Adrienne Rich's challenge to the "dualism of the positive-negative polarities between which most of our intellectual training has taken place" (*Of Woman Born: Motherhood as Experience and Institution* [New York: Norton, 1976], 64; quoted in Aptheker, 18). Likewise, the feminist theologian Rosemary Radford Ruether began in her book, *Sexism and God-Talk: Toward a Feminist Theology* (Boston: Beacon Press, 1983), to develop a feminist theology that challenges the dualistic premises of patriarchal intellectual discourse by legitimating "relational modes of thought" and integrating them with "rational capacities" (112).

49. The title of this section is Lucretia Mott's translation of 2 Timothy 3:16. As Cromwell retells the story, at one woman's rights meeting, a gentleman "sought to embarrass Lucretia Mott by injecting Scriptural quotations into the discussions. 'All scripture is given by inspiration of God,' he said, 'and is profitable. . . . ' To this seemingly redoubtable argument, Lucretia replied, 'If thou will look at that passage thou will see that the 'is' is italicised, which signified that it is put in by the translators. The passage should read 'All scripture given by inspiration of God is profitable,' etc. At a proper time I would like to discuss the subject with thee'" (*Lucretia Mott*, 29).

50. Lucretia Mott to James Miller McKim, 1 Jan. 1834, Hallowell, *James and Lucretia Mott,* 118.

51. William Ellery Channing, Quoted in Mendelsohn, *Channing,* 152.

52. Lucretia Mott to Richard Webb, 4 May 1871, RBD/BPL.

53. Lucretia Mott "Abuses and Uses of the Bible," Sermon delivered at Cherry Street Meeting, Philadelphia, 4 Nov. 1849, Greene, *Lucretia Mott: Speeches and Sermons,* 125.

54. This anecdote is recorded in the *Proceedings, American Anti-Slavery Society,* 1854, and is found in Cromwell, *Lucretia Mott,* 159. The biblical passages cited in this paragraph is from Isaiah 61:1

55. Lucretia Mott, "Likeness to Christ," Greene, *Lucretia Mott: Speeches and Sermons,* 111.

56. Lucretia Mott to George Julian, 14 Nov. 1848, FHL; reprinted in Hallowell, *James and Lucretia Mott,* 305–8.

57. Lucretia Mott, "Religious Aspects of the Age," Sermon delivered at Friends Meeting, Race Street, Philadelphia, 3 Jan. 1869, Greene, *Lucretia Mott: Speeches and Sermons,* 322.

58. Lucretia Mott to George Julian, 14 Nov. 1848, FHL; reprinted in Hallowell, *James and Lucretia Mott,* 307.

59. Lucretia Mott, "Likeness to Christ," Greene, *Lucretia Mott: Speeches and Sermons,* 109, 111.

60. Lucretia Mott to "you all," 6 Jan. 1858, Garrison Family papers, Sophia Smith Collection, Smith College, Northampton, Massachusetts.

61. Angelina Grimké to Theodore Weld and John Greenleaf Whittier, 20 Aug. 1837, CLMT.

62. Angelina Grimké to Sarah Grimké, [10 July 1836], CLMT.

63. Sarah Grimké, *Letters on the Equality of the Sexes and the Condition of Woman, addressed to Mary S. Parker, President of the Boston Female Anti-Slavery Society* (Boston: Isaac Knapp, 1838), reprinted in part in Larry Ceplair, ed., *The Public Years of Sarah and Angelina Grimké: Selected Writings, 1835–1839* (New York: Columbia Univ. Press 1989) 204–72. Quotations from page 205.

64. Sarah Grimké to Sarah Wattles, 23 Dec. [1853], CLMT.

65. Sarah Grimké to Gerrit Smith, 13 Mar. 1866, CLMT.

66. Extracts from a private note by Sallie Holley, printed in the *Liberator,* 14 Dec. 1855, p. 198, col. 6.

67. Mott reminiscences, FHL.

68. Lucretia Mott, "Religious Instincts in the Constitution of Man," Greene, *Lucretia Mott: Speeches and Sermons,* 244.

69. Lucretia Mott to Martha Coffin Wright, 19 Mar. 1866, SMTH.

70. Lucretia Mott, "Likeness to Christ," Greene, *Lucretia Mott: Speeches and Sermons,* 112–13.

71. Lucretia Mott, "Progress of the Religious World," Greene, *Lucretia Mott: Speeches and Sermons,* 61.

72. Abby Kelley Foster, comment summarized by Sargent, *Sketches,* 182. Scriptural passages are from Matt. 19:19, 1 John 4:20, and Matt. 7:12.

73. Angelina Grimké to Sarah Grimké, 31 July 1836, CLMT.

74. Angelina Grimké to Jane Smith, 18 Sept. 1836, CLMT.

75. Ann Taves, ed., *Religion and Domestic Violence in Early New England: The Memoirs of Abigail Abbot Bailey* (Bloomington: Indiana Univ. Press, 1989).

76. See chapter 4, "The Meaning of Mediumship," in Braude, *Radical Spirits.* Both Braude and Douglas, in *Feminization,* have explored this phenomenon in the particular case of the spiritualist movement, but arrive at different conclusions regarding its effectiveness as a tool of liberation for women. Douglas concluded that spirit mediums weakly chose to surrender their claims to individual agency thereby impeding progress towards women's equality. Braude disagrees, citing the numbers of women who claimed the right to speak through divine authority who would otherwise have kept silence, and concludes that "the identification of piety with femininity could aid in the expansion of women's options and contribute to the potency of a comprehensive moral idealism" (201).

77. Up to the 1840s, the Grimké sisters manifested their faith in divine will in different ways. Angelina seemed to take more initiative in acting, but then claimed divine authority for her actions. Sarah was more inclined to wait on events and then ascribe divine providence to them.

78. Abby Kelley to Ann[e] Warren Weston, 29 May 1839, RBD/BPL.

79. Sarah Grimké to Weld, 11 June 1837, quoting Hebrews 12:14, CLMT, reprinted in *B&D,* 1:402.

5. "ABOLITION IS CHRISTIANITY APPLIED TO SLAVERY": AN ACTIVIST FAITH

1. Abby Kelley to Samuel Drummond Porter, 13 Sept. 1842, Porter Family papers, UR. Kelley was paraphrasing Matthew 16:18 in which Jesus says, "thou art Peter, and upon this rock I will build my church; and the gates of hell shall not prevail against it."

2. Sallie Holley to Gerrit Smith, 31 Mar. 1852, Syracuse University, quoted in Herbig, "Friends for Freedom," 121.

3. The ongoing use of scripture raises some issues of consistency within these women's intellectual framework. On the one hand, they rejected the concept of scriptural inerrancy in favor of the notion of human authorship. The Bible, then, was necessarily a historically relativistic document. On the other hand, as discussed here, they also used the Bible as a foundation for their antislavery position by positioning themselves and other abolitionists as prophets. Likewise, they denied clergy the right to dictate scriptural interpretation, but were insistent that their own interpretations of scripture were correct. Lucretia Mott was probably the most cognizant of this contradiction, indicating her reservations about using scripture as an authority, but even so, she insisted that scripture could be correctly interpreted under the guidance of the holy spirit. This contradiction is perhaps the most critical theological problem for these women and for the other radical

reformers of their day who identified themselves as Christian, and who therefore drew upon the Christian Bible as a significant religious authority, and yet who in other respects had moved away from a religious identity defined by a written canon. It should be noted, though, that as time went on these women relied less on scriptural authority and more on their own judgment to justify their beliefs and actions.

4. *Appeal to the Christian Women*, 1, 3, 4–5.

5. Ibid., 13, 14.

6. Ibid., 2–3, 16.

7. *Epistle to the Clergy of the Southern States* (New York, 1836; reprint Ceplair, *The Public Years*, 90–115). Quotes from Ceplair, 90, 93, 96–97, 115. Scripture quoted is from Exodus 22:1 and 21:16.

8. Angelina Grimké to George S. Chase, 20 Aug. 1837, CLMT. For comment regarding Abraham, see Grimké's letter to Elizabeth Bascom, 18 Apr. 1828, CLMT.

9. Lucretia Mott, "I Am Not Here as a Representative of Any Sect," Greene, *Lucretia Mott: Speeches and Sermons*, 292.

10. Catharine E. Beecher, *An Essay on Slavery and Abolitionism, with Reference to the Duty of American Females, Addressed to Miss A. D. [sic] Grimké* (Boston: Perkins and Marvin, 1837), 13–14.

11. Angelina Grimké, *Letters to Catherine E. Beecher, in Reply to an Essay on Slavery and Abolitionism, addressed to A. E. Grimké*, revised by the author (Boston: Isaac Knapp, 1838), Letter 5, 29–30. Quoting Christ's statement that he came not to bring peace but a sword is an example of what might be taken as arbitrariness in Grimké's scriptural interpretation. She used those words to endorse the aggressive tactics of the abolitionists, but as a subscriber to the doctrine of nonresistance, she declared that they could not be used to support physical aggression.

12. Sarah Grimké to William E. Channing, 19 June 1837, Channing papers, MHS. William Ellery Channing (1780–1842) opposed slavery, but argued in his book, *Slavery* (1836), that although the institution was an evil, it should be left to the South to eliminate in their own time (Ceplair, *The Public Years*, 162n).

13. *Proceedings of the Anti-Slavery Convention of American Women . . . 1837*, 7.

14. Sallie Holley, quoted in Herbig, "Friends for Freedom," 120.

15. Abby Kelley to Samuel Drummond Porter, 13 Sept. 1842, UR.

16. Sallie Holley to Caroline Putnam, 12 Jan. 1854, Holley, *A Life for Liberty*, 134.

17. Sallie Holley to a friend, 6 Feb. 1853. Extract printed in the *Liberator*, 11 Feb. 1853, p. 22, col. 6.

18. In *The War Against Proslavery Religion: Abolitionism and the Northern Churches, 1830–1865* (Ithaca: Cornell Univ. Press, 1984), John McKivigan provides convincing evidence that the idea that the Northern churches were in the forefront of the antislavery movement is a myth. The rejection of churches by some abolitionists (McKivigan also demonstrates that this was not a universal phenomenon) was, however, by no means the first time the phenomenon of comeouterism appeared in American history. As Lewis Perry notes in *Radical Abolitionism* (Ithaca: Cornell Univ. Press, 1973), comeouterism was part of a long-standing tradition of "*Chrétiens sans Église*" (Christians without Church), "religious

ideas which . . . posit that there exists a constant antagonism between the fundamental values of Christianity and ecclesiastical institutions" (93). In America, comeouterism first arose from within the evangelical churches and was embraced by a nonelite, often illiterate population (95–102). The scriptural authority cited for comeouterism was "Come out of her, my people, that ye be not partakers of her sins, and that ye receive not of her plagues" (Rev. 18:4) and "Wherefore come out from among them, and be ye separate, saith the Lord, and touch not the unclean thing; and I will receive you" (2 Cor. 6:17).

19. Lucretia Mott, "Progress of the Religious World," Greene, *Lucretia Mott: Speeches and Sermons*, 63.

20. Lyman Beecher, "The Faith Once Delivered to the Saints. A Sermon Delivered at Worcester, Mass., October 15, 1823, at the Ordination of the Rev. Loammi Ives Hoadly, to the Pastoral Office over the Calvinistic Church and Society in That Place," quoted in Abzug, *Cosmos Crumbling*, 50. This is not to imply that all those with sectarian commitments were uninterested in anything but expressions of piety and the growth of the church. Charles Finney, for example, stressed that conversion was the beginning rather than the end of religious life and that it was then a believer's task to make him or herself "useful" within the world. (Barnes, *Antislavery Impulse*, 11.)

21. Lucretia Mott, "Likeness to Christ," Greene, *Lucretia Mott: Speeches and Sermons*, 107. Mott had found this quote in the writings of the revered Quaker William Penn and used it frequently in her addresses. After one such occasion, she reported that she had been visited by two Friends who came to admonish her for spreading this heresy. Upon hearing who had coined the aphorism, they retreated immediately with no comment.

22. Lucretia Mott, "One Standard of Goodness and Truth," Sermon delivered at Bristol, Pennsylvania, 6 June 1860, Greene, *Lucretia Mott: Speeches and Sermons*, 256.

23. Sallie Holley to Mr. Jackson, 16 Feb. 1858, BPL. This anecdote is particularly interesting, for the incident it described took place considerably after the Methodist Church took a stand against slavery, having refused in 1844 to appoint a slaveowning minister as a bishop. This led, as had been feared, to a schism within the denomination along North-South lines. (See Edwin Scott Gaustad, *A Religious History of America*, rev. ed. [San Francisco: HarperSanFrancisco, 1990], 171.)

24. Sallie Holley to Mr. Porter, 3 Sept. 1857, Holley, *A Life for Liberty*, 156–57.

25. Ibid.

26. This was probably the most controversial resolution to be debated at any of the three national women's antislavery conventions. After its passage, a dissenting group of delegates issued a statement. These women agreed "that slaveholders and their apologists are guilty before God, and that, with the former, Northern Christians should hold no fellowship; but as it is their full belief that there is still moral power sufficient in the church, if rightly applied, to purify it, they cannot feel it their duty to withdraw until the utter inefficacy of the means used, shall constrain them to believe the church totally corrupt" (*Proceedings of the Anti-Slavery Convention of American Women . . . 1838*, 5–6).

27. Abby Kelley to the editor of the *Anti-Slavery Standard*, 19 June 1840. Reprinted in the *Liberator*, 10 July 1840, p. 110, col. 3.

28. Abby Kelley to E. D. Hudson, 7 Feb. 1843, UMASS.

29. The New Organization was the name applied to the American and Foreign Anti-Slavery Society formed in 1840 when a group of abolitionists broke away from the American Anti-Slavery Society. This was the non-Garrisonian wing of the movement, which rejected the Garrisonian no-government position and instead, primarily through the Liberty Party, endorsed antislavery candidates for public office. The precipitating factor in the schism had been the New Organization's objection to the nomination of a woman—Abby Kelley—to the Business Committee of the American Anti-Slavery Society, and in keeping with that position, that branch then proved to be less open to women's public leadership roles within the antislavery movement.

30. Braude, *Radical Spirits*, 62.

31. Mott reminiscences, FHL. Emphasis added.

32. Sargent, *Sketches*, 181–82.

33. In *They Who Would Be Free: Blacks' Search for Freedom, 1830–1861* (New York: Atheneum, 1974), Jane and William Pease make the point that whites "understood slavery and freedom as polar absolutes" but for blacks these two concepts "were rather terminal points on a continuous spectrum." They note, for example, that on the one hand, some slaves were allowed to sell their services out and save the proceeds; and on the other, the liberty of free Northern blacks was limited in many ways (4).

34. Sarah Mapps Douglass to Abby Kelley, 18 May 1838, AAS.

35. Maria Stewart, Lecture at Franklin Hall, 21 Sept. 1832, in Marilyn Richardson, ed., *Maria W. Stewart: America's First Black Woman Political Writer: Essays and Speeches* (Bloomington: Indiana Univ. Press, 1987), 45.

36. Maria Stewart, "Religion and the Pure Principles of Morality," and "An Address Delivered at the African Masonic Hall," in Richardson, *Stewart*, 39–40; 30; 38; 60.

37. Samuel E. Cornish, "Responsibility of Colored People in the Free States," 4 Mar. 1837 reprinted in Peter C. Ripley, ed., *The Black Abolitionist Papers*, vol. 3, *The United States, 1830–1846* (Chapel Hill: Univ. of North Carolina Press, 1991), 220. Samuel Cornish (1795–1858?) was a free-born African American from Delaware. In 1827 he became the first senior editor of the first black newspaper, *Freedom's Journal*, a publication dedicated to "the moral, religious, civil and literary improvement of our injured race." In 1837 he founded the *Colored American*. He was also a minister and founded the First Colored Presbyterian Church in New York City. See David E. Swift, *Black Prophets of Justice: Activist Clergy Before the Civil War* (Baton Rouge: Louisiana State Univ. Press, 1989).

38. Sarah Mapps Douglass to William Bassett, December 1837, included in "Colorphobia."

39. See Pease and Pease, *They Who Would Be Free*, 284. Also, Carol George's essay, "Widening the Circle: The Black Church and the Abolitionist Crusade, 1830–1860," is an excellent analysis of the importance of the work of many black clergy who were not part of the abolitionist elite, but who "built Sunday schools, raised money, and joined or sponsored local groups responsive to community needs, all efforts which had the effect of heightening the racial consciousness and collective identity of black people." (George's essay in Lewis Perry and Michael Fellman, *Antislavery Reconsidered:*

New Perspectives on the Abolitionists [Baton Rouge: Louisiana State Univ. Press, 1979], 75–95), quotation on 79. Shirley Yee (*Black Women Abolitionists: A Study in Activism, 1828–1860* [Knoxville: Univ. of Tennessee Press, 1992]) notes that black women also worked to create a self-sufficient and educated community as well as supporting anti-slavery efforts.

40. Augustine [Lewis Woodson], Essay in *Colored American*, New York, New York, 29 Nov. 1839, reprinted in Ripley, *Black Abolitionist Papers*, 3:323–24.

41. Maria Stewart, "Religion and the Pure Principles of Morality" Richardson, *Stewart*, 34.

42. Augustine [Lewis Woodson], Essay, reprinted in Ripley, *Black Abolitionist Papers*, 3:324.

43. Angelina Grimké to Elizabeth Pease, 17 Mar. 1837, BPL.

44. *Proceedings of the Anti-Slavery Convention . . . 1837*, 13.

45. Ibid., 17. Note, however, that in the language of the resolutions, "we," referring to abolitionists, always means "we white abolitionists," despite the fact that the convention was attended by black women, some of whom even served as officers of the convention. Although the white women were conscious of prejudice, they still remained largely unaware of their condescending attitudes toward their African American peers.

46. Ibid., 14 and 17.

47. *Proceedings of the Fourth New-England Anti-Slavery Convention, held in Boston, May 30, 31, and June 1 and 2, 1837* (Boston: Isaac Knapp, 1837), 122–23.

48. *Proceedings of the Anti-Slavery Convention . . . 1838*, 8.

49. *Proceedings of the Third Anti-Slavery Convention of American Women . . . 1839*, 8.

50. Ibid., 6

51. Angelina Grimké to Abby Kelley, 15 Apr. 1837, AAS.

52. Sarah Grimké, Grimké sisters' history, "Colorphobia."

53. Sarah Grimké and Angelina Grimké Weld to Sarah Mapps Douglass, 8 Sept. 1839, CLMT.

54. Abby Kelley to William Lloyd Garrison, 30 Sept. 1841, BPL.

55. Robert Purvis was a well-to-do Philadelphia businessman and a prominent black leader and abolitionist. The Remonds, from Salem, Massachusetts, were another prominent family active in the antislavery movement. Both Charles Remond and his sister Sarah Parker Remond were antislavery lecturers.

56. Sallie Holley to Caroline Putnam, 12 Jan. 1854, Holley, *A Life for Liberty*, 134.

57. Sallie Holley to Caroline Putnam, 26 Nov. 1852, Ibid., 101.

58. Sallie Holley to Abby Kelley Foster, 26 Oct. [1862?], WHM.

59. Holley also extended her critique of racism to include treatment of native Americans, believing that it was "high time to recognise [sic] the truth that the Indian holds a common heritage with the Pilgrim Father or any of his descendants, as a child of God. I cannot see," she continued, "why all good minded people, will not agree with us, to repudiate the idea so sedulously cultivated by writers of books, dignified with the name of Histories, that in all the hostilities between the Indians and the colonists, the

Almighty invariably took sides and sympathies with the Whites" (Sallie Holley to William Lloyd Garrison, 26 Feb. 1855, BPL).

60. Yellin, *Women and Sisters,* 78–79. Chapters 1 and 2 provide a history and analysis of the appropriation by white women of the emblem of the kneeling, bound slave. Gerda Lerner has recently challenged Yellin's critique, at least in the case of Sarah Grimké. She argues that Grimké "took the step into social analysis by showing that wherever power is exercised over a group of people someone benefits and someone is exploited. She had learned this from living within the slave system; now she made the intellectual leap of reasoning from the power/oppression model of slavery to the power/oppression of woman. This is quite different from the use of the metaphor of 'white woman' as sister. . . . Sarah Grimké . . . never made the mistake of equating the white woman's position with that of the slave, and she always emphasized the greater suffering, exploitation and oppression of the black woman" (*The Feminist Thought of Sarah Grimké* [New York: Oxford Univ. Press, 1998], 24).

61. Angelina Grimké to Theodore Weld and John Greenleaf Whittier, 20 Aug. [1837], CLMT.

62. Sallie Holley to Mrs. Miller, 30 Dec. 1878, Holley, *A Life for Liberty,* 229–30.

63. Sallie Holley to Miss Tyler, 15 Aug. 1884, Holley, *A Life for Liberty,* 238.

64. Lucretia Mott, "Unity of Spirit in the Bond of Peace," Sermon delivered at Cherry Street Meeting, Philadelphia, 2 Sept. 1849, Greene, *Lucretia Mott: Speeches and Sermons,* 98.

65. Abby Kelley to Stephen Foster, 14 Mar. 1843, AAS.

66. Lucretia Mott, undated fragment, FHL.

67. Abby Kelley to Olive Darling, 3 Nov. 1845, WHM.

68. Sallie Holley to Mrs. Miller, 30 Dec. 1878, Holley, *A Life for Liberty,* 229. See also her printed letter, 3 Aug. 1875, *A Life for Liberty,* 212–13.

69. Sallie Holley to Miss Tyler, 7 Dec. [1892?], Holley, *A Life for Liberty,* 280.

70. Sallie Holley to Caroline Putnam, 29 Sep. 1861, Holley, *A Life for Liberty,* 183.

71. Sallie Holley to Caroline Putnam, 22 Mar. 1853, Holley, *A Life for Liberty,* 117.

72. Angelina Grimké Diary, 15 Aug. 1829.

73. Sarah Grimké to Ellis Gray Loring, 29 Feb. 1856, Alma Lutz Collection, SCHL.

74. Sarah Grimké to Theodore Weld, 17 Dec. 1837, in *B&D,* 1:498.

75. Condescension of white to black abolitionists was quite common. The white abolitionists who embraced Frederick Douglass as a lecturer were dismayed at his eloquence and asked him to speak only of his experiences in slavery; they would, they assured him, "take care of the philosophy." They also criticized his language as too learned and counseled him to use "plantation speech" in his remarks (Leon F. Litwack, "The Emancipation of the Negro Abolitionist," in *The Antislavery Vanguard: New Essays on the Abolitionists,* ed. Martin Duberman [Princeton: Princeton Univ. Press, 1965], 147). William Lloyd Garrison, too, made a significant comment in a letter to his son, Wendell Phillips Garrison (5 Aug. 1874, BPL). Commenting on two of his son's recent visitors, Sojourner Truth and Angelina Grimké Weld, he said, "The turning up of Sojourner Truth at the Park must have been a surprise to you all. She is indeed a remarkable woman,

and always deserving of considerate and kind treatment; but, at her extreme age, . . . it is a pity that she cannot remain quiet at her home in Battle Creek, instead of perambulating about the country, compelling hospitality whether or no." He was, however, enthusiastic about Grimké Weld's visit: "It must have been very gratifying to dear Mrs. Weld to have enjoyed your hospitality and society at the Park. Like her departed sister Sarah, she is a saintly woman, without any thought of or pretension to saintship. Give my affectionate remembrances to her and Theodore."

76. Sallie Holley to Caroline Putnam, 17 Feb. 1870; Sallie Holley to Porters, 23 Nov. 1869; Sallie Holley to Miss Porter, 30 Sept. 1887. Holley, *A Life for Liberty,* 209–10; 252.

6. "IT IS NOT THE CAUSE OF THE SLAVE ONLY WHICH WE PLEAD": FAITH IN ACTION FOR WOMEN'S RIGHTS

1. Abby Kelley, 1838 Album, Western Anti-Slavery Society papers, LC, as quoted in Hersh, *Slavery of Sex,* 34.

2. Angelina Grimké to Jane Smith, 29 May 1837, CLMT.

3. Sallie Holley to William Lloyd Garrison, 26 Feb. 1855, BPL.

4. Sarah Grimké to Elisabeth Pease, 18 Dec. 1837, BPL.

5. "The General Association of Massachusetts (Orthodox) to the Churches Under Their Care," 1837, reprinted Ceplair, *The Public Years,* 211.

6. See letters from Phebe to Amos A. Phelps, n.d., n.p., reprinted in the *Liberator,* 22 June 1838 (p. 98, col. 5), and H. C. Wright to Amos A. Phelps, 6 June 40, reprinted in the *Liberator,* 24 July 1840, (p. 120, col. 2).

7. Angelina Grimké to Jane Smith, 10 Aug. 1837, CLMT.

8. Sarah Grimké to Amos A. Phelps, 3 Aug. 1837, BPL.

9. Beecher, *Essay,* 100–101, 103; 6. For more on Beecher, see Kathryn Kish Sklar's insightful biography, *Catherine Beecher: A Study in American Domesticity* (New Haven: Yale Univ. Press, 1976).

10. Angelina Grimké, *Letters to Beecher,* Letter 6, 104–5.

11. Lerner, "One Thousand Years of Feminist Bible Criticism," in *Feminist Consciousness,* 166.

12. Sarah Grimké, *Letters on the Equality of the Sexes,* Letter 1, 4.

13. Angelina Grimké to George S. Chase, 20 Aug. 1837, CLMT. Scripture quoted is from Genesis 1:26.

14. Maria Stewart had made the same point in her lectures in the early 1830s.

15. Lucretia Mott, "An Encouraging View as to What Has Already Been Effected," Remarks delivered at the Seventh National Woman's Rights Convention, New York, 25–26 Nov. 1856, Greene, *Lucretia Mott: Speeches and Sermons,* 229.

16. Elizabeth Cady Stanton, Susan B. Anthony, and Matilda Joslyn Gage, *History of Woman Suffrage* (New York: Fowler & Wells, 1881), 1:76.

17. Sarah Grimké, *Letters on Equality,* Letters 1, 4.

18. Lucretia Mott, "The Truth of God," Greene, *Lucretia Mott: Speeches and Sermons,* 28.

19. Lucretia Mott, "The Principles of the Co-Equality of Woman with Man," Remarks delivered at the Woman's Rights Convention, New York, 6–7 Sept. 1853, Greene, *Lucretia Mott: Speeches and Sermons*, 208.

20. Lucretia Mott, "Discourse on Women," Delivered in Philadelphia, 17 Dec. 1849, Greene, *Lucretia Mott: Speeches and Sermons*, 145.

21. *Letters on Equality*, Letter 3, 16; Letter 14, 98.

22. Angelina Grimké to L. Dodge [and the Olive Branch Circle], 14 July 1836, Theodore Weld papers, LC.

23. Angelina Grimké, *Letters to Beecher*, Letter 12, 118.

24. Angelina Grimké to Petrie, [c. 1828], CLMT. See also Lucretia Mott, "The Truth of God," Greene, *Lucretia Mott: Speeches and Sermons*, 26–7.

25. Lucretia Mott to Elizabeth Cady Stanton, 23 Mar. 1841, LC; Lucretia Mott, "Principles of Co-Equality," Greene, *Lucretia Mott: Speeches and Sermons*, 209. See also Lucretia Mott, "An Encouraging View," Greene, 230. Scriptural references are from 1 Corinthians 7:1–8.

26. Angelina Grimké to Jane Smith, 4 Feb. 1837, CLMT.

27. Sarah Grimké, *Letters on Equality*, Letter 1, 8.

28. Angelina Grimké, *Letters to Beecher*, Letter 12, 119–20.

29. Sarah Grimké to Elisabeth J. Davis, 18 Mar. 1838, BPL.

30. *Proceedings of the Anti-Slavery Convention of American Women . . . , 1837*, 9

31. Angelina Grimké to Jane Smith, 26 Oct. 1837, CLMT.

32. Lewis Tappan to the editor, *Liberator*, 20 Mar. 1840, p. 44, col. 6.

33. John Greenleaf Whittier to Sarah and Angelina Grimké, 14 Aug. 1837, reprinted in *B&D*, 1:424.

34. Theodore Weld to Sarah and Angelina Grimké, 15 Aug. 1837, CLMT, reprinted in *B&D*, 1:426–27.

35. Ibid.

36. Theodore Weld to Sarah and Angelina Grimké, 26 Aug. 1837, reprinted in *B&D*, 1:436.

37. Angelina Grimké to Theodore Weld, 12 Aug. [1837], reprinted in *B&D*, 1:415.

38. Sarah Grimké to Amos A. Phelps, 3 Aug. 1837, RBD/BPL

39. Angelina Grimké to Jane Smith, 26 Aug. 1837, CLMT.

40. Angelina Grimké to Theodore D. Weld and John Greenleaf Whittier, 20 Aug. [1837], CLMT.

41. Abby Kelley to William Lloyd Garrison, 20 Oct. 1837, BPL.

42. Buckingham Female Anti-Slavery Society to Sarah and Angelina Grimké, 27 July 1837, UT.

43. Sarah Grimké to Amos A. Phelps, 3 Aug. 1837, RBD/BPL

44. Sarah Grimké to Elizabeth Pease, May 1840, RBD/BPL.

45. Abby Kelley Foster to Lucy Stone, 10 Feb. 1867, NAWSA collection, LC. The quotation from Lucy Stone is contained in this letter.

46. Sallie Holley to Abby Kelley Foster, 13 Mar. 1854, AAS.

47. Herbig, "Friends for Freedom," 150–51.

48. Sallie Holley to Porters, 30 Aug. 1865, Holley, *A Life for Liberty,* 199.

49. J. D. Bridge to the editor of the *New England Christian Advocate,* July 1841. Reprinted in the *Liberator,* 27 Aug. 1841, p. 137, col. 1.

50. Lucretia Mott, undated fragment, FHL.

51. Lucretia Mott to Edmund Quincy, 24 Aug. 1848, reprinted in the *Liberator,* 6 Oct. 1848, p. 159, col. 2.

7. EMBRACING THE CAUSE OF WOMAN AND HUMANITY: THE "PRIVATE YEARS" OF THE GRIMKÉS

1. Henry Blackwell to Lucy Stone, 1853, quoted in Alice Stone Blackwell, *Lucy Stone* (1930; reprint, New York: Kraus Reprint Company, 1971), 126–29.

2. Of the 368 pages of Lerner's book, nearly 300 of them focus on events up to 1841, with the remaining 75 pages dealing with the last half of Angelina Grimké's life, and the last 32 of Sarah Grimké's 81 years. Although Birney sees the events of their later lives as more congruous with their earlier lives (probably because that is when she knew them), her book also reflects this bias, with 242 pages devoted to events up to the Grimké/Weld marriage, and 77 pages for the remaining years.

3. Introduction to *B&D,* xxvi.

4. For example, in the broader sense, a woman's leaving her abusive husband would be considered a political as well as a personal act, whether or not she also became involved in some movement to protest spousal abuse or to enact legislation against it.

5. Angelina Grimké to Jane Smith, 15 Apr. 1838, CLMT.

6. Angelina Grimké Weld to Anne Warren Weston, 15 July [1838], BPL.

7. Abby Kelley to Stephen Foster, 13 Aug. 1843, AAS; Alla Foster, "Reminiscences."

8. Sarah Grimké to Abby Kelley, 15 June 1838, AAS.

9. Theodore Weld, *American Slavery as It Is: Testimony of a Thousand Witnesses* (1839; reprint, New York: Columbia Univ. Press, 1960).

10. Angelina Grimké Weld to Theodore Weld, 20 Feb. 1842, CLMT.

11. Lerner, *Grimké Sisters,* 292–93.

12. Angelina Grimké to Jane Smith, 27 Mar. 1838, CLMT.

13. See the following letters: Angelina Grimké Weld to Theodore Weld, [5 Sept. 1852], CLMT; Sarah Grimké to Samuel and William Allinson, 12 May 1847, Allinson Family papers, HVFD; Angelina Grimké Weld and Sarah Grimké to Lucy Stone, 13 July [1852?], LC.

14. Sarah Grimké to Ann Fitzhugh Smith, 26 May 1848, CLMT.

15. Angelina Grimké to Jane Smith, 27 Mar. 1838, CLMT.

16. Their mother grew weary of what she felt to be her daughters' harping on this issue and wrote in 1839: "Now the only way to carry on our correspondence with affection and satisfaction is to agree to disagree; and not to expect from me more than I do from you. I hope therefore that you will no longer fill your letters with such matter as you well know is offensive; so far from its making any alteration in my opinion respect-

ing the People that you patronize, has only served to confirm me in the belief, that generally speaking, they are at present fit for no other condition" (M. S. Grimké to Sarah Grimké, 10 Mar. 1839, CLMT).

17. Letter from Angelina Grimké Weld to the National Woman's Rights Convention held in Syracuse in 1852, quoted in Stanton, Anthony, and Gage, *History,* 1:540–41.

18. Ibid, 540.

19. Angelina Grimké Weld to Harriot Kezia Hunt, undated, CLMT. Grimké Weld was quite specific about the time and type of usefulness of organizations. They were, she said in the same letter, "the instrumentalities which belonged to the first half of this century not to the last, upon which we have entered. They were preeminently useful in drawing together congenial minds out of divirs [sic] creeds and Churches and breaking down the massive walls of sectarianism and forming a nucleus of power out of which has now arisen germs strong enough to stand alone each by himself and herself true to the sacred intuitions of their own being untrammelled by too close a juxtaposition with others."

20. Angelina Grimké, autobiographical manuscript, 1828.

21. Comment made by Lucy Stone at the National Woman's Rights convention, Syracuse, New York, 1852, quoted in Stanton, Anthony, and Gage, *History,* 1:541. Stone appears to have abandoned her anti-organizationism in 1869 when she formed the American Woman Suffrage Association.

22. Angelina Grimké to Jane Smith, 18 Sept. 1836, CLMT.

23. Lerner, *Grimké Sisters,* 315, 337.

24. Herbig, "Friends for Freedom," 198.

25. Sarah Grimké to Elizabeth Smith Miller, 18–27 Sept. [1852], CLMT.

26. Sarah Grimké to Her Sister, 22 Oct. 1840, reprinted in the *Liberator,* 27 Nov. 1840, p. 190, col. 4.

27. Angelina Grimké Weld to Theodore Weld, c. 1 Feb. 1842, CLMT.

28. Angelina Grimké Weld to Theodore Weld, Feb. 1842, CLMT.

29. Angelina Grimké Weld to Theodore Weld, 1 Jan. 1843, CLMT.

30. Angelina Grimké to Thomas S. Grimké, 3 June [1832?], CLMT.

31. Angelina Grimké Weld to Theodore Weld, 3 [Jan.] 1842, CLMT.

32. Angelina Grimké Weld to Theodore Weld and Sarah Grimké, 1 May [1842], CLMT. Also see Angelina Grimké to Jane Smith, 8 Feb. 1842, CLMT.

33. Angelina Grimké Weld to Theodore Weld, 2 Feb. 1843, CLMT.

34. Lerner, *Grimké Sisters,* 306–308. The Welds' third and last child, Sarah Grimké Weld, was born 22 Mar. 1844.

35. The passage from which this quotation is taken is as follows: "During this summer of 1836 she [Angelina Grimké] certainly made every effort to convert Sarah to her viewpoint. One reason the letters from Shrewsbury to Burlington were so full of theological argument may have been Angelina's awareness that these were the kind of arguments best designed to win a response from Sarah. As for herself, theological problems could not long absorb her interest" (*Grimké Sisters,* 136).

36. Angelina Grimké to Sarah Grimké, 19 July 1836, CLMT.

37. Contrary to common opinion, Miller himself did not set a specific date for the end of the world. He predicted its destruction for the period between 21 Mar. 1843 and 21 Mar. 1844. Later, another date was selected, 22 Oct. 1844; Miller endorsed this date although he was not its originator. See Ruth Alden Doan, *The Miller Heresy, Millennialism, and American Culture* (Philadelphia: Temple Univ. Press, 1987), 47–53.

38. Angelina Grimké Weld to Jane Smith, 15 [Mar. 1843], CLMT.

39. Angelina Grimké Weld to Sarah, Jan. 1845, LC. Lerner believes that this "Sarah" is Sarah Grimké (307). While this is plausible, from the less intimate tone of the letter, I suggest the possibility of it being directed to some other acquaintance. (Sarah Mapps Douglass, perhaps?) If the recipient was Sarah Grimké, the tone may shed some light on the state of their relationship at the time.

40. Angelina Grimké Weld to Theodore Grimké Weld, 12 Dec. [1860], CLMT.

41. Grimké claimed to receive frequent comfort from the presence of her departed mother (see for example, Sarah Grimké to Sarah Wattles, 10 Dec. 1861, CLMT). She also consulted a clairvoyant about the health of her nephew, Theodore Grimké Weld. (See letters from Sarah Grimké to him, 7 July 1860 and 2 Dec. 1860; also C. A. Coleman (a spirit medium) to Sarah Grimké, 17 July 1860, CLMT.)

42. Sarah Grimké to Sarah Wattles, 4 July [1861?], CLMT.

43. Sarah Grimké to Gerrit Smith, 13 Mar. 1866, CLMT.

44. Sarah Grimké to Augustus [Wattles], 22 Jan. 1865, UT.

45. Braude, *Radical Spirits,* 41–44.

46. Sarah Grimké to Harriot Kezia Hunt, 16 Dec. [1849?], CLMT.

47. Sarah Grimké to Preston Day, 19 Jan. 1869, CLMT.

48. Sarah Grimké to Harriot Kezia Hunt, 16 Dec. [1849?], CLMT.

49. Sarah Grimké to Sarah Wattles, 4 July [1861?], CLMT.

50. See the letter from Angelina Grimké Weld to Theodore Weld, [18 Apr. 1841], CLMT. As the years go by there is less correspondence extant from Angelina Grimké Weld, so one cannot say with any certainty how she resolved her spiritual crisis of the 1840s.

51. Sarah Grimké to Rebecca Black, 1 Apr. [1850], CLMT.

52. Sarah Grimké to Harriot Kezia Hunt, 5 Apr. 1853, CLMT; Lerner, *Grimké Sisters,* 321. See Lerner, *Grimké Sisters,* 323–27, for a discussion of the conflict between Angelina Grimké Weld and Sarah Grimké.

53. Sarah Grimké to Harriot Kezia Hunt, 20 Dec. [1854], CLMT.

54. Martha Coffin Wright to Lucretia Mott, 17 May 1858, SMTH.

55. Lucretia Mott to Martha Coffin Wright, 27 May 1858, SMTH.

56. Sarah Grimké to Harriot Kezia Hunt, 28 June 1857, CLMT. Other sources have mentioned this document, but I was unable to locate a copy.

57. Sarah Grimké to Theodore Grimké Weld, 17 May 1863, CLMT. Lerner, *Grimké Sisters,* 351–55. The Women's Loyal National League was formed in 1863 to further the goal of emancipation. For more on this group, see Venet, *Neither Ballots nor Bullets.*

58. Birney, *The Grimké Sisters,* 296.

8. "A GREAT WHILE GROWING TO BE SIXTY": HOLLEY, KELLEY, AND MOTT

1. The quotation that appears in the chapter title is from a letter from Lucretia Mott to Martha Coffin Wright, in which Mott criticized Sarah Grimké for not yielding her place to younger activists, 27 May 1858, SMTH.

2. Abby Kelley Foster to Samuel May, Jr., 15 Sept. 1853; Sallie Holley to Samuel May, Jr. [July 1859?], RBD/BPL.

3. Sallie Holley to Caroline Putnam, 1 Oct. 1861, Holley, *A Life for Liberty*, 184.

4. Sallie Holley and Caroline Putnam to Abby Kelley Foster, 1858?, AAS, as quoted in Herbig, "Friends for Freedom," 166.

5. Sarah Clay to William Lloyd Garrison, *Liberator*, 22 Oct. 1852, p. 171, col. 3; S.W.W. to Friend Garrison, *Liberator*, 4 Feb. 1853, p. 20, col. 3; C. B. to Friend Garrison, *Liberator*, 24 Dec. 1858, p. 206, col. 6.

6. H. W. Carter to Samuel J. May, Jr., 2 Apr. 1860, RBD/BPL; Samuel May, Jr. to James Miller McKim, 29 Nov. 1860, (BPL), as quoted in Herbig, "Friends for Freedom," 209.

7. Sallie Holley to Abby Kelley Foster, 26 Oct. [1862], as quoted in Herbig, "Friends for Freedom," 217; Holley to C. H. Dall, 27 Feb. [1864], MHS, quoted in Herbig, 223. General biographical information from Herbig, 221–25.

8. Sallie Holley to Abby Kelley Foster, 26 Oct. [1862?], WHM. The quotation from Foster is contained in this letter.

9. Sallie Holley to Abby Kelley Foster, 30 Sept. 1862, WHM.

10. Sallie Holley to the Porters, Farmersville, 22 Jan. 1863, Holley, *A Life for Liberty*, 189.

11. Sallie Holley to Abby Kelley Foster, 26 Oct. [1862?], WHM.

12. See Herbig, "Friends for Freedom," 238–41. Quotation taken from letter from Sallie Holley to Caroline Putnam, 16 Dec. 1867, Holley, *A Life for Liberty*, 206.

13. Sallie Holley to Caroline Putnam, 17 Feb. 1870, Holley, *A Life for Liberty*, 209–10. Wendell Phillips was the president of the American Anti-Slavery Society.

14. Sallie Holley to Caroline Putnam, 21 Feb. 1870, Holley, *A Life for Liberty*, 210.

15. I am using the name of the town as Holley inscribed it on her letters; today the town is known as "Lottsburg," not Lottsburgh.

16. Sallie Holley, 3 Aug. 1875, printed letter apparently for general distribution, Chadwick, *Theodore Parker*, 212–13. Also see Herbig, "Friends for Freedom," 304–9.

17. Sallie Holley to Porters, 28 Aug. 1870, Holley, *A Life for Liberty*, 220.

18. Sallie Holley to Miss Porter, 30 Sept. 1887, Holley, *A Life for Liberty*, 252.

19. Sallie Holley to Miss Tyler, 29 Nov. 1884, Holley, 245. A peri is a figure from Persian folklore, a descendant of fallen angels, not permitted to enter Paradise until adequate penance has been done.

20. Sallie Holley to unnamed correspondent, 12 Jan. 1892, Holley, *A Life for Liberty*, 281.

21. Sallie Holley to William Lloyd Garrison, 26 Feb. 1855, BPL; Sallie Holley to Porters, 16 June 1851, Holley, *A Life for Liberty,* 70; Sallie Holley to Elizabeth Smith Miller, 28 Jan. 1875, Holley, 225.

22. Sallie Holley to Caroline Putnam, 6 Dec. 1853, Holley, *A Life for Liberty,* 127.

23. Sallie Holley to Theodore Weld, 12 Nov. 1879, CLMT; Sallie Holley to Mrs. [Elizabeth Smith] Miller, 27 Feb. 1888, Holley, *A Life for Liberty,* 254.

24. Holley, *A Life for Liberty,* 266. Sallie Holley to Mrs. [Elizabeth Smith] Miller, 24 Feb. 1888, Holley, *A Life for Liberty,* 254.

25. Sallie Holley to Mrs. [Elizabeth Smith] Miller, 26 Jan. 1892, Holley, *A Life for Liberty,* 263.

26. Sallie Holley to Robert Morville, 19 Nov. 1888, Holley, *A Life for Liberty,* 257.

27. Sallie Holley to Miss Tyler, 23 Oct. 1890, Holley, *A Life for Liberty,* 259.

28. Abby Kelley Foster to Maria Weston Chapman, 18 Feb. 1846, RBD/BPL;

29. Abby Kelley Foster to Dear Friend, Wolcott's Mills, Indiana, 25 Apr. 1854, reprinted in the *Liberator,* 26 May 1854, p. 82, col. 2.

30. Abby Kelley Foster to Stephen Foster, 10 Sept. [1850s], AAS. This did not mean that she did not have an opinion on the type of home she wanted. Stephen wrote to describe the farm near Worcester that he had selected for them; Abby's dismay, and her conviction that she was making the best of the situation are comical. She responded: "How idle it is to lay plans. The very reverse of all ours, in relation to a home, is realized. Instead of a *few* acres, very many. For *first* rate soil, *third or fourth*—for *good* buildings or *very poor,* not poor enough to pull down, could we afford it—instead of *near* W[orcester] three or four miles out—instead of *fruit* land, what will hardly bear any at all. But I presume you have done the best you could, as you say, under the circumstances—although you talk about *two* families in one house. But you will not find me a grumbler, altho' my air-castles are all demolished with one blow. I am too much a philosopher to take any such disappointment to heart, but think it best to go to work and make the best of things. And again—of all the neighborhoods in Worcester, Tatnuck is most repulsive to me except that called 'Hell County.' Pray dont mention this last fact, as we can get along well enough with the bigots—if we do our duty. But I will say no more about the place, as you will think me uncomfortable about it. But believe me quite calm and comfortable for I am so" (7 Apr. 1847, AAS).

31. Abby Kelley Foster to Lucy Stone, 15 Aug. [1846?], OBRLN. This letter was a transcript of the original, which was located in private hands at the time of transcription.

32. Abby Kelley Foster to Stephen Foster, 9 Sept. 1847, AAS.

33. Correspondence between Jane Elizabeth Hitchcock Jones and Abby Kelley Foster, quoted in Nancy Hall Burkett, *Abby Kelley Foster and Stephen S. Foster* (Worcester, Mass.: Worcester Bicentennial Commission, 1976), 26.

34. In one of the rare moments of introspection recorded in her correspondence, she wrote to her husband: "I have discyphered [sic] the cause of my *lawlessness,* as you seem to consider it, in my manners among folks. It consists in the fact of my feeling that I am as much unobserved as if I were entirely alone. I dont *feel* the presence of the multitude, even when I am crowding among them. They are nothing to my feeling. No more than

so many images in a museum. I find, on looking into my inner man, that this has *always* been the fact with me. I feel the presence only of those whom I intimately know. How then can I carry myself towards them otherwise than I do?" (3 Apr. 1848, AAS).

35. Sarah Pugh to Maria Weston Chapman, 15 June 1844, RBD/BPL quoted in Sterling, *Ahead of Her Time*, 202.

36. Sarah Hallowell Willis to Amy Kirby Post, 6 Mar. 1852, Post Family papers, UR.

37. Abby Kelley Foster to Stephen Foster, 2 Dec. 1851, AAS.

38. Abby Kelley Foster to Wendell Phillips, 24 June 1859, quoted in Jane Pease, "The Freshness of Fanaticism: Abby Kelley Foster: An Essay in Reform," (Ph.D. diss., University of Rochester, 1969), 213.

39. Abby Kelley to Maria Weston Chapman, 10 Oct. 1843, BPL.

40. Lucy Stone to the Fosters, 3 July 1846, AAS.

41. Abby Kelley Foster to Stephen Foster, 18 Aug. 1847, AAS.

42. See correspondence between Abby Kelley Foster and Wendell Phillips, June and July 1859; and with William Lloyd Garrison, July through September 1859, AAS. Sterling reports that the first amicable encounter between Kelley and Garrison after this took place at the Radical Club some time after 1867 (*Ahead of Her Time*, 363). Sterling is again inclined, in my view, to be overly charitable to Kelley, accepting her version of the story, that Garrison had accused her of fraud. Although Sterling admits Kelley was oversensitive, she seems to place most of the blame for the feud on Garrison, referring to him as "stiff-necked" because he would not offer the public apology Kelley insisted she deserved (322–23).

43. Kelley conducted a correspondence with Smith that she reported to Maria Weston Chapman. In one of her letters, she rather maliciously confided, "You would laugh to see his last [letter], in which he has enumerated his great services and sacrifices to the cause in order 'to make me somewhat ashamed of the proud scorn with which you (I) have treated my (his) abolition.' He is struggling most delightfully and I hope it will not be in vain, yet I greatly fear. I have not finished my answer to him in which I am showing him how much more mischief he is doing to the cause from the very fact of his great services. And altho' he denies his real position to be that which *he* takes but which others choose to give him, and tries to throw off his share of the responsibility in the slanders against our society, he evidently feels it as he never before has, and I am doing what I can to up the [ ] on his conscience so that it will not rub off even with [ ] salve" (12 Aug. 1843, BPL).

44. Abby Kelley to Friend Jackson, 22 July 1842, reprinted in the *Liberator*, 12 Aug. 1842, p. 126 col. 6.

45. Abby Kelley to Stephen Foster, 13 Nov. 1844, AAS. Sterling glosses over this less attractive aspect of Kelley's personality, emphasizing instead her skill as a tactician.

46. Melder, "Abby Kelley and the Process of Liberation," 239, 244.

47. Abby Kelley to Stephen Foster, 28 Mar. 1843, AAS.

48. Abby Kelley Foster to Sallie Holley, 17 July, no year, Emily Howland papers, CRNL.

49. Quotation by Caroline Severance, author of *Mother of Clubs*, in Hersh, *Slavery of*

Sex, 144. For more information on the Free Religious Association, see W. J. Potter, *The Free Religious Association: Its Twenty-five Years and Their Meaning* (Boston, 1892); also chapter 3 of Stow Persons's book, *Free Religion: An American Faith* (New Haven: Yale Univ. Press, 1947).

50. Sargent, *Sketches,* "Origins of the Club." She noted also that the club "was composed of members of all religious denominations. Thirty persons were present at its first meeting; and at the closing sessions, in 1880, nearly two hundred were in attendance. In its earlier years, the papers were chiefly confined to theological and religious questions; but during the last decade they were generally upon scientific and educational problems."

51. Sargent, *Sketches,* 153.

52. Alla Foster, quoted in Wyman, "Reminiscences," 538. This contradicts her earlier remark in which she claimed that she hoped to enjoy the luxury of leisure in the afterlife.

53. One major exception was a two-year period, 1844–46, when Mott had contracted an illness she described as affecting her nervous system. Margaret Bacon suggests it was encephalitis. During that period she did very little, including reading and keeping up with her correspondence. See Lucretia Mott to Elisabeth Pease, 28 Apr. 1846, FHL.

54. Lucretia Mott to Martha Coffin Wright, 9 Feb. 1856, Garrison Family papers, SMTH.

55. Lucretia Mott to Richard Webb, 10 Sept. 1848, RBD/BPL.

56. Lucretia Mott to Phebe Post Willis, 10 Mar. 1835, UR.

57. Lucretia Mott to Martha Coffin Wright, 7 Sept. 1857, SMTH.

58. Lucretia Mott, undated fragment, FHL.

59. Lucretia Mott to Webbs, 14 May 1849, BPL.

60. Lucretia Mott, "Quarterly Meetings, No Ordinary Occasions," Sermon delivered at Cherry Street Meeting, Philadelphia, 6 Nov. 1849, in Greene, *Lucretia Mott: Speeches and Sermons,* 135.

61. Lucretia Mott, "We Have Food While Others Starve," Sermon delivered at Cherry Street Meeting, Philadelphia, 31 Mar. 1850, in Greene, *Lucretia Mott: Speeches and Sermons,* 184.

62. Cromwell's biography is the best and most straightforward account of Mott's life. Margaret Bacon's *Valiant Friend : The Life of Lucretia Mott* is also very good. For an example of one of the most uncritical and celebratory biographies, see Lloyd Custer Mayhew Hare's work, *The Greatest American Woman, Lucretia Mott.* (New York: American Historical Society, 1937).

63. Lucretia Mott to Susan B. Anthony, 6 June 1869, FHL.

64. Bacon, *Valiant Friend,* 197.

65. Lucretia Mott, "Worship in Spirit and in Truth," Greene, *Lucretia Mott: Speeches and Sermons,* 275–76.

66. Lucretia Mott to Martha Coffin Wright, 4 Nov. 1868, Garrison Family Papers, SMTH. Thomas, also called Didymus, was the Doubting Thomas who refused to believe in Christ's wound for himself. For brief, general remarks indicating Mott's support for spiritualism, see Sargent, *Sketches,* 22–23.

67. Wendell Phillips to Elizabeth Pease Nichol, 9 Mar. 1851, RBD/BPL, quoted in Bacon, *Valiant Friend,* 137.

68. Lucretia Mott to Adeline Roberts, 5 July 1852, Salem Anti-Slavery Society papers, Peabody and Essex Museum, Salem, Mass.

69. Lucretia Mott to Webbs, 5 Apr. 1852, BPL, quoted in Bacon, *Valiant Friend,* 147.

70. Lucretia Mott, quoted in the *Free Religious Index,* 25 Nov. 1880.

71. Bacon, *Valiant Friend,* 188.

72. Ibid., 229.

CONCLUSION: "THE GOSPEL OF TRUTH AND FREEDOM"

1. The quotation in the title is taken from a letter dated 31 May 1861, from Lucretia Mott to James Miller McKim, introducing Christopher Hussey to McKim, in which she expressed the hope that "'if way opens' for free conversation between you, thy own experience, out of the darkness of orthodoxy, into the 'marvellous light' of the Gospel of truth and freedom may encourage him in this hour of his trial" (Misc. Letters, CRNL).

2. Holley, *A Life for Liberty,* 197. Chadwick does not identify the source of these remarks but it was probably Caroline Putnam.

3. Sarah Parker Remond to Abby Kelley Foster, 21 Dec. 1858, AAS.

4. Reprinted in the *Free Religious Index,* 25 Nov. 1880. Dickinson apparently had a rather different outlook on her lecturing than her forerunners, being concerned to make a profit out of her work. She wrote to Abby Kelley Foster, asking "What plan must I adopt to speak—to make myself heard, and to be paid? . . . I should like to speak in Worcester, could I do it—that is would I have an audience, and would it pay" (21 Oct. 1862, AAS). This was an interesting query to put to Kelley Foster, who, embracing the Quaker free ministry tradition, preferred to "work for nothing and trust consequences" (Abby Kelley to Maria Weston Chapman, 17 July 1845, BPL). Upon Stephen Foster's urging, Kelly Foster reluctantly began to accept a salary after their marriage.

5. The correspondence between the Grimkés and their nephews, Archibald H. Grimké and Francis J. Grimké, is maintained at the Moorland-Spingarn Research Center at Howard University. Archibald Grimké graduated from Harvard Law School and was an important black leader; Francis Grimké (who married Charlotte Forten) served as pastor of the 15th Street Presbyterian Church in Washington, D.C., for almost fifty years (Lerner, *Grimké Sisters,* 364–65.)

6. According to Nancy Burkett (*Abby Kelley Foster and Stephen S. Foster* [Worcester: Worcester Bicentennial Commission, 1976]), Thomas Higginson, author of "Cheerful Yesterdays," states that the Foster home was also an Underground Railroad station.

7. Abby Kelley Foster to Betsy Mix Cowles, 28 Jan. 1846, OBRLN. Original in Betsy Mix Cowles collection, Kent State University.

8. Sarah Grimké to Augustus Wattles, 1 June [1856], CLMT.

9. Ibid.; Sarah Grimké to Harriot Kezia Hunt, 31 May [1854], CLMT.

10. Letter to Harriot Kezia Hunt, 24 Apr. [1853], CLMT.

11. Lucretia Mott, "Discourse on Woman," Greene, *Lucretia Mott: Speeches and Sermons,* 147.

12. Lucretia Mott, quoted in Margaret H. Bacon, "Lucretia Mott: Holy Obedience and Human Liberation," paper read at the Symposium on Quaker Women, Guilford College, 16–18 Mar. 1978.

13. Ibid.

14. Sarah Grimké to Preston Day, 19 Jan. 1869, CLMT.

15. Lucretia Mott, "To Speak Out the Truth," Greene, *Lucretia Mott: Speeches and Sermons,* 57.

16. Abby Kelley to William Lloyd Garrison, 20 Oct. 1837, BPL.

17. Abby Kelley Foster to Stephen Foster, 28 Sept. 1847, AAS.

18. Abby Kelley to the Uxbridge Meeting of the Society of Friends, included with a letter from Kelley to William Lloyd Garrison, 30 Sept. 1841, BPL.

19. Sallie Holley to Mrs. Porter, 1 Sept. 1872, Holley, *A Life for Liberty,* 222.

20. Sarah Grimké to Gerrit Smith, 13 Mar. 1866, CLMT.

21. Angelina Grimké to Amos A. Phelps, 2 Sept. [1837?], BPL.

22. Lucretia Mott, "One Standard of Goodness and Truth," Greene, *Lucretia Mott: Speeches and Sermons,* 259.

APPENDIX

1. Colman, *Reminiscences,* 13.

2. *NAW* records Craft's death as having occurred in 1897; *BWA* lists her year of death as 1891.

3. Brown, *Mary Grew,* 39.

4. Ibid., 64, 67.

5. Sterling, *Ahead of Her Time,* 261.

6. See James Oliver Horton, "Freedom's Yoke: Gender Conversations among Antebellum Free Blacks," *Feminist Studies* 12, no. 1 (spring 1986): 51–76; Emma Jones Lapsansky, "Feminism, Freedom, and Community: Charlotte Forten and Women Activists in Nineteenth-Century Philadelphia," *Pennsylvania Magazine of History and Biography* 113, no. 1 (Jan. 1989): 3–19.

7. Shirley Yee, *Black Women Abolitionists: A Study in Activism, 1828–1860* (Knoxville: Univ. of Tennessee Press, 1992), 115.

8. Stewart, "An Address Delivered at the African Masonic Hall," 27 Feb. 1833, quoted from Marilyn Richardson, *Stewart,* 57.

Bibliography

MANUSCRIPT COLLECTIONS

American Antiquarian Society, Worcester, Massachusetts
    Abby Kelley Foster Papers
    Gardner Family Papers
Boston Public Library, Boston, Massachusetts
    Antislavery Manuscripts
The Center for American History, University of Texas at Austin
    Sarah Moore Grimké Papers
Cornell University, Library, Division of Rare and Manuscript Collections,
        Ithaca, New York
    Fowler Wells Papers
    Florence Hazzard Papers
    Emily Howland Papers
    Miscellaneous Letters of Lucretia Mott
Friends Historical Library of Swarthmore College, Swarthmore, Pennsylvania
    Mott Family Papers
Haverford College Library, Quaker Collection, Haverford, Pennsylvania
    Allinson Family Papers
    Howland Papers
    Talcot Family Papers
Kent State University Libraries, Special Collections and Archives, Kent, Ohio
    Betsy Mix Cowles Papers
Library of Congress, Washington, D.C.
    Sarah M. Grimké Papers
    Lucretia Mott Papers
    National American Woman Suffrage Association Papers
    Elizabeth Cady Stanton Papers
    Theodore Weld Papers

Massachusetts Historical Society, Boston, Massachusetts
    George Bancroft Papers
    William E. Channing Papers
    Samuel May Papers
    Norcross Papers
Moorland-Spingarn Research Center, Manuscript Division, Howard
    University, Washington, D.C.
    Archibald H. Grimké Papers
Oberlin College, Oberlin, Ohio
    Papers of Robert S. Fletcher
Phillips Library, Peabody Essex Museum, Salem, Massachusetts
    Salem Anti-Slavery Society Papers
Schlesinger Library, Radcliffe College, Cambridge, Massachusetts
    Abby Kelley Foster Papers
    Alma Lutz Papers
    Lucretia Mott Papers
    Miscellaneous Letters
    Poor Family Papers
    Women's Rights Papers
    Theodore Weld Papers
Smith College, Sophia Smith Collection, Northampton, Massachusetts
    Garrison Family Papers
Syracuse University Library, Department of Special Collections, Syracuse,
    New York
    Gerrit Smith Papers
University of Massachusetts at Amherst, Special Collections and Archives,
    W. E. B. DuBois Library
    Hudson Family Papers, M5332
University of Rochester Library, Department of Rare Books and Special
    Collections, Rochester, New York
    Abby Kelley Foster Papers
    Samuel Drummond Porter Papers
    Isaac and Amy Post Papers
William L. Clements Library, University of Michigan, Ann Arbor, Michigan
    Weld and Grimké Papers
Worcester Historical Museum, Worcester, Massachusetts
    Kelley and Foster Papers

NEWSPAPERS AND JOURNALS

Free Religious Index
The Liberator
National Anti-Slavery Standard
The Woman's Journal

PUBLISHED BOOKS, ARTICLES, AND REPORTS

Abzug, Robert H. *Cosmos Crumbling: American Reform and the Religious Imagination.* New York: Oxford Univ. Press, 1994.

Albanese, Catherine L. *America Religions and Religion.* Belmont, Cal.: Wadsworth Publishing Company, 1981.

————, ed. *The Spirituality of the American Transcendentalists.* Macon, Ga.: Mercer Univ. Press, 1988.

Allen, Gay Wilson. *Waldo Emerson: A Biography.* New York: Viking Press, 1981.

Andolsen, Barbara Hilkert, Christine E. Gudorf, and Mary D. Pellauer, eds. *Women's Consciousness, Women's Conscience.* Minneapolis: Winston Press, 1985.

Andrews, William L. *Sisters of the Spirit: Three Black Women's Autobiographies of the Nineteenth Century.* Bloomington: Indiana Univ. Press, 1986.

Anti-Slavery Convention of American Women. *Proceedings of the Anti-Slavery Convention of American Women, Held in the City of New York, May 9th, 10th, 11th, and 12th, 1837.* New York: William S. Dorr, 1837.

Anti-Slavery Convention of American Women. *Proceedings of the Anti-Slavery Convention of American Women, Held in Philadelphia, May 15th, 16th, 17th, and 18th, 1838.* Philadelphia: Merrihew and Gunn, 1838.

Anti-Slavery Convention of American Women. *Proceedings of the Third Anti-Slavery Convention of American Women, Held in Philadelphia, May 1st, 2d and 3d, 1839.* Philadelphia: Merrihew and Thompson, 1839.

Aptheker, Bettina. *Tapestries of Life: Women's Work, Women's Consciousness, and the Meaning of Daily Experience.* Amherst: Univ. of Massachusetts Press, 1989.

Bacon, Margaret. *I Speak for My Slave Sister: The Life of Abby Kelley Foster.* New York: Thomas Y. Crowell, 1974.

————. *Valiant Friend: The Life of Lucretia Mott.* New York: Walker, 1980.

Barnes, Gilbert Hobbs. *The Antislavery Impulse, 1830–1844.* 1933. Reprint, Gloucester, Mass.: Peter Smith, 1957.

Barnes, Gilbert H., and Dwight L. Dumond, eds. *Letters of Theodore Dwight Weld, Angelina Grimké Weld and Sarah Grimké 1822–1844.* 2 vols. Gloucester, Mass.: Peter Smith, 1965.

Bartlett, Elizabeth Ann. *Liberty, Equality, Sorority. The Origins and Interpretation of American Feminist Thought: Frances Wright, Sarah Grimké, and Margaret Fuller.* Brooklyn, New York: Carlson Publishing, 1994.

Bartlett, Irving H. *Wendell and Ann Phillips: The Community of Reform, 1840–1880.* New York: W. W. Norton, 1979.

Beecher, Catharine E. *An Essay on Slavery and Abolitionism, with Reference to the Duty of American Females, Addressed to Miss A. D. Grimké.* Boston: Perkins and Marvin, 1837.

Beecher, Lyman. "The Faith Once Delivered to the Saints. A Sermon Delivered at Worcester, Mass., October 15, 1823, at the Ordination of the Rev. Loammi Ives Hoadly, to the Pastoral Office over the Calvinistic Church and Society in That Place." In *Sermons Delivered on Various Occasions.* Boston, 1828.

Berg, Barbara. *The Remembered Gate: Origins of American Feminism.* New York: Oxford Univ. Press, 1978.

Bethune, Rev. George W., ed. *Memoirs of Mrs. Joanna Bethune.* New York: Harper and Brothers, Publishers, 1863.

Birney, Catherine H. *The Grimké Sisters: Sarah and Angelina Grimké, The First American Women Advocates of Abolition and Women's Rights.* 1885. Reprint, Westport, Conn.: Greenwood Press, 1969.

Blackwell, Alice Stone. *Lucy Stone.* 1930. Reprint, New York: Kraus Reprint Company, 1971.

Blassingame, John W., ed. *Slave Testimony: Two Centuries of Letters, Speeches, Interviews, and Autobiographies.* Baton Rouge: Louisiana State Univ. Press, 1977.

Bonomi, Patricia. *Under the Cope of Heaven: Religion, Society, and Politics in Colonial America.* New York: Oxford Univ. Press, 1986.

Boston Female Anti-Slavery Society. *Report of the Boston Female Anti-Slavery Society; with a Concise Statement of Events, Previous and subsequent to the Annual Meeting of 1835.* 2nd ed. Boston: Boston Female Anti-Slavery Society, 1836.

Boston Female Anti-Slavery Society. *Annual Report of the Boston Female Anti-Slavery Society, with a Sketch of the Obstacles thrown in the way of Emancipation by certain Clerical Abolitionists and Advocates for the subjection of Woman, in 1837.* Boston: Isaac Knapp, 1837.

Braude, Ann. *Radical Spirits: Spiritualism and Women's Rights in Nineteenth-Century America.* Boston: Beacon Press, 1989.

Brown, Ira. *Mary Grew, Abolitionist and Feminist, 1813–1896.* Selinsgrove, Penn.: Susquehanna Univ. Press, 1991.

Bruce, Dickson. *And They All Sang Hallelujah: Plain-Folk Camp-Meeting Religion, 1800–1845.* Knoxville: Univ. of Tennessee Press, 1974.

Burkett, Nancy Hall. *Abby Kelley Foster and Stephen S. Foster*. Worcester, Mass.: Worcester Bicentennial Commission, 1976.

Butler, Jon. *Awash in a Sea of Faith: Christianizing the American People*. Cambridge: Harvard Univ. Press, 1990.

Carter, Stephen L. *The Culture of Disbelief: How American Law and Politics Trivialize Religious Devotion*. New York: BasicBooks, 1993.

Cassara, Ernest. *Hosea Ballou. The Challenge to Orthodoxy*. Boston: Universalist Historical Society and Beacon Press, 1961.

Cazden, Elizabeth. *Antoinette Brown Blackwell: A Biography*. Old Westbury, N. Y.: Feminist Press, 1983.

Ceplair, Larry, ed. *The Public Years of Sarah and Angelina Grimké: Selected Writings, 1835–1839*. New York: Columbia Univ. Press, 1989.

Chadwick, John White. *Theodore Parker: Preacher and Reformer*. 1900. Reprint, St. Clair Shores, Mich.: Scholarly Press, 1971.

Chambers-Schiller, Lee. *Liberty, a Better Husband: Single Women in America: The Generations of 1780–1840*. New Haven: Yale Univ. Press, 1984.

———. "The Single Woman Reformer: Conflicts Between Family and Vocation, 1830–1860." *Frontiers* 3, no.3 (1978): 41–48.

Chester, Giraud. *Embattled Maiden: The Life of Anna Dickinson*. New York: Putnam, 1951.

Christ, Carol P., and Judith Plaskow. *Womanspirit Rising: A Feminist Reader in Religion*. 2nd ed. New York: HarperSan Francisco, 1992.

Cogan, Frances. *All-American Girl: The Ideal of Real Womanhood in Mid-Nineteenth Century America*. Athens: Univ. of Georgia Press, 1989.

Colman, Lucy N. *Reminiscences*. Buffalo, New York: H. L. Green, 1891.

Conrad, Susan Phinney. *Perish the Thought: Intellectual Women in Romantic America, 1830–1860*. New York: Oxford Univ. Press, 1976.

Cott, Nancy F. *The Bonds of Womanhood: "Woman's Sphere" in New England, 1780–1835*. New Haven: Yale Univ. Press, 1977.

———, ed. *The Root of Bitterness: Documents of the Social History of American Women*. New York, E. P. Dutton, 1972.

———. "Young Women in the Second Great Awakening in New England." *Feminist Studies* 3 (1975): 15–29.

Cromwell, Otelia. *Lucretia Mott*. Cambridge: Harvard Univ. Press, 1958.

Daly, Mary. *Beyond God the Father*. Boston: Beacon Press, 1973.

Degler, Carl N. *At Odds: Women and the Family in America from the Revolution to the Present*. New York: Oxford Univ. Press, 1980.

Dillon, Merton L. *The Abolitionists: The Growth of a Dissenting Minority*. De Kalb: Northern Illinois Univ. Press, 1974.

Doan, Ruth Alden. *The Miller Heresy, Millennialism, and American Culture.* Philadelphia: Temple Univ. Press, 1987.

Douglas, Ann. *The Feminization of American Culture.* New York: Avon Books, 1977.

Duberman, Martin, ed. *The Antislavery Vanguard: New Essays on the Abolitionists.* Princeton: Princeton Univ. Press, 1965.

DuBois, Ellen Carol. *Elizabeth Cady Stanton, Susan B. Anthony: Correspondence, Writings, Speeches.* New York: Schocken Books, 1981.

———. "Struggling into Existence: The Feminism of Sarah and Angelina Grimké." *Women: A Journal of Liberation* (spring 1970): 4–11.

Epstein, Barbara Leslie. *The Politics of Domesticity: Women, Evangelism and Temperance in Nineteenth-Century America.* Middletown, Conn.: Wesleyan Univ. Press, 1981.

Farrar, Eliza W. R. *The Young Lady's Friend.* 1836. Reprint, New York: Arno Press, 1974.

Filler, Louis. *The Crusade Against Slavery 1830–1860.* New York: Harper and Row, 1960.

Fletcher, Robert Samuel. *A History of Oberlin College: From Its Foundation Through the Civil War.* 2 vols. Chicago: R. R. Donnelley and Sons, 1943.

Flexner, Eleanor. *Century of Struggle.* New York: Atheneum, 1974.

Friedman, Lawrence J. *Gregarious Saints: Self and Community in American Abolitionism, 1830–1870.* New York: Cambridge Univ. Press, 1982.

Frost, J. William, ed. *The Quaker Origins of Antislavery.* Norwood, Penn.: Norwood Editions, 1980.

Gaustad, Edwin Scott. *A Religious History of America.* Rev. ed. San Francisco: HarperSanFrancisco, 1990.

Geary, Linda L. *Balanced in the Wind: A Biography of Betsey Mix Cowles.* Cranbury, N. J.: Associated Univ. Presses, 1989.

George, Carol. *Segregated Sabbaths: Richard Allen and the Emergence of Independent Black Churches, 1760–1840.* New York: Oxford Univ. Press, 1973.

———. "Widening the Circle: The Black Church and the Abolitionist Crusade, 1830–1860." In *Antislavery Reconsidered: New Perspectives on the Abolitionists,* edited by Lewis Perry and Michael Fellman, 75–95. Louisiana State Univ. Press, 1979.

Gillespie, Joanna Bowen. "'The Clear Leadings of Providence': Pious Memoirs and the Problems of Self-Realization for Women in the Early Nineteenth Century." *Journal of the Early Republic* 5 (summer 1985): 197–221.

Ginzberg, Lori D. "'Moral Suasion is Moral Balderdash': Women, Politics, and Social Activism in the 1850s." *Journal of American History* 73 (Dec. 1986): 601–22.

———. *Women and the Work of Benevolence: Morality, Politics, and Class in the Nineteenth-Century United States*. New Haven: Yale Univ. Press, 1990.

Gold, Ellen Reid. "The Grimké Sisters and the Emergence of the Woman's Rights Movement." *Southern Speech Communication Journal* 46, no. 4 (1981): 341–360.

Graham, Maureen. *Women of Power and Presence: The Spiritual Formation of Four Quaker Women Ministers*. Wallingford, Penn.: Pendle Hill Publications, 1990.

Greaves, Richard L, ed. *Triumph over Silence: Women in Protestant History*. Westport, Conn.: Greenwood Press, 1985.

Green, Ashbel. "The Christian Duty of Christian Women. A Discourse Delivered in the Church of Princeton, New Jersey, August 23rd, 1825, before the Princeton Female Society, For the Support of a Female School in India." *Christian Advocate* 4 (1828). In *Women and Religion in America*. Vol. 1, *The Nineteenth Century*, edited by Rosemary Radford Ruether and Rosemary Skinner Keller. San Francisco: Harper and Row, 1981.

Greene, Dana, ed. *Lucretia Mott: Her Complete Speeches and Sermons*. New York: Edward Mellen Press, 1980.

———. "Quaker Feminism: The Case of Lucretia Mott." *Pennsylvania History* 48, no. 2 (1981): 143–154.

Grimké, Angelina E. *Appeal to the Christian Women of the South*. New York: American Anti-Slavery Society, 1836.

———. *Letter from Angelina Grimké Weld, to the Woman's Rights Convention*. Syracuse: Masters' print, 1852.

———. *Letters to Catherine E. Beecher, in Reply to an Essay on Slavery and Abolitionism, Addressed to A. E. Grimké*. Revised by the Author. Boston: Isaac Knapp, 1838.

Grimké, Sarah M. *An Epistle to the Clergy of the Southern States*. New York: American Anti-Slavery Society, 1836.

———. *Letters on the Equality of the Sexes and the Condition of Woman, addressed to Mary S. Parker, President of the Boston Female Anti-Slavery Society*. Boston: Isaac Knapp, 1838.

Gutiérrez, Gustavo. *A Theology of Liberation*. Translated and edited by Sister Caridad Inda and John Eagleson. Maryknoll, New York: Orbis Books, 1973.

Hall, David D. *Worlds of Wonder, Days of Judgment: Popular Religious Belief in Early New England*. Cambridge: Harvard Univ. Press, 1990.

Hallowell, Anna Davis, ed. *James and Lucretia Mott: Life and Letters*. Boston: Houghton, Mifflin, 1884.

Hansen, Debra Gold. *Strained Sisterhood: Gender and Class in the Boston Female Anti-Slavery Society*. Amherst, Mass.: Univ. of Massachusetts Press, 1993.

Hare, Lloyd Custer Mayhew. *The Greatest American Woman, Lucretia Mott*. New York: American Historical Society, 1937.

Hatch, Nathan. *The Democratization of American Christianity*. New Haven: Yale Univ. Press, 1989.

Hersh, Blanche G. *The Slavery of Sex: Feminist-Abolitionists in America*. Urbana: Univ. of Illinois Press, 1978.

———. "To Make the World Better: Protestant Women in the Abolitionist Movement." In *Triumph over Silence: Women in Protestant History*, edited by Richard L. Greaves. Westport, Conn.: Greenwood Press, 1985.

———. "The 'True Woman' and the 'New Woman' in Nineteenth-Century America: Feminist-Abolitionists and a New Concept of True Womanhood." *Maryland History* 9, no.2 (1978): 27–38.

Hewitt, Nancy. *Women's Activism and Social Change: Rochester, New York, 1822–1872*. Ithaca: Cornell Univ. Press, 1984.

Hine, Darlene Clark, ed. *Black Women's History*. 2 vols. Brooklyn: Carlson Publishing, 1990.

Hine, Darlene Clark, Elsa Barkley Brown, and Rosalyn Terborg-Penn, eds. *Black Women in America. An Historical Encyclopedia*. 2 vols. Bloomington: Indiana Univ. Press, 1993.

Holley, Sallie. *A Life for Liberty, Antislavery and Other Letters of Sallie Holley*. Edited by John White Chadwick. New York: G. P. Putnam's Sons, 1899. Reprint: New York, Negro Universities Press, 1969.

Horton, James Oliver. "Freedom's Yoke: Gender Conventions among Antebellum Free Blacks." *Feminist Studies* 12, no. 1 (Spring 1986): 51–76.

Horton, James Oliver, and Lois E. Horton. "Black Theology and Historical Necessity." In *Transforming Faith: The Sacred and the Secular in Modern American History*, 25–37. New York: Greenwood Press, 1989.

Hudson, Winthrop S. *Religion in America*. 3rd ed. New York: Charles Scribner's Sons, 1981.

Hyde, Rev. Charles. *Memoir of Caroline Hyde*. New York: American Tract Society, 1836.

Ingle, H. Larry. *Quakers in Conflict: The Hicksite Reformation*. Knoxville: Univ. of Tennessee Press, 1986.

Irie, Yukio. *Emerson and Quakerism*. Tokyo: Kenkyusha, 1967.

James, Edward T., and Janet Wilson James, eds. *Notable American Women. A Biographical Dictionary*. 3 vols. Cambridge: The Belknap Press of Harvard Univ. Press, 1971.

James, William. *The Varieties of Religious Experience*. Edited by Martin E. Marty. New York: Penguin Books, 1982.

Japp, Phyllis M. "Esther or Isaiah: The Abolitionist-Feminist Rhetoric of Angelina Grimké." *Quarterly Journal of Speech* 71, no. 3 (1985): 335–48.

Juster, Susan. *Disorderly Women: Sexual Politics and Evangelicalism in Revolutionary New England.* Ithaca: Cornell Univ. Press, 1995.

———. "'In a Different Voice': Male and Female Narratives of Religious Conversion in Post-Revolutionary America." *American Quarterly* 41, no. 1 (Mar. 1989): 34–62.

Kerber, Linda. "Separate Spheres, Female Worlds, Woman's Place: The Rhetoric of Women's History." *Journal of American History* 75 (June 1988): 9–39.

Kerr, Andrea Moore. *Lucy Stone.* New Brunswick, N. J.: Rutgers Univ. Press, 1992.

Kessler-Harris, Alice. *Out to Work: A History of Wage-Earning Women in the United States.* New York: Oxford University Press, 1982.

———. "Women and Individualism in American History." *Massachusetts Review* 30 (winter 1987): 589–609.

Kirkpatrick, Frank G. "From Shackles to Liberation: Religion, the Grimké Sisters and Dissent." In *Women, Religion, and Social Change,* edited by Yvonne Yasbeck Haddad and Ellison Banks Findly. Albany: State Univ. of New York Press, 1985.

Kraditor, Aileen. *Means and Ends in American Abolitionism: Garrison and His Critics on Strategy and Tactics, 1834–1850.* New York: Pantheon Books, 1967.

Lapsansky, Emma Jones. "Feminism, Freedom, and Community: Charlotte Forten and Women Activists in Nineteenth-Century Philadelphia." *Pennsylvania Magazine of History and Biography* 113 (Jan. 1989): 3–19.

———. "'Since They Got Those Separate Churches': Afro-Americans and Racism in Jacksonian Philadelphia." *American Quarterly* 32 (spring 1980): 54–78.

Lasser, Carol. "'Let Us Be Sisters Forever': The Sororal Model of Nineteenth-Century Female Friendship." *Signs* (autumn 1988): 158–181.

Lasser, Carol, and Marlene Deahl Merrill, eds. *Friends and Sisters: Letters Between Lucy Stone and Antoinette Brown Blackwell, 1846–93.* Urbana: Univ. of Illinois Press, 1987.

Lerner, Gerda. *The Creation of Feminist Consciousness.* New York: Oxford Univ. Press, 1993.

———. *The Creation of Patriarchy.* New York: Oxford Univ. Press, 1986.

———. *The Feminist Thought of Sarah Grimké.* New York: Oxford Univ. Press, 1998.

———. *The Grimké Sisters from South Carolina: Pioneers for Woman's Rights and Abolition.* New York: Schocken Books, 1971.

———. "The Grimké Sisters and the Struggle Against Race Prejudice." *Journal of Negro History* 48, no. 4 (1963): 277–91.

———. "The Lady and the Mill Girl: Changes in the Status of Women in the Age of Jackson, 1800–1840." In *A Heritage of Her Own: Toward a New Social History of American Women,* 182–96. New York: Simon and Schuster, 1979.

———. *The Woman in American History.* Menlo Park, Cal.: Addison-Wesley, 1971.

Litwack, Leon F. "The Emancipation of the Negro Abolitionist." In *The Antislavery*

Vanguard: New Essays on the Abolitionists, edited by Martin Duberman, 137–55. Princeton: Princeton Univ. Press, 1965.

Litwack, Leon, and August Meier, eds. *Black Leaders of the Nineteenth Century.* Urbana: Univ. of Illinois Press, 1988.

Loewenberg, Bert, and Ruth Bogin. *Black Women in Nineteenth-Century American Life.* University Park: Pennsylvania State Univ. Press, 1976.

Lumpkin, Katherine DuPre. *The Emancipation of Angelina Grimké.* Chapel Hill: Univ. of North Carolina Press, 1974.

Lutz, Alma. *Crusade for Freedom: Women of the Antislavery Movement.* Boston: Beacon Press, 1968.

Mabee, Carleton. *Sojourner Truth: Slave, Prophet, Legend.* New York: New York Univ. Press, 1993.

MacKinnon, Catherine A. *Toward a Feminist Theory of the State.* Cambridge: Harvard Univ. Press, 1989.

Magdol, Edward. *The Antislavery Rank and File: A Social Profile of the Abolitionists' Constituency.* New York: Greenwood Press, 1986.

Maniha, John K., and Barbara B. Maniha. "A Comparison of Psychohistorical Differences among Some Female Religious and Secular Leaders." *Journal of Psychohistory* 5, no. 4 (1978): 523–49.

Manning, Beverley. *Index to American Women Speakers, 1828–1978.* Metuchen, N. J.: Scarecrow Press, 1980.

Mathisen, Robert R., ed. *The Role of Religion in American Life.* Washington, D.C.: Univ. Press of America, 1982.

May, Samuel J. *Some Recollections of Our Antislavery Conflict.* 1869. Reprint, New York: Arno Press, 1968.

McKivigan, John. *The War Against Proslavery Religion: Abolitionism and the Northern Churches, 1830–1865.* Ithaca: Cornell Univ. Press, 1984.

Melder, Keith. "Abby Kelley and the Process of Liberation." In *The Abolitionist Sisterhood: Women's Political Culture in Antebellum America,* edited by Jean Fagan Yellin and John C. Van Horne. Ithaca: Cornell Univ. Press, 1994.

———. *The Beginnings of Sisterhood: The American Woman's Rights Movement, 1800–1850.* New York: Schocken Books, 1977.

Mendelsohn, Jack. *Channing: The Reluctant Radical.* Boston: Little, Brown, 1971.

Merrill, Walter, ed. *The Letters of William Lloyd Garrison.* vol. 1. *I Will Be Heard! 1822–1835.* Cambridge: Harvard Univ. Press, 1971.

Midgley, Clare. *Women Against Slavery: The British Campaigns, 1780–1870.* New York: Routledge, 1992.

Moore, R. Laurence. *Religious Outsiders and the Making of Americans.* New York: Oxford Univ. Press, 1986.

Moseley, James G. *A Cultural History of Religion in America*. Westport, Conn.: Greenwood Press, 1981.

Mott, James. *Three Months in Great Britain*. Philadelphia: James Miller McKim, 1841.

O'Connor, Lillian. *Pioneer Women Orators: Rhetoric in the Ante-Bellum Reform Movement*. New York: Columbia Univ. Press, 1954.

Olmstead, Clifton E. *History of Religion in the United States*. Englewood Cliffs, N. J.: Prentice-Hall, 1960.

Painter, Nell Irvin. *Sojourner Truth: A Life, A Symbol*. New York: W. W. Norton, 1996.

Papachristou, Judith. *Women Together*. New York: Alfred A. Knopf, 1976.

Pease, Jane H., and William Pease. *They Who Would Be Free: Blacks' Search for Freedom, 1830–1861*. New York: Atheneum, 1974.

Perry, Lewis. *Childhood, Marriage, and Reform: Henry Clarke Wright, 1797–1870*. Chicago: Univ. of Chicago Press, 1980.

————. *Radical Abolitionism: Anarchy and the Government of God in Antislavery Thought*. Ithaca: Cornell Univ. Press, 1973.

Perry, Lewis, and Michael Fellman, eds. *Antislavery Reconsidered: New Perspectives on the Abolitionists*. Baton Rouge: Louisiana State Univ. Press, 1979.

Persons, Stow. *Free Religion: An American Faith*. New Haven: Yale Univ. Press, 1947.

Peterson, Carla. *"Doers of the Word": African-American Women Speakers and Writers in the North (1830–1880)*. New York: Oxford Univ. Press, 1995.

Porterfield, Amanda. *Feminine Spirituality in America: From Sarah Edwards to Martha Graham*. Philadelphia: Temple Univ. Press, 1980.

Potter, W. J. *The Free Religious Association: Its Twenty-Five Years and Their Meaning*. Boston: n.p., 1892.

Quarles, Benjamin. *Black Abolitionists*. New York: Oxford Univ. Press, 1967.

Raboteau, Albert J. *Slave Religion: The "Invisible Institution" in the Antebellum South*. New York: Oxford Univ. Press, 1978.

Richardson, Marilyn, ed. *Maria W. Stewart, America's First Black Woman Political Writer: Essays and Speeches*. Bloomington: Indiana Univ. Press, 1987.

Ripley, C. Peter, ed. *The Black Abolitionist Papers*. Vols. 3–5. Chapel Hill: The Univ. of North Carolina Press, 1991.

Robinson, David. *Apostle of Culture: Emerson as Preacher and Lecturer*. Philadelphia: Univ. of Pennsylvania Press, 1982.

Rose, Willie Lee. *Slavery and Freedom*. New York: Oxford Univ. Press, 1982.

Ruether, Rosemary Radford. *Sexism and God-Talk: Toward a Feminist Theology*. Boston: Beacon Press, 1983.

————. "The Subordination and Liberation of Women in Christian Theology: Saint Paul and Sarah Grimké." *Soundings* 61, no. 2 (1978): 168–81.

Ruether, Rosemary Radford, and Rosemary Skinner Keller, eds. *Women and Religion in America*. Vol. 1, *The Nineteenth Century*. San Francisco: Harper and Row, 1981.

———. *Women and Religion in America*. Vol. 2, *The Colonial and Revolutionary Periods*. San Francisco: Harper and Row, 1983.

Ruether, Rosemary Radford, and Eleanor McLaughlin, eds. *Women of Spirit: Female Leadership in the Jewish and Christian Traditions*. New York: Simon and Schuster, 1979.

Ryan, Mary P. "The Power of Women's Networks: A Case Study of Female Moral Reform in Antebellum America." *Feminist Studies* 5, no. 1 (1979): 66–86.

———. *Womanhood in America: From Colonial Times to the Present*. 3rd ed. New York: Franklin Watts, 1983.

Sargent, Mrs. John T. (Mary Elizabeth). *Sketches and Reminiscences of The Radical Club of Chestnut Street, Boston*. Boston: James R. Osgood, 1880.

Segundo, Juan Luis. *The Liberation of Theology*. Trans. John Drury. Maryknoll: Orbis Books, 1976.

Silverman, Jason. "Mary Ann Shadd and the Search for Equality." In *Black Leaders of the Nineteenth Century*, edited by Leon Litwack and August Meier, 87–100. Urbana: Univ. of Illinois Press, 1988.

Sklar, Katherine Kish. *Catharine Beecher: A Study in American Domesticity*. New York: W. W. Norton, 1976.

Smith, Dorothy E. *The Everyday World as Problematic: A Feminist Sociology*. Boston: Northeastern Univ. Press, 1987.

Smith-Rosenberg, Carroll. "The Female World of Love and Ritual." In *Disorderly Conduct: Visions of Gender in Victorian America*. New York: Oxford Univ. Press, 1986. Originally published in *Signs: Journal of Women in Culture and Society* 1(1) (1975).

Snay, Mitchell. *Gospel of Disunion: Religion and Separatism in the Antebellum South*. New York: Cambridge Univ. Press, 1993.

Soderlund, Jean R. *Quakers and Slavery: A Divided Spirit*. Princeton: Princeton Univ. Press, 1985.

Stanton, Elizabeth Cady, Susan B. Anthony, and Matilda Joslyn Gage. *History of Woman Suffrage*. 2 vols. New York: Fowler and Wells, 1881.

Sterling, Dorothy. *Ahead of Her Time: Abby Kelley and The Politics of Antislavery*. New York: W. W. Norton, 1991.

———. *Lucretia Mott, Gentle Warrior*. Garden City, New York: Doubleday, 1964.

Stewart, Maria. *Meditations from the Pen of Mrs. Maria W. Stewart*. 1832. Reprinted, Washington, by author, 1879.

Stone, Lucy. *Loving Warriors: Selected Letters of Lucy Stone and Henry B. Blackwell*. Edited by Leslie Wheeler. New York: Dial Press, 1981.

Swift, David E. *Black Prophets of Justice: Activist Clergy Before the Civil War.* Baton Rouge: Louisiana State Univ. Press, 1989.

Tanner, Leslie B., comp. and ed. *Voices from Women's Liberation.* New York: Signet, 1970.

Taves, Ann, ed. *Religion and Domestic Violence in Early New England: The Memoirs of Abigail Abbot Bailey.* Bloomington: Indiana Univ. Press, 1989.

Thayer, Caroline Matilda. *Religion Recommended to Youth in a Series of Letters Addressed to a Young Lady.* 2nd ed. New York: J. Soule and T. Mason, 1818.

Thomas, Cordelia. *The Sheaf: The Work of God in the Soul; as Illustrated in the Personal Experience of Mrs. Cordelia Thomas.* Boston: Henry V. Degen, 1852.

Tolles, Frederick B. *Slavery and "The Woman Question," Lucretia Mott's Diary of Her Visit to Great Britain to Attend the World's Antislavery Convention of 1840.* Haverford, Pa.: Friends Historical Association, 1952.

Tyler, Alice Felt. *Freedom's Ferment: Phases of American Social History to 1860.* Minneapolis: Univ. of Minnesota Press, 1944.

Venet, Wendy Hamand. *Neither Ballots nor Bullets: Women Abolitionists and the Civil War.* Charlottesville: Univ. Press of Virginia, 1991.

Vielhaber, Mary E. "An Abandoned Speaking Career: Angelina Grimké." *Michigan Academician* 17, no. 1 (1984): 59–66.

Weisberger, Bernard, ed. *Abolitionism: Disrupter of the Democratic System or Agent of Progress?* Chicago: Rand McNally, 1963.

Weld, Theodore. *American Slavery As It Is: Testimony of a Thousand Witnesses.* 1839. Reprint, New York: Columbia Univ. Press, 1960.

Wellman, Judith. "Women and Radical Reform in Antebellum Upstate New York: A Profile of Grassroots Female Abolitionists." In *Clio Was a Woman: Studies in the History of American Women,* 113–27. Washington, D.C.: Howard Univ. Press, 1980.

Wells, Mary. *Memoir of Mrs. Joanna Turner, as Exemplified in Her Life, Death, and Spiritual Experience.* Baltimore: John Midwinter, 1830.

Welter, Barbara. "The Cult of True Womanhood." *American Quarterly* 18 (1966): 151–75.

———. "The Feminization of American Religion: 1800–1860." In *Clio's Consciousness Raised,* 137–57. New York: Octagon Books, 1976. Originally published in *Problems and Issues in American Social History,* ed. William O'Neill, 1974.

Whicher, Stephen E., ed. *Selections from Ralph Waldo Emerson.* Boston: Houghton Mifflin, 1957.

Williams, Peter. *Popular Religion in America: Symbolic Change and the Modernization Process in Historical Perspective.* Chicago: Univ. of Illinois, 1989.

Williman, William H. "The Grimké Sisters: Prophetic Pariahs." *South Carolina History Illustrated* 1, no. 2 (1970): 15–17, 56–58.

Woolman, John. *A Journal of the Life, Gospel Labors, and Christian Experiences of that Faithful Minister of Jesus and Christ, John Woolman, to which are added his last Epistles and Other Writings*. New York: Collins, 1845.

——. *Some Considerations on the Keeping of Negroes, 1754* and *Considerations on Keeping Negroes, 1762*. New York: Grossman Publishers, 1976.

Wyman, Lillie Buffum Chace. "Reminiscences of Two Abolitionists." *New England Magazine* (Jan. 1903): 536–50.

Yee, Shirley J. *Black Women Abolitionists: A Study in Activism, 1828–1860*. Knoxville: Univ. of Tennesee Press, 1992.

Yellin, Jean Fagan. *Women and Sisters: The Antislavery Feminists in American Culture.* New Haven: Yale Univ. Press, 1989.

Yellin, Jean Fagan, and John C. Van Horne, eds. *The Abolitionist Sisterhood: Women's Political Culture in Antebellum America*. Ithaca: Cornell Univ. Press, 1994.

UNPUBLISHED PAPERS, DISSERTATIONS, AND THESES

Bacon, Margaret H. "Lucretia Mott: Holy Obedience and Human Liberation." Paper presented at the Symposium on Quaker Women, Guilford College, 16–18 Mar. 1978.

Bartlett, Elizabeth Ann. "Liberty, Equality, Sorority: Origins and Interpretations of American Feminist Thought: Frances Wright, Margaret Fuller, and Sarah Grimké." Ph.D. diss., Univ. of Minnesota, 1981.

Bass, Dorothy C. "'The Best Hopes of the Sexes:' The Woman Question in Garrisonian Abolitionism." Ph.D. diss., Brown Univ., 1980.

Bruland, Esther Louise Byle. "Great Debates: Ethical Reasoning and Social Change in Antebellum America—The Exchange Between Angelina Grimké and Catherine Beecher." Ph.D diss., Drew Univ., 1990.

Clark, Elizabeth Battelle. "The Politics of God and the Woman's Vote: Religion in the American Suffrage Movement, 1848–1895." Ph.D diss., Princeton Univ., 1989.

Coleman, Willie Mae. "Keeping the Faith and Disturbing the Peace: Black Women from Anti-Slavery to Women's Suffrage." Ph.D. diss., Univ. of California at Irvine, 1982.

DeBlasio, D. M. "Her Own Society: The Life and Times of Betsy Mix Cowles, 1810–76." Ph.D. diss., Kent State Univ., 1980.

Fitzgerald, Maureen Anne. "Religion and Feminism in Elizabeth Cady Stanton's Life and Thought." M.A. Thesis, Univ. of Wisconsin-Madison, 1985.

Hansen, Karen. "Transcending the Public/Private Divide: The Local Dimension of Laborers' Lives, 1810–1860." Ph.D. diss., University of California at Berkeley, 1989.

Herbig, Katherine. "Friends for Freedom: The Lives and Careers of Sallie Holley and Caroline Putnam." Ph.D. diss., Claremont Graduate School, 1977.

Isenberg, Nancy Gale. "'Co-Equality of the Sexes': The Feminist Discourse of the Antebellum Women's Rights Movement in America." Ph.D. diss., Univ. of Wisconsin-Madison, 1990.

Lewis, Janice Sumler. "The Fortens of Philadelphia: An Afro-American Family and Nineteenth-Century Reform." Ph.D. diss., Georgetown Univ., 1978.

Pease, Jane H. "The Freshness of Fanaticism: Abby Kelley Foster: An Essay in Reform." Ph.D diss., Univ. of Rochester, 1969.

Soderlund, Jean R. "The Philadelphia Female Anti-Slavery Society: Priorities and Power." Paper presented at the Annual Meeting of the Organization of American Historians, 1991.

Williams, Carolyn. "The Philadelphia Female Anti-Slavery Society and the Conventions of Anti-Slavery Women: Women's Rights and African-American Rights in Antebellum America." Paper presented at the Annual Meeting of the Organization of American Historians, 1991.

_____. "Religion, Race, and Gender in Antebellum American Radicalism: The Philadelphia Female Anti-Slavery Society, 1833–1870." Ph.D diss., Univ. of California at Los Angeles, 1991.

Yoakum, Doris G. "An Historical Survey of the Public Speaking Activities of American Women, 1828–1860." Ph.D diss., Univ. of Southern California, 1935.

Index

Folk healing, 6

Fort Lee (N.J.), 49, 102, 124

Foster, Abby Kelley: abuse of, 53, 55; on afterlife, 155, 156; call to antislavery lecturing, 36–38, 49; on character of abolitionists, 93; defending conduct, 153–55; and domesticity, 125, 150–51; and father's death, 36; on comeouterism, 96–97; early years of, 35–38; first public remarks by, 37; as a Garrisonian, 151, 153–54; and Grimké/Welds, 36, 47–50, 66, 129; and Holley, 47, 52, 72–73, 143, 151; later years of, 150–56, 162–64, 166–67; lecturing of, 38, 50–51; marriage of, 150–51; as mother, 151; and nature of God, 75–76; and obedience to God, 88; public reactions to, 151–54, 177; on racial prejudice, 102; and relationship of faith and social action, 87, 89, 96–97, 154–56; on relationship of reforms, 119–20, 121; and Society of Friends, 2, 67, 72, 102, 166–67; and teaching career, 35–38; on theologizing, 63; on truth, 166; on women's rights and roles, 109, 164. *See* Leadership; New Organization

Foster, Paulina Wright (Alla), 38, 50, 75, 151, 156

Foster, Stephen Symonds, 38, 55, 93, 105, 150, 151, 153, 154, 166

Fox, George, 23, 80, 81

Free Religious Association (Boston), 155, 159

Free Religious Index, 67

Freedman's Hospital (Washington, D.C.), 180

Gannett, Deborah Sampson, 3

Garrison, William Lloyd, 7, 27, 36, 46, 61, 67, 71, 77, 93, 119, 130, 144, 147, 153, 160, 179

Garrisonian abolitionism. *See* Abolitionism: radical/Garrisonian

Gleason, Dr. Silas and Rachel Brooks, 141

God, nature of, 63, 75–76, 84–85, 88, 137–38, 155, 166

God's will. *See* Divine will

Gould, Miss, 55–56

Grahamism, 36

Great Awakening, Second, 75

Green, Rev. Ashbel, 3–4

Grew, Mary, 174–75

Griffing, Charles, 175

Griffing, Josephine White, 175

Grimké, Angelina Emily. *See* Weld, Angelina Grimké

Grimké, Charles, 24–25

Grimké, Judge John Faucheraud, 13

Grimké, Mary Smith, 13, 25

Grimké, Sarah Moore: and association with African Americans, 100, 102; and call to ministry, 15–21; on character of abolitionists, 92; on Christian doctrine, 62–64; and class prejudice, 107; and communitarianism, 138–39; and criticisms of her speaking style, 16, 139; death of, 140; and domesticity, 125–27, 130; early years of, 13–15; on equality of women and men, 112–14, 164–65; and Holley, 47, 129; and human nature, 78; on intuition, 81–82; and Kelley Foster, 47, 49, 129; later years of, 124–27, 129–30, 136–40, 162–66; and lecturing, 18, 116; and Mott, 47; and nature of God, 76; and nature of Jesus, 79–80; and organized religion, 72; on racial prejudice, 102; on relationship of reforms, 119, 120–21; and rejection of marriage proposal, 17; and religious conversion, 14–15; on scripture, 85; and the Society of Friends, 14–18, 65–66, 72–73, 102; and spiritualism, 78, 136–38, 166; on teaching, 129; and women's rights, 139–40. *See also* "Colorphobia exemplified," Divine will; Episcopalianism; Leadership; Society of Friends

Grimké, Thomas Smith, 13, 133

Hamilton, William, 165

Harper, Fenton, 176

Harper, Frances Ellen Watkins, 176

Hartford (Conn.), 174, 179

Haviland, Charles, Jr., 177

Haviland, Laura Smith, 177

Hicks, Elias, 33, 81. *See also* Society of Friends: and schism of 1827

Hicksites, 33, 54, 66, 160. *See also* Society of Friends: and schism of 1827

Hints to the Colored People of the North (1849), 171

Hitchcock, Jane Elizabeth. *See* Jones, Jane Elizabeth Hitchcock

Holley, Myron, 2, 41–42
Holley, Sallie: on African-American religious forms, 104–5; on afterlife, 148; on associating with African Americans, 103, 107; call to antislavery lecturing, 44–45; on character of abolitionists, 93–94; Christian aspirations, 44; and class prejudice, 105–6; early years of, 38–45; and father's death, 42; and Kelley Foster, 44–45, 47, 52, 72–73, 143, 151; and Garrisonianism, 44, 93–94; and Grimké/Welds, 47–48, 148, 162–63; later years of, 141–50, 162–63, 166–67; and lecturing, 44–45, 141–43; and *National Anti-Slavery Standard*, 144; and nature of Jesus, 80; and Oberlin College, 42–45, 122; on racial prejudice, 103, 107, 143–44; reactions of people to, 142–43; and relationship with Caroline Putnam, 44–45, 51–53, 141–43; on relationship of faith and social action, 89, 95–96; on relationship of religion and truth, 167; on scripture, 85; and Society of Friends, 67–68; and Unitarianism, 42, 45, 67, 96; and water cure, 141; and women's rights, 121–22. *See also* Holley School; Leadership; Mission, call to
Holley, Sally House, 41–42
Holley School, 145–47, 149
Howard Law School, 171
Howland, Emily, 145
Huldah (biblical prophetess), 3, 113
Human nature, 76–78, 136
Hunt, Harriot Kezia, 138

Individual autonomy: and women's rights organizations, 127–29; spiritual, 18–21, 23–24, 28, 80–83, 154–55
Intuition, 81–83: relationship to reason, 82–83. *See also* Individual autonomy: spiritual; Inward light
Inward light, 5, 23, 36, 77, 82
Isabella. *See* Truth, Sojourner
Isaiah (biblical prophet), 80

Jacobs, Harriet, 103
Jeremiah (biblical prophet), 80
Jesus, 81: nature of, 61, 78–80; in scripture, 17, 86, 90, 114; Second Coming, 133–36
Joan of Arc, 80, 81–82
Jones, Benjamin Smith, 177

Jones, Jane Elizabeth Hitchcock, 177
Judd, C. B., 61

Kelley, Abby. *See* Foster, Abby Kelley
Kelley, Diana Daniels, 35
Kelley, Olive. *See* Darling, Olive Kelly
Kelley, Wing, 35
Kimber, Abby, 59
Kolloch, Rev. Henry, 14

Lane Seminary (Cincinnati), 43
Leadership, 10–11: during Anti-Slavery Conventions of American Women, 57; in the coalescence of the antislavery community, 59–60; effect on other individuals, 55–60
Lerner, Gerda: on Grimké lecture tour, 29; on religiosity of Grimké sisters, 4, 9n. 18; on women and religion, 8–9
Letters on the Equality of the Sexes (1837–38), 85, 112–13
Letters to Catherine E. Beecher, in Reply to an Essay on Slavery and Abolitionism, addressed to A. E. Grimké (1838), 112, 115–16
Liberator, 27, 67, 122, 142, 144, 179
Liberty Party, 41, 42, 44, 154
Lincoln, Abraham, 143, 172
Litchfield (Ohio), 44, 175
Longwood (Pa.), 46
Lottsburgh (Va.), 145
Lowell (Mass.), 142
Lynn (Mass.), 36–37, 49
Lynn Female Anti-Slavery Society, 36–37
Lyons (N.Y.), 41

Macon (Ga.), 172
Massachusetts state legislature: addressed by Angelina Grimké, 29, 46; reactions to Grimké's address, 55
Massachusetts Woman Suffrage Association, 140
Matthias, 181
May, Samuel, Jr., 142
May, Samuel J., 1
McDowell, Rev. William, 23
McKim, James Miller, 79, 143, 160
Mental Science, 149
Methodism, 15, 23, 41, 64, 67, 68, 95–96; camp meeting, 62
Micah (biblical prophet), 86

Middle Passage, 30
Millbury (Mass.), 36
Miller, Elizabeth Smith, 51, 72, 106, 129, 148–49
Miller, William, 135
Millerism, 74, 80, 133–36
Mission, call to, 2: Angelina Grimké, 25–28; Sarah Grimké, 15–21; Sallie Holley, 44–45; Abby Kelley, 36–38, 49–50; Lucretia Mott, 30–34
Monroe (Mich.), 42
Moore, Esther, 56
Moral Argument Against Calvinism (1820), 82
Moral reform, 3: within African-American community, 98–100
Morris, Catherine, 15, 26
Morris, Isaac, 17
Moses, 84
Mott, Anna, 33
Mott, James, 31–35, 59
Mott, Lucretia Coffin: on African American religious forms, 105; and associating with African Americans, 72, 101, 103; and call to ministry, 33; on Christian doctrines, 62–64; on comeouterism, 96; on conditions of the working class, 105; and death of son, 33; and development of antislavery conviction, 30, 34; early years of, 29–35; on equality of women and men, 30, 113–14, 165; and friendship with Richard and Hannah Webb, 59; and Grimkés, 48–49, 129, 139; health of, 156, 160–61; and Holley, 47, 163; and hospitality, 51, 158; and human nature, 77–79; and intuition, 81–82; later years of, 156–61, 165; marriage of, 31–32; and nature of Jesus, 78–79; and nature of God, 75–76; and participation in various social causes, 34, 156; and Sarah Pugh, 59, 178; on relationship of faith and social action, 86; on relationship of religion and truth, 165, 167; on relationship of reforms, 122; on religious association, 160; on Ernestine Rose, 159; on salvation, 86, 94; and scripture, 83–84; on sectarianism, 94; sheltering fugitive slaves, 158; and Society of Friends, 2, 4, 33–34, 53–54, 66–67, 72–73, 159–60; on spiritualism, 160; on theology, 74, 86, 159; at World's Anti-Slavery

Convention, 54; and worship, 72, 159–60. *See also* Mission, call to; Society of Friends; Women, rights of
Mott, Maria. *See* Davis, Maria Mott.
Mott, Thomas, 33
Mysticism, Christian, 76, 81

Nantucket, 29–30
National Anti-Slavery Standard, 96, 144, 154
National Colored Orphan Asylum, 172
National Freedman's Bureau, 175
National Freedman's Relief Association, 175
Neall, Daniel and Rebecca, 53–54
New England Anti-Slavery Convention (1838), 49
New England Friends Boarding School, 35
New Organization (antislavery faction), 97, 154
New York: city of, 36, 145–46, 149–50, 180; state of, 28
New York Anti-Slavery Society, 42
New York Commercial Advertiser, 54
New York State Assembly, 41
Nine Partners Boarding School, 30–31
Northampton Association, 181

Oberlin College, 42–45, 56, 74, 100, 143, 153, 173, 180: Ladies' Board of, 45
Occult, religious dimensions of, 6
Odeon (Boston), 29
Oneida Institute, 100
Onesimus, 90
Original sin. *See* Human nature

Parker, Theodore, 78, 80, 83
Pastoral Letter of the Congregational Churches of Massachusetts. *See* Congregational Churches of Massachusetts, Pastoral Letter
Paul (biblical apostle), 3, 43, 80, 81, 84, 90, 114–15
Peace: Abby Kelley's position on, 36; Lucretia Mott's involvement, 34
Pease, Elizabeth, 58–59, 99, 102, 110, 127
Pelham, Massachusetts, 35
Pennsylvania Anti-Slavery Society, 174
Pennsylvania Hall, 174
Perfectionism, 75
Peter (biblical apostle), 80, 84
Petitions, antislavery, 36–37
Phebe (New Testament apostle), 3

Phelps, Amos A., 111, 167
Philadelphia: Angelina Grimké's move to, 26; Angelina Grimké's visit to, 24; as home of Lucretia and James Mott, 33; as home of Sarah Pugh, 177–78; and Sarah Grimké's visit with father, 14; Sarah Grimké's move to, 15
Philadelphia Female Anti-Slavery Society, 27, 34, 130, 174
Philemon, 90
Phillips, Wendell, 144, 153, 154
Pillsbury, Parker, 67, 93
Pintor, Lazarro, 181
Pittsburgh Manufacturer, 55
Poems on Miscellaneous Subjects (1854), 176
Poole, H. M., 149
Porter, Samuel Drummond, 89, 93
Porter family, 42
Post, Amy, 172
Poughkeepsie (N.Y.), 30
Prayer, 44, 46, 58, 70. *See also* Society of Friends
Prejudice, racial: among abolitionists, 97–98, 107; among clergy, 69; duty of abolitionists to combat, 57, 99–101, 144; and link with slavery, 57, 97–101; within the Society of Friends, 49, 59, 101–102.
Premillennialism, 5
Presbyterianism, 21–22, 63, 64, 97
Productions of Mrs. Maria W. Stewart (1835), 180
Progressive Friends, 160
Protestantism: conversion to, 14; critiques of, 5, 68–69. *See also* African Methodist Episcopal Church; Baptists; Beecher, Lyman; Book of Common Prayer; Calvinism; Congregational Churches; Conversion, religious; Creeds, Christian; Doctrines, Christian; Ecumenism; Episcopalianism; Methodism; Presbyterianism; Puritans; Rituals, Christian; Sacraments, Christian; Sectarianism; Society of Friends; Theology; Unitarianism; Unitarians; Universalism
Providence (divine). *See* Divine will
Providence (R.I.), 35
Provincial Freeman, 171
Pugh, Sarah, 59, 151, 177–78
Puritans, 71
Purvis, Robert, 103, 107
Purvis family, 103

Putnam, Caroline: antislavery activism of, 51–52; as publicist for Holley, 51; and travels with Holley, 45. *See also* Holley, Sallie; Holley School

Radical Club (Boston), 150, 159
Religion: African American, 7, 104–5; and afterlife, 148–49; as disempowering, 6–7; as distinct from the secular world, 7–8; as liberating, 6–7; New Age, 8; organized, 4, 61–62, 71–73, 80–81, 94–95; relationship to social activism, 8, 86–88, 97; as search for truth, 166–67; as synonymous with reform, 4–5, 154–56. *See also* Baptists; Beecher, Lyman; Book of Common Prayer; Calvinism; Clergy, authority of; Congregational Churches; Conversion, religious; Creeds, Christian; Divine will; Doctrines, Christian; Ecumenism; Episcopalianism; Folk healing; God, nature of; Jesus: nature of; Methodism; Presbyterianism; Puritans; Religiosity; Rituals, Christian; Sacraments, Christian; Scripture, biblical; Sectarianism; Society of Friends; Spiritualism; Theology; Unitarianism; Universalism
Religion and the Pure Principles of Morality (1831), 179
Religiosity: difficulty of defining, 4–5, 9; as distinct from organized religion, 5; as integrated with the secular, 7, 8. *See also* Individual autonomy, spiritual; Lerner, Gerda; Mission, call to; Mott, Lucretia Coffin
Remond family, 103
Remond, Charles Lenox, 178
Remond, Sarah Parker, 169, 178–79
Rights of Man (newspaper), 42
Rituals, Christian, 69–72, 86, 90
Roadside, 158
Rochester (N.Y.), 42, 122, 171–72
Rochester (Ohio), 173
Rose, Ernestine, 148, 159
Ross, Benjamin, 182
Ross, Harriet Greene, 182
Ruritan Bay Union, 129, 139

Sabbatarianism, 70–71
Sacraments, Christian, 23; Baptism, 23, 70, 71, 86; Communion, 22, 44, 70, 86, 96, 160

Salem (Mass.), 178
Sampson, Deborah. *See* Gannett, Deborah
    Sampson
Sandusky (Ohio), 45
Sarah (biblical matriarch), 90
Sargent, Mary Elizabeth, 155
Scripture, biblical: and arguments against
    slavery, 89–92; as authority, 7, 61,
    83–86, 113; mistranslations in, 113–14
Sectarianism: critiques of, 22, 61, 67, 94–95;
    as evidenced by competition among
    denominations, 6, 22, 64–65
Secularism, 7
Seneca Falls (N.Y.), 122
Shadd, Abraham, 170
Shadd, Harriet, 170
Shadd, Mary Ann. *See* Cary, Mary Ann Shadd
Shakespeare, William, 79
Slavery: economic basis for, 57; Grimké
    family views of, 25–26; range of views
    on, 2; religious foundation of, 57; sec-
    tarian passivity on, 57, 94–97. *See also*
    Women, rights of: and relationship to
    slavery
Smith, Gerrit, 51, 85, 129, 136, 154
Smith, James, 15
Smith, Jane, 51, 69, 87, 124, 133
Society of Friends, 4: Arch and Fourth Street
    meeting, 15; and authority, 16–18, 28,
    65–66; in Charleston, 25; and dress,
    16–17; and equality of spiritual gifts
    for men and women, 30; in Great
    Britain, 59; and ministry, 68–69; and
    opposition to slavery, 65, 94; and pre-
    pared speeches, 16, 69; and public
    prayer, 17, 71; and schism of 1827,
    33–34; and separation from the world,
    26, 65–67; Twelfth Street meeting, 33;
    Uxbridge meeting, 35; and women as
    ministers, 15. *See also* "Colorphobia
    exemplified," Foster, Abby Kelley; Fox,
    George; Grimké, Sarah Moore; Holley,
    Sallie; Inward Light; Mott, Lucretia
    Coffin; Weld, Angelina Grimké
Sorosis (women's club), 149
Spiritualism, 5, 6–7, 74, 136–37, 160, 172
Stanton, Elizabeth Cady, 49, 51, 129, 181
Stewart, James W., 179
Stewart, Maria W., 3, 98, 99, 103, 169–70,
    179–80
Still, William, 176
Stone, Francis, 180

Stone, Hannah, 180
Stone, Lucy, 43, 51, 82, 121, 128, 151, 153,
    169, 173, 180–81
Suffrage, women's. *See* Women, rights of

Tappan brothers, 43
Tappan, Lewis, 43, 117
Tatnuck (Mass.), 35, 151
Temperance, 34, 36, 87, 113
Theology, 63, 74–88
Thompson, George, 27, 178
Tracy, John Martin, 173
Transcendentalism, 5, 81
Trial (whaling vessel), 29–30
Trinity, 63–64
Truth, Sojourner, 9, 103, 107, 169, 172, 181
Tubman, Harriet, 182
Tubman, John, 182
Twelfth Street Meeting Friends' School, 178

Underground Railroad, 164, 176, 182
Union Free School (Lockport, N.Y.), 177
Union Seminary (later Wilberforce Univ.),
    176
Unitarianism, 159: as changing over time,
    62, 70; as element of subjects' views, 5;
    and Myron Holley, 41; and reason, 82.
    See also Holley, Sallie; Parker, Theodore
Universalism, 5, 64, 171
Uxbridge (Mass.), 35

Victoria, Queen of England, 51

Washington, D.C. *See* District of Columbia
Water cure (Elmira, N.Y.), 141, 143
Watkins, Frances Ellen. *See* Harper, Frances
    Ellen Watkins
Watkins, William, 176
Wattles, Esther, 43
Wattles, Sarah, 137
Webb, Richard and Hannah, 59, 72, 73, 77
Weld, Angelina Grimké: and antislavery
    activism in Philadelphia, 27–28; and
    arguments against slavery, 90–91; and
    association with African Americans,
    102; on character of abolitionists, 92;
    and class prejudice, 106; death of, 140;
    and development of antislavery con-
    viction, 25–28; and domestic responsi-
    bilities, 124–27; early years of, 21–29;
    on equality of women and men, 103–4,
    109, 112–13, 114, 115–17; on formation